From Lordship to Stewardship

Religion and Society 15

GENERAL EDITORS

Leo Laeyendecker, *University of Leyden*
Jacques Waardenburg, *University of Utrecht*

MOUTON PUBLISHERS · THE HAGUE · PARIS · NEW YORK

From Lordship to Stewardship

Religion and Social Change in Malta

MARIO VASSALLO
The University, Malta

MOUTON PUBLISHERS · THE HAGUE · PARIS · NEW YORK

ISBN: 90 - 279 - 7967-7

@ 1979, Mouton Publishers, The Hague, The Netherlands

Printed by Veritas Press, Zabbar, Malta

For my parents

Preface

This book examines the effect of the processes of rapid social change that have occurred in recent decades on the religious life and practice of the Maltese people. It seeks to trace how modernization has affected, and continues to affect, the traditional attachment of the Maltese to Catholicism.

As an occupied colonial territory, Maltese society had experienced relatively little separation of institutional orders before the Second World War. Rural life had for long been the characteristic mode of life for the large proportion of the population, and even in the urban areas, the institutions and practices of rural life persisted, so that the social organization of the towns was, in many respects, like that of the villages. Community was the characteristic mode for activities and relationships of the islanders, and life was superintended in the greater part by the domineering position of the Church and the clergy.

Vast changes have taken place since the end of the war: attempts by a new type of indigenous political leadership led to the gradual dismantling of Malta's centuries old role as a 'fortress', to be replaced by a new mode of living based on industry and tourism. The important changes that became possible as a result of Malta's changed constitutional standing affected all areas of social life. Traditional values and customs gradually got abrogated, literacy was extended, and rational procedures took over social organization to an increasing degree. This was not without effect on the Church, traditionally the focus of national identity, and in many respects an almost surrogate form of political expression and nationalism. With the acquisition of Independence in 1964, and the gradual emergence of the indigenous welfare state the Church lost its traditional claims to exclusive representation. New social needs, directly related to the new social forces generated by the new openings in Maltese society as it developed *gesellschaftlich* characteristics, required new structures, and some of these arose within the Church itself, even though it was not easy for the Church to shed the additional roles that had been ascribed to it over the centuries.

Because of its size and location at the centre of a number of cultures, Malta offers a particularly interesting, almost laboratory-like case for a study of both modernization and secularization — two very common themes in sociological literature. In its attempt to study both these phenomena and the way they are linked to each other in the Malta case, this book is divided into three main sections. After a general introduction, the process of social change, as manifested in political, economic and educational structures in traced in chapters One and Two. Chapters Three and Four dwell on Religious Institutions in Malta, whilst chapters Five and Six attempt to sound the response of Religious Leadership in Malta to a new type of society. The Conclusion draws the various strands together into a synthesis.

This book is a shortened, revised version of a thesis I wrote for the degree of D.Phil. at the University of Oxford between 1972 and 1974. Because of space constraints, many details had to be left out from chapters Four and Five of the original work. As it now stands, the book deals with events as they took place until December 1978.

Throughout my work, so many individuals contributed, through their work and ideas, towards the completion of this book that it is really impossible for me even to attempt to list them all. The many persons I mention in the text I heartily thank: without them life in Malta would not have been what it is, and neither would this book. Particular thanks is due to the University of Malta which supported my studies, to the various officials in the civil service who provided me with important data, to the Directors and Staff of the various diocesan commissions for the time they gave me, to the many members of the clergy for kindly consenting to be interviewed, to Professors J. Boissevain and P. Serracino Inglott for their valuable comments, and to Fathers A. Depasquale and B. Tonna for a critical reading of the manuscript. Enormous patience was exhibited by Mrs P.A. Broadbent who typed the first draft, by the Misses R. Agius M. Borg and V. Grech who produced subsequent versions and helped with the proofs, and especially by the management and workers of *Veritas Press* and *Interprint* in Malta who printed and bound the book. My most sincere thanks goes to Mr Antoon J. van Vliet for his great care in designing the book's lay-out and cover.

My last thanks is to three major benefactors: Professor L. Laeyendecker and Professor D. Martin were most encouraging when I started to think about the publication. But without the continued inspiration and very close support of my supervisor, Dr Bryan Wilson of All Souls College, Oxford, this book would not even have been conceived. I do not think I shall ever be absolved of my debts to such a good teacher.

Tal-Qroqq, Malta   Mario Vassallo
January 1979

Contents

List of Tables

List of Abbreviations

AAC	Archives of the Archbishop's Curia
AAPSO	Afro Asian Peoples' Socialist Organization
AOM	Archives of the Order in Malta
BICAL	Bank of Industry, Commerce and Agriculture
CP	Constitutional Party
CPA	Cassa Pie Amministrazioni
CWP	Christian Workers' Party
DNP	Democratic Nationalist Party
GWU	General Workers Union
MLP	Malta Labour Party
MUSEUM	*Magister Utinam Sequatur Evangelium Universus Mundus*
MVARC	Archives of Author
NP	Nationalist Party
PCP	Progressiv Constitutional Party
PRS	Pastoral Research Services
RAM	Research Agency Malta
RBAC	Religious Broadcasting Authority Committee (later RBAB — Board)
RUM	Royal University of Malta

Introduction

I

The relationship of traditional ideology and contemporary rapid social change has been given considerable attention in recent sociological studies. The sources of this interest are, of course, diverse — from that of development studies, investigations concerned to isolate influences that promote or retard the process of modernization, to the study of the religionist, concerned to trace the effects of changing social organization, productive activities, the introduction of new techniques, on the influence, operation, and perhaps the viability of a received religious ideology or an ecclesiastical system. The juxtaposition of religion and social change has become almost a commonplace in sociology.[1] Many studies have been concerned with the Third World, but there is a growing interest in the sociology of religion in western countries, which is also fed by the concern of theologians to understand the origins and course of the changing patterns of religious belief, practice, and institutional activity in advanced societies. This book takes up various aspects of this relationship in one specific context, that of Malta since the end of the Second World War. Malta is, in some ways, an almost ideal-typical laboratory where one of Durkheim's 'well-conducted experiments' might have been set. The total population, although scattered between urban and rural contexts, is that of only a moderately large town in the western world. It has a strong religious tradition — perhaps one of the most homogenously strong traditions in Christendom. The religious situation is virtually that of monopoly, and the absence not only of pluralistic traditions, but even of denominations within one tradition, or of variants on the dominant theme, provides a context for analysis found in only a limited number of similar islands in the western world.[2] Until recent times there has been very little anti-clericalism, scarcely any history of freemasonic hostility to the Church, and, again until recently, no political expression of religious differences.

It is of course true that, ideal as Malta is for examining a 'pure' case of interrelation of social change and religion, no society can claim to be typical or salient, except insofar as the absence of complications enables the analyst to distinguish more clearly the factors at work. Malta would not, obviously, yield much that might be of value to a study of a large-scale social system undergoing industrialization; nor to the analysis of the replacement of specific religious tenets by ideologies more conducive to modern productive processes; nor again to an assessment of religion as itself a powerful agency promoting a restructuring of the factors of production — since in Malta, religion has been first the recipient of reactions to changed conditions occurring elsewhere, rather than itself an innovatory agency in the productive process. There is, in effect, hardly any 'Protestant Ethic' effect to be discerned in the Maltese case.

But Malta combines specifically the virtues of being both an 'isolated' community and a total society. It is nearer to a community in the classic sense in which the word has had currency in sociology — consisting, that is, of persons in social interaction within a geographical area and having one or more additional common ties [3] — than perhaps any other nation-state could claim to be. Its size, and a long history of rule by powerful foreign nations, has caused the people to live necessarily close to one another both physically and emotionally, in a tightly-knit web of interrelations that offered the best prospect of common defence. Even now that the population is almost three times as big as that of the last century, the Maltese live lives in which inter-personal relationships colour every aspect of social involvement. In the villages, most especially in the smaller ones furthest away from Valletta, practically everybody knows everyone else, and friendship and kinship ties are of the greatest importance. And even though the same could not be said of relationships on the level of the 'total society', there is an important sense to the idea that one can know about everyone whom one needs to know about, that such information can be quickly acquired, and is indeed acquired inadvertently, and all the time. [4] Obviously enough, in such a society, gossip, the exchange of information, and the recurrent attempt to 'locate' individuals in some sort of network which everyone apprehends in part, are important dimensions of social reality, and these should be borne in mind in the following pages. At the basis of all this, of course, lies another important fact: until very recently literacy was very limited, and the slow tempo of rural or pre-industrial society allowed the Maltese to avoid the preoccupation with time and its use characteristic of an industrial and automatized society. Time was not the automatic measure of activity in everyday life which it has become in advanced nations. Work and play were less sharply differentiated, since time was less often a commodity which one sold as such. Even when people were employed with the Services, and in the Dockyard, the frequent fact of over-recruitment allowed an atmosphere of unhurried ease to prevail even at work, and this attitude reflected both the rhythms of the pre-industrial world, and the importance attached to the cultivation and maintenance of interpersonal relationships.

On the other hand, Malta has gradually acquired a political structure, social institutions, integrated throughout society, agencies of control and incentive systems, which make it structurally very much like much larger social entities, and unlike the ordinary community within a nation-state, which is the location of the normal 'community study'. Despite its size, if it was to survive, Malta had to develop links with other, bigger nations, on various levels, and to consolidate these links by the appropriate institutions at home. Even though they exist only in miniature, Malta has had to evolve, for example, a communications system, a diplomatic corps, a currency, and financial institutions of its own. These and many other institutions which are a normal feature of a nation-state, but not of a town or city, at times not even of a metropolis, Malta had to create as it developed itself as a state society. Race, language, distinctive social and political institutions, and — perhaps most important — sustained aspirations to self-determination, existed in Malta, and distinguished it from other bigger islands in the Mediterranean. Sicily, less than sixty miles north, eighty-one times larger, and with a population fifteen times that of Malta, has had a not dissimilar experience of foreign control, but it lacks racial and linguistic distinctiveness, and in spite of the various attempts to affirm its independence has never succeeded in attaining full nationhood. Other Mediterranean islands, such as Corsica and Ibiza, [5] inhabited by people with direct ethnic connections with mainland nations, related their fortunes to their mother country. Tendencies similar to those evident in the ethnically mixed island of Cyprus did exist in Malta, when a section of local intellectuals averred that Malta's survival depended exclusively on Italy's fate, and that the Italian language was indigenous to Malta, [6] but with the Second World War and the rise of universal education, these beliefs melted away. The existence of a native language spoken by a mono-lingual majority, and of strong indigenous traditions in family life and other basic social institutions, made it necessary for successive ethnic accretions to become integrated in a general pattern of social life. Thus, despite a variety of origins — evident even from the widely divergent surnames [7] — the Maltese may now be said to form a homogenous ethnic group. In more ways than one, therefore, Malta is simultaneously the microcosm and the macrocosm, not only for the sociologist, but also for those involved in Maltese social life itself.

II

Malta unites some of the most important features of Mediterranean communities and in some respects this book seeks to add something to the field that has developed in Mediterranean studies. Most of those studies have been undertaken by anthropologists, and their focus has been very much on the ethnographic aspects of the life of Mediterranean communities. This book has been conceived as a study in the sociology of religion, and the emphasis is less explicitly on the ethnological analysis of culture than on the analysis of social institutions. Nonetheless, social life and social institutions are in various respects similar to those of other communities in the area. There are however also differences. In the Mediterranean, the ecological setting facilitated the relative isolation of different communities and of their civilization and culture: the mountainous peninsulas and the many islands provided continuous and natural protection to their inhabitants, prevented cross-fertilization, and fostered among the people, by way of self-defence, a sense of communal cohesion not readily paralleled in larger communities. J. Pitt-Rivers has summarized the situation:

> the geographical form favours unification by military force, settlement, and, as soon as the commanding power relaxes, rebellion, but not integration into a homogenous culture... [8]

Yet, this diversity does not entail total isolation and exclusiveness. Comparative Mediterranean sociology is still in its infancy, but the results of research in the area indicate that ecological factors did not prevent similar patterns from taking shape. Perhaps it was precisely the similarity of prevailing conditions, with which every community had to come to terms, that gave rise to such patterns. Not only was man's response to the problems of cultivation similar among 'Mediterranean Countrymen', [9] but even such apparently volatile traditions as those related to honour and shame [10] were found to be strikingly alike. Village traditions, organization, networks, and the villagers' world views are readily comparable in Mediterranean societies, as is evident from the findings of, for example, Christian and Boissevain, the former in his research on the Nansa Valley in Spain, [11] the latter in one of Malta's smallest villages: Hal-Farrug. [12] It is this unity in diversity that is so striking in the Malta case; and that fully vindicates a further remark by Pitt-Rivers:

> the communities of the Mediterranean possess both more similarities between different countries and more diversities within their national frontiers than the tenets of modern nationalism would have us believe ... and behind the diversities there is room to discover continuities which run counter to the varying political hegemonies observing the exigencies of the ecology or the entrenched conservatism of the local settlements ... [13]

This book is less directly concerned with the analysis of culture than with the interrelation of specific facets of social structure, most particularly of the relation of other social institutions to religion. Although some of the same type of considerations that are the focus of concern in other Mediterranean studies find their place in the pages that follow, it is less an attempt to articulate the nuances of changing cultural conditions than a broader, more sociologically conceived, essay in the transformation of social structure that is the principal burden of discussion. Thus there is no attempt to discuss the Maltese adaptation of such Mediterranean cultural stereotypes as *machismo*; no discussion of the relationship of concepts of honour, shame, guilt, of the operation of status striving. Although changes in occupational activity are reviewed, there is no attempt to discuss such matters of land utilization, inheritance laws, competition and co-operation between neighbours or kinsfolk, such as are emphasized in Cooper's study of Ibiza. [14] The focus is much more on the macrocosmic aspects of social structure, and the relationship of structural change to religious practice and institutions. What this book might, then, have to contribute to the comparative anthropological study of Mediterranean cultures is slight, although the writer is sensitive to the importance of these studies as part of the cultural background against which his own attempt to interpret religious change in Malta must be set.

III

The religious uniformity of Malta has already been alluded to: but that uniformity is not merely the virtual absence of competing Christian denominations. It is also the absence of a folk religion with an independent existence. In many Mediterranean communities, official religion, whilst well enough entrenched, has never wholly eliminated or absorbed facets of folk culture that are, in all probability, pre-Catholic, or which have grown alongside and outside the religious practice of the faithful. The Maltese have, of course, their superstitions, but the remarkable thing is the extent to which those superstitions have acquired a specifically Catholic flavour. The long continuance of the Church in the island, the complete conquest of the Maltese by Christianity, the juxtaposition of Christianity with Islamic conquerors for centuries, and, later, the juxtaposition of Catholicism with an alien branch of Christianity, Anglicanism, are part of the background of this deep penetration of social life with religious intimations of a uniform and unchallenged kind. Certainly, Maltese religion is not indigenous. It was from the beginning an import, and insofar as the spiritual direction of the Church lies outside the islands, it remains an import, relying on edicts and directions that come, ultimately, from without. Yet the process of religious socialization has been long and thorough, steadily absorbing the preoccupations of folk culture into a Catholic matrix. In large measure, the monopoly of religious education, and the focus of education as a religious concern, for religious ends, and the maintenance of a religious establishment, have been the factors responsible for this result. The island has, of course, been insulated until recent times from the technological and industrial developments that have threatened the process of religious socialization, but even in earlier periods Catholicism has embedded itself into the national life, and the ubiquity of the clergy and the religious has undoubtedly been the primary cause of this intensive effect. Priests have for so long been involved so intimately with the affairs of everyday life that there was no space for folk-cultural elements untouched by religion to persist. This is not to suggest that all the magical elements were eliminated from the consciousness of the Maltese peasantry, since magic is a persistent preoccupation of rural classes, but that such dispositions were canalized into more specifically Catholic formulations. Faith was often simple, and the apprehensions of religious truth of the countrymen were not always those of the seminary professor, nor even of the priest himself, but they were always couched in acceptable Catholic terms, and incorporated into the wider Catholic world-view, and ultimately were subject to the discipline of the established religious institution and its functionaries.

Catholicism, then, easily became very much a re-statement of Maltese national identity, particularly in the years when Malta was occupied by conquerors of a different religious persuasion, and those circumstances served both to bolster nationalism by religious claims, and religion by national claims — so much so, that the years of rupture between these two demands, in the final stages of the struggle for independence, were seriously traumatic for many Maltese. [15] Religion, for a relatively weak and small people, was for a long time a surrogate for political identity in the face of an alien conquering power. The clergy were the 'natural' leaders of the people in very large part, and the Church was the nursery of the indigenous intelligentsia. In these circumstances, not only was religion entrenched, and its prescriptions reinforced, but the Church itself, as an institution, strengthened its significance for the Maltese in their interpretation of their world vis-a-vis the stranger who occupied the land.

It is for these reasons that any analysis of social change in Malta would need to pay special attention to religion. [16] In this book, religion is chosen as the specific focus of analysis, and the foregoing considerations justify this emphasis in the Maltese case. The attempt to interpret the recent history of Malta within a sociological frame of reference would demand in any case some detailed analysis of the role of religion and the nature of the Church in Malta if, for example, the political events of the decades since the Second World War were to be understood. Thus, it is suggested here that religion is not merely an item to be taken into account in the interpretation of social change in Malta, but is a particularly important item.

The study of religion in Malta necessarily encompasses two broad, analytically distinguishable, but empirically intricately interwoven, areas — that of religious belief and practice, and the effect of religion in everyday life; and that of the institution of the Church itself, and the operation through its functionaries of its own organizational life. Catholicism affects everyday life through a complex body of clearly articulated norms, intended to regulate both behaviour and ritual. The viability of these norms within a changing social structure are a primary focus of this study. Their maintenance has been affected not only by the changing pattern of work and leisure activities in Malta, but also by the changing interpretation of moral life, and the changing expectations of men (and of the Church itself) issuing from Rome since the Second Vatican Council. Malta, as a traditionalist centre of Catholicism, is a particularly interesting example of relatively late development in the autonomous process of Catholic change. The changes of the Vatican Council were introduced from outside, and although Malta had not been uninfluenced by the unarticulated currents within the Church in previous years — transmitted in some measure by her own returning 'emigrant' [17] priests — nonetheless, the country was one of those the Catholicism of which was, until the Council, cast in a traditional mould. The very strength of the Church in Malta, and the fact that it had not had to face any really prolonged challenge at home, ensured that. Malta's traditionalism in religion related of course to her size and relative isolation, to the fact that religion fulfilled basically communal (in contradistinction to societal) functions in Malta. Malta was a small-scale society, and within it the Church could operate in separate local communities, as a communal institution. Attention is given in the second section of this book to the operation of the Church in the everyday life of the local community.

If the operation of the Church among the laity has been affected by the decisions of the Vatican Council, it has also necessarily been modified by the changing patterns of social life that have arisen as a consequence of a measure of industrialization, of political independence, of the introduction and extension of the use of the mass media, and all these items are considered as the basic elements in the analysis of social change which follows, and in its effects on religion. Many of these developments occurred in Malta at much later dates than in mainland Catholic Europe, and have been more closely coincidental with the changes introduced in the Church by the Council. What in other countries appeared as the process of induced religious change displaying a characteristic 'cultural lag', in Malta appeared as a much more simultaneous process of change within the religious and social sectors. If at times some of the changes in liturgy — especially those relating to the traditional festas — were in some way shocking to the older laity in Malta, they may to other have appeared to be a much more immediate and responsive adjustment to changed conditions than, because they were belated, they could have done in other Catholic countries. In this circumstance, a difference of response to these changes, and a difference in attitudes to the Church may be anticipated.

In the final section of the book, attention is given to the effects of change on the institution of the Church itself. No detailed description of the operation within the hierarchy is attempted in this book, and no analysis of the administrative and fiscal branches of the hierarchy (since these are the areas perhaps most insulated from the effects of wider social change), and indeed, in present conditions, information adequate for the study of these branches of the Church is not available. But attention is devoted to the changes in the functions and activities of the priesthood, to the traditional relationship within the local community of the various types of priests, to training and the pattern of vocational choice. The effects of wider changes in the country as a whole on the role of the clergy, on the attractiveness of the profession, and on its relation to other groups of professionals, are all given attention. Unlike most other professionals, the Catholic clergy, operating as they do as officials of an ideology that has turned into a church, and one which, through its structures of communication and control, seeks to perpetuate itself indefinitely and to remain coterminous with society, seem to have to exercise their professional techniques within the framework of a 'total institution', described by Goffman in the following terms:

> A basic social arrangement in modern society is that the individual tends to sleep, play, and work in different places, with different co-participants, under different authorities, and without an overall rational plan. The central feature of total institutions can be described as a breakdown of the barriers ordinarily separating these three spheres of life. [18]

The concept of 'total institution' has to be further developed to be applicable to the study of clergymen, the more so in the case of Malta where priests do not live in presbyteries, but with their next of kin. What matters most in our case is not co-habitation under the same roof, or the fact that work is stereotyped and repetitive, but the fact that the legitimacy of the values of the clergy derives from the same source. After recruitment, socialization follows a unique pattern (at the Seminary) and initiation in the exercise of the professional ethos — though varying in small degrees from one individual to the next — easily falls within certain well-defined categories. Hall and Schnieder [19] lament the paucity of research so far carried out on the priests' relationship with the organizational set-up in which they work. Even though this criticism is only partially valid — as is evident from the works of Fichter on wh'ch the Hall and Schneider work itself so heavily leans, [20] and from the works of Brion Michel in France, [21] Schreuder in Holland, [22] on the different attitudes adopted by the clergy to social situations, and to some extent research into the roles of the clergy (Blizzard, [23] Anfossi, [24] World Council of Churches, [25] and Russell's historical study [26]) — much remains to be done if the clergy's position in the context of social change is to be understood. Basically, the priests' position has a double implication: as official carriers of an ideology, and the controllers of the institutional set-up, they have to measure the implication of social change and pattern their lifestyles accordingly. Their intellectual training, however, may sometimes impose upon them not only the role of carriers of an institutional ethos, but also that of the primary actors in the process of change.

The formal expectations about the role of the priest had not, of course, changed very much in recent western history, despite the widespread experience of industrialization and urbanization. In many respects, the priest's role, the conception of which derived from an essentially agrarian society, had remained formally much the same over centuries. Industrialization and the changes in the distribution of the population, in work activities and lifestyles, the changes in social structure, and the increasingly conscious and articulated character of other social institutions had, naturally, affected the effectiveness of the priesthood and the place of religion in society, but until Vatican II changes in the selection, training, socialization, and functioning of the priesthood had been partial, incidental and mainly informal. Neither did Vatican II itself do much by way of 'reforming' the priesthood. It was specifically the intention of the Council Fathers to reform the training for the priesthood, and to move away from the defensive attitude incorporated into the Tridentine decree which had introduced priestly formation as a requisite for Ordination. But bursting open clerical isolation did not necessarily entail that clear conceptions of the priesthood and its role had been worked out. The various stages that the schema on the priesthood underwent, and especially the various names which were attached to it from time to time, demonstrate the uneasy atmosphere that prevailed at the Council whenever the priesthood was discussed. In the end, a clear departure from the previous juridical approach was registered, but the final document did not in any way reach the levels, and discuss the problems intimated in the interventions of such prominent Council Fathers as Cardinals Döpfner and Alfrink. [27] It was precisely this uncertainty on the theological relevance of the priesthood within Catholicism, especially at a time when the episcopacy and the role of the laity had received such attention, that bore the seed for the 'crisis of the priesthood' that was soon to erupt in the Catholic Church. Each country, whether it had a Catholic majority or not, experienced a substantial rate of drop-outs in the years following Vatican II. Problems related to the private lives of the clergy, to celibacy, as well as others more related to the social significance of their chosen way of life, came to be discussed openly; priests began to experiment in areas — such as the liturgy — that had previously been shrouded in an aura of mystery and 'untouchableness', and at times also openly to adopt positions in social and political life. Almost suddenly, it seemed as if the world realised that it had no further place for the traditional priesthood, and seminaries which had previously been full suddenly became like the empty mansions of the past, uninhabited except by memories of a lost civilization. [28] Such widespread patterns did not prevail in Malta, and whatever pent-up feelings there might have been there on the inadequacy of the priest's role or facilities, and whatever discontent there was about church restraints on the priesthood, these were apparently much less than elsewhere. Society had not, after all, changed as quickly or as much, and the politicized call for reform arising among leaders of the Malta Labour Party did not have a mature enough intellectual base to have an immediate effect on social life in Malta. On the contrary, even at that time innovation within the permitted sphere of priestly operations had come from within the Maltese Church itself, particularly in the effort to establish new social service functions. Specific attention to these initiatives is given in the second section of this book, and the reasons for the attempt made by the Church to assume responsibilities normally assumed by the Government in larger societies are examined.

The extent of social change that Malta had experienced by 1974 did not, however, fail to subject the nature and function of the Church and its supporting institutions to serious test. Even though the Maltese still register a high level of religiosity and involvement with religious celebrations and practices, the growing minority who do not concern themselves with the Church is indicative of the loss of the previous all-pervasive influence of the Maltese clergyman. All this was further intensified by the uncertainties surrounding the Church and the priesthood in particular in international circles. The situation which turned Rome from being the previous stable source of information into a blurred sound of disagreement, and the uncertainty at the headship of the Maltese Church itself (when such important matters as financial reform in the Church were mooted) made it necessary to obtain some form of self-appraisal of the priesthood from the people currently engaged in the ministry. This subject is dealt with in the final section of this book.

IV

In some respects the following pages are an account of social change in Malta, particularly since the Second World War, and as such are an account of a process of modernization in a less-developed country. In general the account which is given emphasizes social structural change in Malta, recognizing, where appropriate, and particularly in respect to changes in social facilities, the part played by some significant innovators; but no attempt has been made to marshall these data in accordance with any of the developed theories of social change established in the sociological literature. These general explanations of change obviously have their own uses, and the writer's decision not to order his material in accordance with one of these conceptual schemes is not intended to deny their general value, but as a doubt about the appropriateness of such theoretical formulations for the task in hand. It seemed more sensible to set out the actual evidence of change in Maltese social structure, following a broad historical procedure, and to indicate the relationships between these changes in society in general and the changes occurring in religion, than to attempt to describe concrete situations in more abstract terms merely for the sake of paying lip-service to specific sociological theories. Clearly, the general insights derived from sociology are employed, as the focus on social structure must make apparent, but the purpose of this book is to discuss change in related institutions in one particular context (with appropriate if brief comparative allusions where necessary) rather than to test a particular theory of social change by the Maltese evidence.

The process of social change over the past three decades which an analytical social history of Malta reveals is one which might be called structural differentiation, although it differs in significant respects from that process as it has occurred in the major advanced nations. Malta had experienced relatively little separation of institutional orders before the Second World War. Community was the characteristic mode for activities and relationships, and in this context the priesthood and the Church continued to superintend the greater part of social arrangements. The social pattern was still a 'synthetic' pattern, modelled on the idea of a synthesis, rather than an 'analytic' pattern, with social life parcelled out into functionally distinguishable areas of activity. Life was still 'of a piece', and much of its activity fell directly under the control of the church. The Church alone had formal agencies that operated effectively at all levels of social life, and the Church alone had a universal presence — perhaps more universal than in most other societies at any time.

V

The development of relatively autonomous institutional orders in Malta came belatedly, as the following pages reveal, and in part as an almost conscious process of structural differentiation. The operation of the new independent state itself created more formalized expectations and the attempt (in some instances perhaps premature) to wrest from religious control activities that had been, in the earlier dispensation, very much under the charge of the Church. Over the past few decades, therefore, the institutions of society swiftly grew apart, and — as a direct result of the increasing number of 'laymen' with the necessary technical quali-fications for the new jobs created by an expanding bureaucracy and the expanding industrial system — religious institutions and functionaries be-gan to lose their previously all-pervasive control of most social activities. Even though this process may not have reached a stage equal to that of larger nations, its incidence is unmistakable. The new society created new needs, many of which could not be satisfied by the structures and services provided by the Church as traditionally organized. Within the Church itself, the need for specialized services began to be felt, and a process of structural differentiation within the Maltese Church can be readily discerned. This itself reflected a basic departure from the tradi-tional 'communal' organization of the Maltese life, and a clear indication that new needs were being created beyond the level of the traditionally self-enclosed parochial community. In some ways, too, this development arises as a direct result of the Church's attempt to come to terms with the basic process of secularization, to disallow, that is, the eventual out-come of a situation in which 'religious thinking, practice and institutions lose social significance'. [29] The precise way in which this came about will be closely scrutinized in this book, and especially the clergy's own appraisal of the process of social change presented in the third section, will suggest that, contrary to what Shiner seems to imply, [30] the process of structural differentiation in Maltese society, as it emerged from a period of centuries-old colonial rule into a young nation, was at the basis of the process of secularization and not in any way an independent phenomenon.

Religion remains strong in Malta. It would be surprising, given the island's history, were it otherwise. Nonetheless, incipient indications of secularization are evident, and these have been closely associated with the almost consciously-induced process of structural differentiation — the process whereby institutional orders acquire relative autonomy — that necessarily occurred in the creation of a nation state from an island community under colonial rule. The influence — external to the island, but internal to the Church in the more 'catholic' sense — of secularization was imported, as it were, from Vatican II. Malta was no longer to be an island in the old sense, isolated from the currents arising in the outer world. But perhaps more dramatic than these changing currents of theological and ecclesiastical thought, liturgical reform and organizational change within the Church, was the process of institutional change in Malta itself. In particular, the priestly role, as traditionally known, was seriously affected by changes in education, industrial organization, and perhaps also in the arrival and expansion of the mass media. The priesthood was perhaps most directly affected by the emergence of other professionals, better qualified in their respective fields, who now took over from the priest activities that had long constituted part of his social role. The process produced something of a crisis of identity among Maltese priests, the more so at a time when the theoretical evaluation of their chosen vocation was not at all clear. The ensuing pluralism of leadership roles inevitably resulted in confusion, at times in an 'alienation' of priests from the Church itself, especially for the older clergy who had been trained for a monolithically organized and ordered society, underpinned in its most important sectors by a religious ideology (and one must remember that, in Malta, 'religious' has always meant 'clerical'). The rapidity of social change in Malta helped only to accentuate tensions among the clergy, much to the concern of the laity in general, who, because of their, at times, not too advanced educational attainments, found themselves at a loss when faced with the new postures adopted by the younger clergy, and, more recently, by talk of the need for 'deep evangelization' of the country — a country which, they had previously been taught, had received and treasured pristine Christian traditions long before the nations from which now flowed the new instructions on how to live a Christian life in a de-christianized world.

This book examines the changes in religion in one well-defined, small country undergoing significant processes of social change. Many of these changes in religion may be described as a process of secularization, or at least as the incipient manifestations of such a process. These manifestations are traced in a variety of social contexts, some related to the changing patterns of church superintendency of various aspects of everyday life; some as facets of moral change; others as changes arising in new, more industrialized and urbanized environments; and yet others in the organization of specific institutional activities (particularly in education). Changes within the Church itself, some of them stimulated by reforms from Rome, and not all of them wholly acceptable to all the Maltese clergy, may be taken as further evidence of a secularizing process. We shall have occasion to notice particular instances, however, of the Church's increased involvement with certain aspects of social life, its availability as a 'service agency' when new facilities are required, or when new tasks have to be undertaken for which no specialized and trained manpower is available. In exploring the context for secularization in Malta, the writer has tried to give due weight to those cases where the evidence requires some modification of the generalizations that are widely accepted about social change and secularization.

Malta in Time and Space

1.1 Historical Developments

The process of social change in Malta has differed considerably from that which has occurred in other parts of Europe. Effectively isolated — at least until recently — from the major currents of production and consumption affecting the industrial centres of the world, Malta nonetheless experienced some of the consequences of these changes through the incursion of occupying powers. As agents of social change, naval and military occupation forces have a highly selective influence, both in the content of what they transmit, and in their influence on the indigenous population. Even in a country as small as Malta, the differential character of impact was always evident. It was always most significant, and at times overwhelmingly so, in the harbour areas of the Valletta conurbation but often of surprisingly little importance in villages even as close as five miles away. Only since Malta became embraced by the media of mass communications has external influence operated with anything approaching equal incidence. Until the period following the Second World War, Malta experienced the influences from the wider world — always and easily the primary source of social change on the island — only as a coveted military base, changing hands with relative frequency as one European or African power eclipsed another. The island received Phoenicians, Carthaginians, Greeks and Romans — the remains of whose cultures may still be found on the island. [1] The Maltese themselves tend to regard the shipwreck at San Pawl il-Baħar of the vessel carrying the apostle Paul to Rome as virtually the starting point of their history. The effect of the apostle's teaching, the miracles that he worked, and his healing of the sick, established Christianity on the island, and thereafter the Christian religion became a vital focus of national identity. The conquest of Malta by the Arabs in 870 A.D., its liberation in the eleventh century by Count Roger, its transmission as part of the Swabian inheritance to Peter I of Aragon, and its subsequent reunification with Castille and Sicily, are remote events that, important as they are for Maltese history and perhaps even for their influence on some aspects of Maltese character and lifestyle, are not the subject of discussion here. A little more must be said of the Knights of St. John. This Order was originally intended as a 'nursing service' to pilgrims to the Holy Land. The Knights had gradually expanded their influence and developed, after the success of the First Crusade, into a military power based in Rhodes, but they could not long withstand the Turkish threat. Grand Master Philippe Villiers de l'Isle Adam capitulated to Sultan Suleiman on Christmas Eve 1522. He was then granted all the honours of war and the chance to leave Rhodes with all possessions of the Order. A new base and abode for the Order had to be sought. Malta was suggested by Charles V as early as 1523 but the Knights were very reluctant to take up residence in what a special commission of Knights reported to be 'an infertile, treeless, waterless and defenseless island'. By 1530, however, much to the discontent of the Maltese, who saw their earlier aspirations for more control over domestic affairs wrecked by the coming of the Order, l'Isle Adam had accepted Malta and Tripoli as the new home for the Order. He set foot on the island on 13 November of that same year with full pomp and majesty.

The arrival of the Knights in Malta severely restricted the prerogatives of the Università, the islanders' own assembly — evolved in the period of Spanish domination. The islanders were looked down upon by the Knights and they were deprived of all their privileges. For almost three centuries Maltese aspirations for freedom and self-government were stifled. Only when a common enemy faced both Maltese and Knights in the form of the Turkish menace was there any extensive collaboration between rulers and inhabitants — as in 1565, when for almost four months (from 18 May till 8 September) the Maltese withstood the longest siege in their history, defending their island from the Turks. When, with help from Don Carcide of Sicily, the siege was over, there was rejoicing throughout Europe. Not only had Malta taken Europe's part but it had also proved itself, as it was to do frequently again, as a bastion of European defence.

The Knights' hold over Malta ceased with the annexation of Malta to France by Napoleon. Paradoxically, this occurred at a time when both England and Russia were vying with each other to be the Order's protector, and hence to have a foothold in Malta. With the help obtained through subversive elements which the French had been cultivating, Napoleon's way into Malta was easy. Ignoring the Grandmaster, he set up his official residence in the very centre of Valletta, and during his brief six-day stay on the island embarked on a programme of far-reaching political and social reforms. Stringent regulations were enforced on the population; the nobility and its privileges were abolished; men were forced to serve in the French army; foreign clergy were banished; the rights of ecclesiastics were severely curtailed; and the population was systematically disarmed.

The people were ordered to wear the tricolour cockade, and all escutcheons on the interior and exterior of buildings were removed. The University was to be closed down, and a new form of school system was to be introduced. Sixty young men, selected from the richest families, were to proceed immediately to Paris, at the expense of their parents to be educated there. Heavy taxes, designed to levy at least 720,530 francs annually, were also introduced to provide means for the administration to effect its programme. The Church was worst hit. The Bishop had his jurisdiction reduced to the simple control of ecclesiastics. Religious marriages were declared illegal, and civil marriage was instituted. The Pope was denied all power in the island, even in matters related to religion, and appeal to him was declared unlawful. Churches were pillaged, and their gold and silver treasures — the pride of a deeply religious community — were desecrated and loaded on to the *Orient* in time for Napoleon's departure for Egypt.

On 2 September 1798, the Maltese rose against their oppressors, and 'penned them up in Valletta and the Three Cities'. [2] Under the leadership of the trio, Canon Francesco Caruana, Vincenzo Borg, and Emmanuele Vitale, resistance continued — in spite of the execution of Dun Mikiel Xerri and his group of anti-French plotters within the walls of Valletta on 17 January, 1799. All Maltese realized they could not stand alone. It was to Nelson, then Master of the Mediterranean, that they turned. The Maltese leaders implored King Ferdinand, whom they still considered their rightful king, 'allow us to appeal to an allied power — that of His Britannic Majesty — in order that we may obtain his special protection and powerful co-operation'. [3] In the circumstances permission by the king of the Two Sicilies could not be withheld.

Nelson did come to the rescue but it was not until two years later that any real effort to oust the French was made. Finally, however, the French capitulated on 5 September, 1800. A period of uncertainty followed. According to the Peace of Amiens, Malta was to be restored to the Knights, but to this the Maltese were deeply opposed. They turned to the British to protect them, and they reasserted the principles expressed in the Declaration of Rights drawn up by their leaders in the National Assembly which had functioned during the French siege. Lord Hobart finally announced the annexation of Malta to the Empire. The annexation was undertaken primarily in furtherance of Britain's policy on India. This last period of foreign sovereignty continued until 1964.

1.2 Demographic Patterns

In the context of a small society such as Malta, a brief note

Table 1.2-1 Demographic Developments of the Maltese Islands

Year	Population	Crude Birth Rate	Still Birth Rate	Neo-Natal Death Rate	Infant Mortality Rate	Crude Death Rate	Net Rate	Emigrants	Returned Migrants	Crude Marriage Rate
1842	113,864									
1911	211,564									
1917	223,741									
1927	228,574									
1937	264,662									
1947	303,356	38.9	25.5	38.0	120.3	12.6	26.3	2,446	304	6.0
1948	308,929	36.0	23.0	37.7	113.0	12.2	23.8	3,150	131	6.4
1949	312,722	34.0	23.1	36.1	83.8	10.4	23.6	5,368	108	5.8
1950	311,970	32.9	26.5	35.9	88.5	10.3	22.6	8,503	493	5.6
1951	312,648	30.4	21.1	37.3	99.8	11.1	19.3	7,692	470	6.1
1952	316,764	29.3	23.4	30.1	71.7	10.7	18.6	5,345	1,009	5.8
1953	320,613	28.3	20.5	34.3	64.8	9.0	19.3	4,532	949	6.4
1954	315,952	28.1	21.1	33.1	66.9	9.6	18.5	11,447	950	6.7
1955	313,955	27.2	22.8	25.5	45.0	8.5	18.7	9,007	861	7.0
1956	316,239	26.8	21.8	25.3	42.7	9.3	17.5	4,492	338	6.4
1957	319,957	27.6	19.7	24.5	40.7	9.3	18.3	3,285	1,671	6.3
1958	323,667	26.5	22.2	23.2	40.0	8.6	17.9	3,152	899	6.7
1959	327,218	26.2	22.2	22.4	34.7	8.7	17.5	3,265	465	6.2
1960	328,938	26.1	19.5	25.7	38.3	8.6	17.5	3,841	362	5.9
1961	329,763	23.3	20.2	20.6	31.8	8.9	14.4	3,580	451	5.9
1962	329,326	22.8	21.6	23.3	35.0	8.6	14.2	3,641	525	5.7
1963	326,130	20.3	22.4	23.1	34.2	9.1	12.2	6,579	536	6.1
1964	320,620	19.8	17.4	25.0	34.3	8.5	11.2	8,989	495	6.3
1965	316,440	17.6	17.1	24.2	34.8	9.4	11.3	8,090	530	6.2
1966	318,109	16.8	12.2	25.3	30.1	9.0	8.2	4,340	193	6.1
1967	317,926	16.7	11.9	18.6	27.3	9.4	7.8	3,971	36	6.3
1968	318,158	16.1	13.8	21.2	27.2	9.0	7.3	2,992	343	6.7
1969	322,353	15.8	13.2	18.1	24.3	9.4	7.1	2,646	282	6.8
1970	322,187	16.3	13.0	22.2	27.8	9.4	6.4	2,960	317	7.3
1971	322,070	17.1	11.2	18.7	23.9	9.5	6.9	2,798	143	8.3
1972	318,530	16.9	9.6	12.3	16.7	9.1	7.6	3,163	202	9.2
1973	318,481	17.7	9.2	19.5	23.1	9.8	7.8	4,059	230	11.5
1974	317,980	18.3	7.7	14.2	19.9	9.2	7.5	4,189	535	11.4
1975	319,885	19.0	9.9	11.8	17.5	9.6	9.1	1,624	2,957	8.7
1976	322,016	18.7	9.2	12.6	15.0	9.7	9.4	1,107	2,472	9.1
1977	325,679	18.8	9.9	9.0	13.8	9.3	9.0	1,237	2,261	9.3

Source: Demographic Review (several issues).

on demographic patterns is relevant. The figures given in *Table 1.2-1* are self-explanatory and need no elaborate elucidation. Three primary factors were operative in Maltese demographic developments over the last few decades:

(a) better medical and hygenic provision resulted in a drastic decrease in neo-natal mortality, in lower infant mortality rates, and in a very marked shift in the epidemiological patterns of the Maltese islands; [4]

(b) new ideas about the ideal composition of a family-unit (compounded by novel economic and educational needs) resulted in a declining birth-rate; and

(c) lack of employment opportunities was offset by mass emigration that reached three very prominent peaks in 1950, 1954 and in 1964. The male component of the local population was thereby extensively depleted.

These factors, some of which will be further clarified in the following pages, led to various changes in the composition of the population structure of the Maltese islands.

Two primary features are worth noting: (a) there is a widening disparity between the male and female ratio of the population; and (b) Malta's population pyramid is dented, with an overall ageing emphasis.

Since 1842, each census revealed an excess of women over men, with the disparity becoming most accentuated in the peak emigration years (958 males for every 1000 females in 1948; 920 males for every 1000 females in 1957; and 936 for every 1000 females in 1977). In actual fact, there has always been an excess of males over females up to the age of puberty; but this is always followed by an increasing excess of females over males as one moves up the age scale. Although more male than female babies are born each year, the tendency for the male mortality rate to exceed that for females of all ages, and for female migrants to lag behind their male counterparts, results in a progressively higher rate of depletion of the male vis-à-vis the female population. In 1969, for example, the number of males aged 0 to 14 years at the end of that year was 47,075 (equivalent to 30.4% of the total male population), whilst the corresponding figures for females were lower, namely 44,725 or 26.7%. The 122,850 females aged 15 years and over exceeded the corresponding figure of 107,703 males by 14%. This imbalance results in surplus women of marriageable age, and the probability of marriage for a girl over twenty-nine is very low.

The fact that Malta has an ageing population results from two considerations. As already indicated, migrants tend to be mainly young people in the 15-30 age bracket, who also have the highest specific fertility rates. Their migration can therefore be viewed as a leakage which simultaneously affects Malta's otherwise heavier young and middle-aged population, and the would-be higher incidence of children in the total population. The recent influx into Malta of elderly people — whether they are returning migrants or foreigners taking up residence on retirement — has further accentuated the imbalance. Secondly, the specific reduction of fertility rates has had negative effects on the proportion of children in the total population. This has certainly had some beneficial effects; and for a time mitigated what had previosuly been an economic burden on the community, but in the long run might well result in social and economic problems. It is disturbing to note that in 1969, for example, the percentage of children aged 0 to 4 years was only 7.9% as compared to the 1931 figures of 11.6%, whilst the proportion of persons aged 60 years and over had increased from the 1931 figure of 9.5% to 13.9% in 1977.

Such disparities may not be at all chronic however. The recent increase in the number of marriages celebrated (partly as a result of the coming to age of the postwar increase in child-birth; 1972, with 2,935 marriages, exceeded the record set in 1944: 2,733), coupled with a low migratory level, already indicate that if economic conditions remain stable, the distribution of persons in the different age brackets will eventually even out. By then, however, important features of Malta's demography would have changed. Individuals will be much less susceptible to the hazards of illnesses and disease than they used to be; and will consequently have a much higher life expectancy. Families too will probably be more numerous; but they will be much smaller than now, with an average number of children comparable to that of other developed countries of the West.

The Experience of Social Change in Malta

The analysis of social change often presents difficulties to the quantitative researcher. Malta is no exception. To a significant extent the incidence of social change in Malta has left its indelible mark on the ecological setting as various parts of the islands had to be adapted or rebuilt to the needs of a self-modernising society. But the sociologist's primary concern is not with the architectural manifestation of change, however significant this tends to be. Unlike the archeologist he has other types of structures and human artefacts available for analysis. Sometimes these structures constitute important 'sub-systems' of a particular society, and as such are made use of in research as the locus of social change. In the following pages attention is focused on broad developments in Maltese politics, in the economy, and in education. These areas have been isolated for independent study, but the interlinkage which necessarily exists among them allows only formal distinction. and only in synthesis it is possible to work out an adequate framework for an eventual discussion on the interaction of religion and social change in Malta.

2.1 Change in Political Institutions

Politics in Malta have focused directly on the matter of the country's constitution. This is, of course, a commonplace for previously dependent and colonial territories, but the constitutional issue in Malta — the division of powers between the indigenous population and the occupying power — has an exceptionally long history. In broad outline, at least since the indigenous population was able to assert its wishes in any significant way, the process has been one of a steady and persistent demand by the locals for more power, which finally led to the attainment of Independence in 1964. Constitutions, and the changes made to them, reflect not only the opinions of their framers, but also the end result of the political, economic, and social forces operative within society at the time of their adoption. They thus provide an important vantage-point from which the process of political emancipation — in our case of the Maltese people — can be studied. Indeed, K. Loewenstein writes of a constitution as the basic instrument for the control of the power process; its purpose being the articulation of devices for the limitations and control of political power and to liberate the power addressees from the absolute control of the rulers and to assign to them their legitimate share in the power process. [1]

C. Lavagna [2] goes further and isolates three different meanings usually adduced from the use of the word 'constitution': (1) the constitution in a *material* sense, as the real and effective structure of a specific society, to which the term 'state' is applicable; (2) the constitution in the *formal* sense, indicating the constitution as a solemnly written act; and (3) the constitution in a *substantial* sense, which Lavagna considers to be equivalent to the constitutional system of the state, and which includes both positive norms and other usages and conventions which together make up constitutional law.

Within the context of Lavagna's distinctions, it is thus suggested that an historical excursus into constitutional law (into *formal* constitution) should provide ample indications of what was actually happening in constitutional reality (in the constitution in the *material* sense). Two preliminary considerations are however necessary for a better understanding of why this is particularly true of Malta: (1) Malta's constitutions, except the last one attained with Independence in 1964, were always enforced from above, by an Order in Council; and, as will soon be quite evident, acted as a form of restraint or relaxation of the British overloads' control over the affairs of Malta, in accordance with their needs, and with their readings of the aspirations of the Maltese for power. In this regard it is extremely important to make clear that Loewenstein's assertion, as well as the philosophy behind constitutional law already referred to, are here only negatively applicable: rather than being an instrument whereby the electorate, as supreme bearer of legislative powers, could control its rulers, the constitutions governing Malta, up to 21 September 1964, were intended as instruments whereby the colonizers could control the colonized. (2) Within this context, a second factor should not pass unmentioned: the frequently mentioned time-lags between constitutional law and constitutional reality operate differently in a country governed by a foreign power — and hence where the supreme bearer of power is not the electorate — from the way in which such time-lags occur in what may be called normal democratic circumstances. In the colonial case, time-lags tend to become unduly extended before the recognition of the aspirations for more freedom among the governed is embodied in constitutional law; but in the reverse instance, when what governors believe to be a dangerous situation has arisen, the aspirations of the indigenous population (or of the politically self-conscious elite in that population) are often suddenly repressed. Thus there is a slow process of relaxation of restraints in certain periods, which alternates — when local feeling becomes too vigorously expressed — with the sudden re-introduction of restraint when the effect of many years of steady progress towards self expression is reversed often almost overnight. Malta's slow process of political indigenization fully vindicates the hard realities endemic in such colonial circumstances where full democratization is bound to run counter to at least some of the essential features of the overall political set-up.

After the Maltese Declaration of Rights, on 15 June 1802, and the annexation and government through the Colonial Office, Maltese aspirations for self-determination were inevitably tempered by the political and military considerations of the British Government. The course of constitutional change was erratic; constitutional progression and retrogression alternating in quick sequence, and in relation both with events occurring in Malta itself [3] and with those generally affecting the political situation across the Mediterranean. [4] This was readily recognized in 1939 by the Royal Commissioners as they wrote,

> It would be almost possible to plot a graph of the Constitutional history of Malta during the last hundred years showing the rise and fall of Constitutions modelled alternatively on the principle of benevolent autocracy and that of representative government. [5]

Commenting thirty-three years later, J.J. Cremona added that, 'if such a graph were to be plotted, it would have to start at the lowest point in the chart, with gubernatorial autocracy'. [6] Upward trends — measured by the extent to which the Maltese were allowed to participate in government — came in 1849 (elective representation in minority); in 1887 (representative system); in 1921 (with semi-responsible government); in 1947 (self-government); and finally in 1964 when full independence was achieved. The years 1813, 1903, 1936 and 1959 mark clear points of retrogression. More extensive details of the various instruments of government are given in *Table 2.1-1*.

Of course one must take a realistic historical view: only in 1832 had Britain, generally, and as a matter of principle, admitted any section of the wider population to participate in elections in Britain itself — and then only a very limited and propertied minority. It was therefore not surprising — given the limited and unreformed character of the franchise in Britain — that the British entertained only the most rudimentary idea of any sort of constitutional rights for the Maltese, and did not do much by way of extending the traditions initiated by such earlier Maltese institutions like the *Università*, the *Consiglio Popolare* and the *National Assembly*.

The constitution of 1921 established a dyarchy, with the old official side separated in its responsibilities from the unofficial side, the former

Table 2.1-1   *Malta's Constitutional Developments*

Date	Details of Instrument	Type of Government	Formation of Governing Body
1813	C.O. 158/19	Gubernatorial Autocracy	(Advisory Council to be composed of 4 ex officio and 4 appointed members never set up by Tom Maitland)
1835	C.O. 159/12 & 161/2 pp. 48 - 64	Advisory Council of Government	Council to advise and assist in the administration of Govt 7 members: 4 *official* (Senior Officer of Forces, Chief Justice, Bishop, & Chief Sec.) *3 unofficial* (2 selected from landed proprietors born in Malta, 1 from among British merchants).
1849	Letters Patent of 11 May 1849	Elective Representation in Minority	Concurrent powers retained by Crown 18-member Council: Governor, 8 elected unofficial members, 9 official members
1883			
1887	Letters Patent of December 12, 1887	Representative System	20-member Council: Governor, 6 official members, 10 elected, 4 representing the clergy, nobility & landed proprietors, graduates, & merchants - to be elected by the special electors
1903	Letters Patent of June 3, 1903	Elective Representation in Minority	Governor, Lieutenant Governor, 9 official members, 8 unofficial
1921	Letters Patent of April 14, 1921	Semi-responsible Government	Dyarchy: *Maltese Imperial Govt.* in charge of "reserved matters" & *Maltese Government* responsible to a bi-cameral legislature: 17 members (corporate); Legislative Assembly: 32 members (Executive & Nominated Councils)

Date	Electorate	Pro/ Retro-gressive	Local Events	European Events
1813	Nil	Retrogressive		
1835	Nil	Progressive	Efforts of George Mitrovich (with the assistance of Liberal W. Ewart)	
1849	Persons over 21 who qualify to act as jurors	Progressive		Revolution in Europe
1883	Qualification changed: persons who pay/ receive £6 p.a. in rent.			
1887	As in 1883, but rent could also be in wife's name (special electors = £60).	Progressive	Efforts by G. Strickland & F. Mizzi	Britain's Naval Supremacy was being challenged by France; Mediterranean Agreement in 1887
1903	As in 1887	Retrogressive (back to 1849	Language issue	England afraid of Italian influence in Malta
1921	Senate: 7 members elected on limitted franchise Assembly: 4 members from each of 8 electoral divisions (£5 rent)	Progressive	National Assembly under Dr F. Sciberras	Aftermath of World War I

Date	Details of Instrument	Type of Government	Formation of Governing Body
1930	Letters Patent of June 26, 1930	Advisory Council	1921 set-up retained, but with no powers
1932	Letters Patent of April 25, 1932	Responsible Government	As in 1921 Police transferred from Maltese Government control to Maltese Imperial Govt.
1933	Proc. No. XIV of November 2, 1933	Gubernatorial Autocracy	Legislation by Ordinance
1936	Letters Patent of August 12, 1936	Advisory council	5-member *ex-officio* Council
1939	Letters Patent of February 14, 1939	Representative Government	20-member Council of Govt. 5 *ex-officio*, 3 official, 10 elected, 2 unofficial, nominated by Governor. The Governor presided Executive Council as in 1936
1947	Letters Patent of September 5, 1947	Self-Government	40-member Legislative Assembly (Uni-cameral system adopted) Dyarchy again (reserved matters)
1959	Letters Patent of February 19, 1959	Consultative Council	Executive Council: 3 ex-officio, and such others, not less than 3 public officers
1961/2	Order in Council of October 24. 1961	Self-Government	Unicameral Legislature, Cabinet, 50-member parliament; Governor Head of the 'State of Malta'; British High Commissioner endowed with vast powers
1964	Order in Council of September 2, 1964	Independence obtained September 21, 1964	Unicameral Legislature, 50 members (enlarged to 55 in 1970). Full power
1974	Act No. LVIII	Establishment of a Republic	Unicameral Legislature (enlarged to 65) full power

Date	Electorate	Pro-/Retro-gressive	Loval Events European Events	European Events
1930	Nil	Retrogressive	Trade-Union senators dispute - Politico-Religious troubles (Strickland)	
1932	As in 1921	Progressive		
1933	Nil	Retrogressive	Language Issue	The Rise of Mussolini
1936	Nil	Progressive on 1933		
1939	As in 1921, but voter must have resided in Malta for 1 year; 2 dis-tricts, each returning 5 members	Progressive		World War II Prelude
1947	Universal suffrage: wo-men vote for the first time; 21 years old 8 constituencies	Progressive		World War II Aftermath
1959	Nil	Retrogressive	Aftermath of Integration claim & politico-re-ligious issue (Mintoff - Gonzi)	Aftermath of Suez
1961/2	As in 1947	Progressive but highly criticised as unsatisfactory by all Maltese	Height of poli-tico-religious disputes	
1964	As in 1947	Progressive: the realization of a dream, long enter-tained by the Maltese		
1974	As in 1947	Progressive		

retaining control of a number of 'reserved matters'. The Maltese government was responsible to a bicameral legislature for internal affairs. The checks and balances of the new arrangement did not satisfy Maltese nationalists, of course, and in the period of discord in the late 1920s the constitution was suspended. Church affairs acquired considerable importance in this period, particularly since the Imperial Party, led by Strickland, regarded church privileges as unnecessary. In this period the Nationalists became identified as the party representing the clerical interest, even though there were at this time clerics among the more prominent members of the Labour Party (which at this time supported Strickland). Under the guise of disputes about the language issue, other problems were emerging, and Malta — little as it was recognized at the time — was experiencing the first indications of a process of secularization.

Throughout the 1930s, Malta oscillated between different types of political solutions to her problems, suffering periods of direct colonial rule, until a new government under a new constitution was won by Strickland just before the outbreak of the Second World War. The war itself precluded any other concerns but defence. but no sooner were the first steps to national rehabilitation begun, than constitutional matters again commanded the country's attention, and in 1947 a new constitution incorporating the dyarchy principle again was introduced, and the bicameral legislative set-up of the 1920s was abandoned, never to re-appear again.

The war produced lasting changes for the Maltese population. The increased interaction of the Maltese among themselves, especially as a result of the organized evacuation of 55,000 people from the bombed towns to the villages, established new and more intimate relationships between the various strata. Ascribed status differences diminished in significance in the common conditions of warfare; and the society which emerged after the war already showed indications of conforming to new patterns. The introduction of universal suffrage was a sign of the new principles of equality, and of the new opportunities for personal and individual advancement. Achievement-orientation did not, of course, emerge as a new value-orientation immediately, but, with hindsight, it can be said that this was one of the nascent patterns of the immediate postwar years. The old educational and property qualifications for the franchise were set aside; differences between the sexes ceased to enjoy constitutional legitimation. And although old patterns of male dominance, deference, and tradition persisted in many areas of life, the political and legal basis for change was now laid, and already there were those who based their ideological appeal to the electorate on the promise of radical reform. Political autonomy was still a goal, and as long as foreign sovereignty prevailed, this item remained the predominant political issue, but behind this particular concern were arising others, which, even if not yet articulated as such, were, in effect, the expectation of a new lifestyle. The appeal of the parties was now increasingly directed to the least-educated sections of the electorate, and although Malta is perhaps too small a community in which to talk of 'mass' parties, nonetheless the implications of political change were of the same type — the inclusion in the political process of the whole adult population, and not simply the articulate, nationally-conscious elite strata who had previously monopolized political debate. As, over time, the national consciousness and the demand for autonomy were articulated, so the masses had to be mobilized for one type of permanent political situation or another. Once that matter was settled, with the acquisition of independence, the implications of the enfranchisement of all sections of society could make itself evident in the development of new structures in Maltese life and society.

An indication of the transformation of political concerns, and in particular of the changing significance of national consciousness, can be seen in the way in which the old language issue, once the nub of national concern, receded into insignificance after the war. The war had itself been the catalyst of course. During the war the Maltese had fought side by side with British soldiers, and the English language gradually came into general use in a natural way. The emerging leaders of the various political parties were, in any case, now more concerned with changing the social circumstances of the yet uneducated and economically undeveloped segments of the population than with the old language issue. The language question had gradually lost its symbolic appeal, and when English and Maltese were recognized as the official languages of the island, no one raised a voice in protest.

Although a variety of social reforms were introduced in the early postwar years, the constitutional issue remained a primary focus of concern — its character increasingly affected perhaps by the changing lifestyle and life-chances of the Maltese (with the development of free primary education, and old-age and unemployment benefits). The debate about dominion status, integration with Britain, complete independence, went through numerous vicissitudes, but underlying the new political demands there were now also demands for economic advancement. [7] The language of Marxist rhetoric was introduced into the nationalist debate, particularly by Dom Mintoff, the rising power in the Labour Party. Mintoff saw Malta as having been exploited by Britain. Since the island was indispensable to the Empire, as everybody (including Mintoff) saw it at that time, its social services, education, and general standard of living should be commensurate with the importance of its role, and it was this type of argument which led him to assert the eventually abortive proposal for complete Maltese integration with Britain. For a time, integration — the policy which returned Mintoff to power for the first time as Prime Minister in 1955 — was the Maltese Labour Party's programme, and with it the implication of complete economic parity in welfare programmes with Great Britain. The Round Table Conference held to discuss Malta's plan for integration favoured the proposal and recommended its implementation. [8]

Integration implied a departure from traditional insularity to direct participation in the fate of a larger nation. The new policy posed a problem for the Catholic Hierarchy, of course. What would happen to the Catholic-inspired — and controlled — institutions such as marriage and education when Malta became part of the United Kingdom? Without guarantees specifically enshrined in the Constitution against the application to Malta of English law not in accordance with the prevailing traditions of a community proud of its Catholic heritage, and as yet with no clear ideas on religious liberty as would eventually evolve within Catholicism itself, Archbishop Michael Gonzi and his assistants considered that integration would threaten the religious life of the island, and the power and influence of the Church. [9]

Although the attitude and fears of the Church were only one item in the integration debate, and perhaps not in any sense a determining one, the cultural costs of integration were one set of factors which some were prepared to throw into the balance against the obvious gains in social welfare. The Catholic hierarchy wanted written guarantees rather than verbal assurances about the Church's future. In the event, both local problems and world affairs operated to make integration seem less plausible to both Maltese politicians and the British. The local issues were the need for subsidization of the Maltese budget, and the international ones, the Suez crisis, and its effect on the prospects of the Maltese dockyard, the mainstay of the country's economy. [10]

The demand for complete independence steadily gained ground, as the most attractive solution for the Maltese. Events came to a head in April 1958. Rapportage on what exactly happened is clouded by evident political bias. The declaration of a state of emergency followed the disturbances, and the revocation of the Constitution meant that once more Malta was to be governed by direct rule from Whitehall.

The years following 1958 were years of continuing internal discord, the Church continuously being attacked by the Labour Party to be working against the interests of the indigenous population and their demands for political freedom. Frequently, the political meetings of all parties degenerated into a discussion of Church-State relationships, with the Malta Labour Party on one side and the 'umbrella' parties (Nationalist Party,

Democratic Nationalist Party, Christian Workers' Party and the Progressive Constitutional Party) on the other.

When, in 1961, a new constitution was presented by an *ad hoc* commission, neither of the two major parties were satisfied. The Nationalists declared that it flouted the basic principles of the United Nations Charter, while the Labour Party regarded the new provisions as 'not worth the paper on which they were written'. When the parties finally accepted to contest general elections, not without reservations, it was already evident that the constitution was soon to be changed once more. Britain eventually appeared to be ready to accede to the proposals for complete independence put forward by the United Nations Special Committee of Twenty-Four on 10th May 1963. [11]

Independence was finally accorded to Malta in September 1964, almost four months after the date earlier set by the British Government. The final months before the declaration of independence were marked by internal troubles among the Maltese parties, and between the Labour Party and the Church. The major parties now both demanded independence, but differed on the specific provisions. There were essentially two points at issue. After its failure to work out the integration of Malta with Britain, the Labour Party had opted for full independence outside the Commonwealth; Labourites clamoured for a Republic, Nationalists for a Constitutional Monarchy. The most delicate area, however, and the one on stitutional Monarchy. The most delicate area, however, and the one on which no agreement could be reached, was the role of the Church and religion in the social life of the island, as to be reflected in the new Instrument of Law. The Malta Labour Party favoured complete separation of Church and State; equality before the Law; a break with the traditional state of affairs in which religion was not merely a private affair but was maintained in an institution of necessity recognized by the State in the planning and organization of society. Gradually Mintoff's tendencies to 'laicism and secularism' emerged in the guise of various points (commonly held to be six) on which he wanted the draft constitution presented by the Nationalist government to be amended. [12] These may be broadly grouped into the so-called 'Corrupt Practices Act', and the principle that the criterion of public morality should not be that of any particular religion, but 'accepted Western standards'.

The independence constitiution did not incorporate any of Mintoff's demands. A referendum on the issue had proved inconclusive, with more than half of those who voted voting in favour of the draft Nationalist constitution. Over 60% of all electors however either voted against it, or boycotted the referendum. The Maltese leaders had failed to agree among themselves on a final draft of the Constitution, and it therefore rested with British representatives to amend the draft presented by the Nationalists to meet some of the demands of the Labourites. The final constitution ensured equal treatment for citizens of different religions, and guaranteed the exercise of human rights as formulated by the United Nations. On 21st September 1964, Malta became independent.

Independence effected a radical change in Malta's standing in relation to the other members of the community of nations. The 'Malta Independence Act 1964', an act of the United Kingdom Parliament, contained provisions 'for and in connection with the attainment by Malta of fully responsible status within the Commonwealth', and finally secured for the Maltese people *equality of status* with the United Kingdom, and *sovereignty* in international law.

Ten years later Malta, now governed by the Labour Party, elected in 1972, became a Republic through the use of provisions that reflect more the political will than standard legal procedures. [13] Most of the amendments of the Constitution now entrenched ideas that had previously been vigorously opposed to. But by then the Labour Party and the Church had long reached an agreement on the mutual interests of the 'two communities' and though the provisions of article 67 were not fully adhered to on the basis of a 'loophole' covering section 6, the constitutional changes introduced in 1974 were voted for also by a significant section of Nationalist representatives in Parliament.

Our concern with constitutional and political change in Malta has been necessitated by the intimacy of the relationship of these spheres of the island's life with the wider processes of social change, and with the place of the Church in the country. Church affairs loomed larger in most European countries in the nineteenth than in the twentieth century, whether in the struggles between religious and anticlerical parties in Catholic countries, or between the established Church and the Nonconformists for control of such institutions as education in Great Britain. It is itself an indication of the retardation of processes of political and social change, that the struggle between the political and religious institutions should have occurred so late in Malta, and it is clear that once effective political expression was achieved one of the important props sustaining the Church in Malta, its importance as a focus of national culture, was seriously weakened. As long as the island was occupied, political expression curbed, and the vital functions of the economy and the defence were in the hands of foreigners, the Church was the natural agency for the preservation of the Maltese way of life, and the custodian of the institutions of socialization and social control. Once a political voice became effective, the Church ceased to have a monopoly of cultural and social custodianship. It ceased to be the obvious focus of indigenous autonomy and Maltese identity.

Alarmed at the prospect of complete integration with a dominant country of a different religious tradition (and a largely irreligious lifestyle), the Church was also somewhat equivocal about its prospects in an entirely autonomous Malta, and particularly in a Malta dominated by politicians tainted with the theories of economic materialism and eager to change the traditional institutional framework of the country's life. Yet, the Church was itself in some measure a symbol of national identity and indigenous pride. The paradox for the Church was that its symbolic effectiveness was more pronounced when no other agency existed to fulfil this function: the attainment of national autonomy, in which national identity — for which the Church had been the symbol — might be realized, was also the occasion for the diminution of the significance of the Church in Maltese national life. Of course, few can have envisaged this possibility in these terms at the time, and yet the reservatons of many of the clergy about at least the terms of independence, or indeed the terms of any sort of change, may be seen as an intimation of the possible loss of functions. Once the Church ceased to be the symbolic (but scarcely in any degree instrumental) agency of nationalism, by the attainment of national autonomy, so the way was open for a process of erosion of its role. As long as culture, tradition, national lifestyle, and religion were intertwined in a complex set of mutually supportive attitudes and values, the Church was the dominant indigenous institution. Once the connections were broken, the way was open for a process of secularization which had occurred in most of the rest of Europe up to a century earlier.

2.21 Constant Adaptation to Economic Needs

Malta's economic condition has always been closely affected by political events, and of these the principal influences have been those arising in the world outside. It is only very recently that economists and politicians in Malta have tried to break 'the artificial cycle determined not by the vicissitudes of the market but by the exigencies of military security'. [14]

Malta's historical role as a coveted stepping-stone from North to South and from West to East led, particularly from the period of the Knights of St John, to the island being transformed into an armed and fortified military base. The Order's naval strength, coupled with Malta's proximity to the main ports of supply, allowed the Maltese to remain unperturbed by problems related to production. [15] Local production was therefore minimal, and exports were limited to cotton. The islanders' needs were satisfied by subsistence-level agriculture, and many Maltese lived from the return for services rendered to the Order. The continuous repairs needed by the Order's galleys absorbed some of the surplus labour whilst the rest, which was quite considerable, was dedicated mainly to the demands of construction as the Knights attempted to change Malta from a barren rock into a stately home. The magnificent churches, palaces, auberges, and all the other public monuments from these times, testify to the art and dedication of the Maltese stonemason of the period. During the three centuries of the Order's absolute hegemony, Malta's economic organization changed very little: the limited needs of the population were satisfied from the Order's treasury.

The British, who had been called in by the Maltese to help oust the French who had taken over the island from the Knights, were for a long time quite uncertain about their future policy. Their eventual decision to stay was determined by Malta's strategic advantage as a fortress from which Britain's navy could continue to command mastery over the whole Mediterranean. The economic plight of Malta was erratic: only in time of war and crisis in the Mediterranean was Malta's population satisfied. The Crimean War, the Opening of Suez in 1869, the development of longer-range ships that did not need to berth in Malta for bunkering purposes all resulted in a very artificially sustained economy. As far back as 1912 a Royal Commission noted that

> For centuries the people of Malta have never been a self-supported community. Their own agriculture, industries and commerce have never supported them. They have always been able to rely on a large expenditure in the island of revenues drawn from outside sources. This has by no means produced a pauperised and parasitic population, but it has diverted industry from production for internal consumption and external trade to work for the Government and the foreign governing class... A sudden withdrawal of the British fleet and garrison would reduce a large section of the population to idleness and starvation... [16]

The two World Wars brought an element of prosperity to Malta as the local population was mobilized to cater for the needs of visiting troops and ships. Even so, detailed analysis of Malta's war economy makes plain that Malta's small size is an important consideration. Changes in any area of production or demand had swift consequences for other areas: the call for ancillary services during the war distracted the Maltese from the productive sector, however undeveloped that was at the time, and made them almost exclusively dependent on the inflow of capital from abroad. The Second World War, with the death and hunger which it brought, was, despite the new wealth that accompanied it, yet another in a long series of instances of the ways in which Malta's livelihood depended on world politics. Peace brought demobilization and a return to high rates of unemployment.

In a 1945 study of the Maltese economy by Sir Wilfred Woods, who had been sent to Malta 'to examine the present and prospective financial position of the Malta Government in the light of the policy of His Majesty's Government that responsible government should be granted to Malta after the war', the structure of the economy was once more deplored, and indications of possible shifts were put forward for the first time:

> if any considerable expansion of Malta's national income apart from employment in the United Kingdom services is possible at all, it will have to come from more intensive exploitation of the land, the production for export markets of a limited range of consumer goods which her resources in labour may make possible or some combination of these possibilities... [17]

Woods had little hope that the manufacturing sector could expand much in Malta. Neither did he expect Malta, erstwhile a battlefield, to carry much lure as a centre of leisure, but he did say that the nature of the economy favoured 'purely commercial operations, concerned with the handling of wealth rather than with its creation'. [18]

Since the Woods report, Malta's economic development went through various vicissitudes. Various factors, mostly political, militated against the implementation of Woods' own proposals. By the mid-1950's a number of reports were produced, but only in 1955, and in connection with the Integration proposal, was serious consideration given to Malta's economic needs. When, for reasons already discussed, the integration proposals were dropped in the late 1950's, Malta had to face the arduous task of economic diversification when it was least prepared for it, both economically and politically. Now a five-year plan was proposed to cushion the effects of the military run-down and the reduction of service establishments. The island's assets were few, and primarily its climate. The development of a tourist industry, together with the conversion of the dockyard to a commercial ship repair base, the development of a competitive manufacturing industry, and the indispensable further exploitation of agriculture, were the main features of Malta's first five-year plan. [19]

Various factors militated against the full success of the first attempt at economic planning in Malta. Political instability and uncertainty in the years of the politico-religious crisis, and the effects of the run-down which began in 1962 on a scale much more massive than had been envisaged, in no way attracted the private sector to act as midwife during the hazard-prone period of Malta's industrial birth. The 1960's were years of change, even though planners had to have recourse to emigration as an important safety-valve for employment opportunities not available at home. In spite of the dull predictions by Stolper and his team of advisers from the United Nations, [20] the Maltese economy managed to grow and to do so on lines which were to remain, despite the ideological differences of successive governments, basic to the island's future. In the late 1960's and early 1970's the effects of pending recession were felt, partly in reflection to international developments related to the oil crisis.

A detailed analysis of Malta's economic development is beyond the scope of the present discussion. The usual set of economic indicators could be utilized to point at, and to measure, the patterns of change. In 1977 an important econometric study of the Maltese economy was published. [21] Even though dissident voices disagreed with the broad policy implications of the projected economic trends as presented by the author, the correctness of the broad outline of Metwally's analysis of previous development are self-evident, and clearly points at the important structural changes that took place in the Maltese economy over the previous two decades. Metwally himself summarized his findings:

(a) The Maltese Economy has changed from a 'fortress' economy with almost 25 per cent of its income derived from Military Services in 1955 to a productive economy, with over 28 per cent of its income derived from Manufacturing and only 5 per cent of income derived from Military Services in 1974.

(b) The 'take-off' would seem to have occurred during the late sixties. Within the context of this important shift, overall progress was continuous even if not constant. As evident from *Table 2.2-1*, the overall contribution of ancillary services like quarrying and construction, which were needed to complete the infrastructure phase of the changeover, did not show the highest fluctuations over the period, even though the percentage amount of labour they absorbed rose heavily during the boom of the mid- and late sixties. The same can be said to have been the case for the banking, insurance and financial sectors of the economy. On the other hand, and despite losses in the labour force, the percentage contribution to GDP of the traditional trades, particularly those of fishing and agriculture, remained more or less stable. Malta's foreign trade and the provision for tourism expanded considerably.

The complexities of Malta's changing economy have been set out, even if so summarily, less for their intrinsic interest, or for their political implications, than to indicate the radical nature of change in the country's life, registered in this the most fundamental institutional sphere. The shift has been from the economy of an island fortress, perhaps not dissimilar from a feudal castle and its surrounding territory to the economy of a small industrialized country, specializing in consumer servicing. Although it is not wholly true, Malta's changing economy can be summarized as involving a shift from the involuntary sale of its strategic significance to the voluntary sale of its sunshine and beaches.

Table 2.2-1 *Percentage Distribution of Sectoral Contribution to GDP*

Sectors	1955	1960	1965	1969	1974	Rate of Change of sectoral share 1955 — 1974
Agriculture and Fishing	5.65	6.94	7.53	7.35	7.01	0.005
Construction and Quarrying	8.36	7.75	5.46	6.76	5.21	-0.167
Manufacturing (including ship-building and repairing)	8.29	16.1	19.34	22.39	28.38	1.000
Transport and Communications	3.13	3.61	4.60	3.84	3.46	-0.020[a]
Wholesale and Retail Trade	22.69	21.95	20.03	17.07	14.93	-0.540
Insurance, Banking and Real Estate	1.00	2.74	3.16	6.16	4.55	0.205
Government Enterprises	3.62	3.21	3.99	4.17	3.81	0.075
Public Administration	9.48	10.81	13.34	13.79	15.46	0.415
Military Services	24.85	16.45	11.75	7.72	5.00	-1.026
Property Income from Domestic sources	6.39	5.52	5.42	4.00	5.85	-0.001[a]
Private Services	6.60	4.92	5.36	6.74	6.34	0.059
GDP at Factor Cost	100.00	100.00	100.00	100.00	100.00	

a = statistically not significant
Source: M.M. Metually, *Structure and Performance of the Maltese Economy* (Table 3.1) p. 50

2.22 The Features of Economic Change

What, then, is the overall picture that emerges from this brief account of Malta's economic history? Two facts definitely stand out: the *fact* of change, and the *rapidity* of change. Although in 1974, Malta was still tied by financial agreements with Britain based on the presence of a foreign military power on the island, it was no longer completely dependent on services spending as it previously was. From 1958, when Britain publicly made known its intention not to retain Malta as a military base, Malta has shown its commitment to change, and to diversify its economy. Gradually, the artificial basis of the Maltese economy was laboriously abandoned by a people fully determined to 'dedicate itself to economic and social progress through peaceful collaboration with all', an objective impossible to realize whilst the 'livelihood of the Maltese people remained dependent on the economic assets of a fortress'. [22]

The second striking feature that emerges very clearly is the *rapidity* of the recent changes towards full economic viability. As late as 1964, Stolper was still referring to Malta's problem as being 'essentially one of complete economic transformation'. In 1964, it was Stolper's considered opinion that 'with a maintained level of 10,000 emigrants per annum', one could forecast that 'unemployment of substantial dimensions would prevail throughout the period [of the second five-year plan]'. [23] The Stolper Mission estimated that with a labour force of 92,500 in 1968/69, unemployment was bound to be in the range of 7,050 in that year. The predictions were not borne out. Despite a further unpredicted diminution of the military, beginning in 1967; despite an increase in the total labour force to 104,273 in 1969; and despite the low emigration figure of 2,648 during that year, nonetheless there were only 3,813 registered unemployed in that year. In the second Progress Report published by the Joint Steering Committee under the chairmanship of Lord Robens on 24 November 1970, it was further stated that

> the problem facing Malta over the next three years may well be not one of mopping up surplus labour shed by the services, or of reducing unemployment or of lessening the compulsion to emigrate, but conceivably of finding the labour resources to match the job opportunities which are likely to arise... [24]

These expectations, for one reason or another, did not fully materialize. In 1973 unemployment and emigration were both rising, but both were still much below the levels forecast by Stolper. Actual unemployment in 1972 was 6,360 (not including the 1,495 persons in the Emergency Labour Corps, which was to be renamed 'Pioneer Corps' and had about 4,000 members the following year) from a total labour force of 106,642, whilst emigration that year reached only the 3,163 mark. Despite the changed rhythm of evolution witnessed in the early 1970s, the rapidity of the continuing change is unquestionable.

Changes in economic activity have inevitably been accompanied by changes in economic organization. The basic shift from subsistence agriculture and small family craft organizations has affected not only the security of the worker and his family, protecting him as never before from the hazards of the past, but simultaneously exposing him in new ways to economic changes occurring in the wider world. Malta has always been sensitive to the European and Mediterranean economic climate, but subsistence agriculture remained as a relatively stable concern unaffected by many of the changes occurring elsewhere which might result in an increase or a decrease in the use of the harbour — and recently of the airport — facilities, or in the demand for the servicing of ships. Today the island's dependence on the outside world is evident in many other departments of its economic life, and particularly in the growing dependence on tourism — itself a luxury trade easily affected by the change in the economic or political stability of the major European countries.

The transformation of this type of Maltese interdependence on other countries has created a new social milieu for almost the entire population. Increasingly, it has become apparent that to survive Malta needed to exploit her natural assets, and sell herself to a client who had a completely different set of values from those of her previous military occupant. Suddenly, folklore, tradition, sandy beaches, local artisanship, and religious pageantry itself became a ware which had to be exploited and sold. This led to new styles in relationships with foreigners, and in particular it has had important implications for the diffusion of values. Tourists may be somewhat insulated, just as military garrisons and the personnel of ships might be, but there are in each case some points of contact, and, together with the media of mass communication and the increased use of English, these points of contact have grown enormously — with attendant effects on Maltese life.

Strikingly enough, developments in this sector, to which in many respects people could easily turn from the previous pattern of employment with the Armed Services, and which was bound to continue the 'servant mentality' that had been engendered by long years of living under foreign administrations, took place at a time when Maltese national identity was becoming increasingly emphasized and expressed, and when a new ethos of a self-asserting Malta was developing. The ambiguity of the resulting situation has implications which are perhaps still not very clearly recognized — and which people are perhaps unwilling to recognize. But these consequences must have a bearing in psychological terms as is borne out by the mixed attitudes currently developing among hoteliers and their staff vis-à-vis the attitudes of tourists from northern countries like Sweden, who come to Malta with minutely organized cheap package tours, but who demand extensive service for the very small payments which they are prepared to make. These feelings of uncertainty in the new venture of tourism are bound to be accentuated when young people working in this industry mix with others working in the new factories, where, despite the still not well-developed practices of participation in control and production, the worker's individuality and contribution to the productive process and to the finished product is a self-evident fact which in many ways con-tributes to his pride and self-assertion.

Viewed from a more global, European, point of view, developments in Mediterranean tourism have wider, if not easily quantifiable, implications. Small islands like Malta, Ibiza, Majorca, Formentera, and Cyprus have had, over the last decade or so, to develop their tourist potential in an attempt to increase their national incomes and thus solve the balance of payments problems that are endemic and potentially catastrophic in econ-omies that depend extensievly on imports. Such a development could occur only when affluence of Western economies, and better means of transport, created the demand — and provided the means by which such demand for a type of service previously unthought of could be satisfied. The dependence of these islands on the western economies is evident: what must also be made evident is the possibility of negative effects on the dispersed communities that are obliged to develop 'a mass servant ethos' if they wish to survive. The fact that today Europe has islands 'full of servants' who provide a service for the relaxation of people caught in the hustle and bustle of the modern metropolis, cannot be ignored. Nor can its effects on the aspirations of the indigenous population be neglected. The rise of nationalism, and the simultaneous cognizance of the fact that this nationalism cannot be fully realized because of problems of size and scale, is certainly one of the most important — if not the most important — effects of economic change, and of a process of rationalization, in these small island communities. In the long run, peoples emerging from a situa-tion of prolonged subjection may now choose a different type of submission to a different sort of colonizer as they learn to live with the tourist, whose primary interest is self-satisfaction in an atmosphere where all the inhibitions of his normal life can be shed without scruple. The alternative, if it could be afforded, might be to affirm their indigenous identity and culture, harbour an exclusive mentality, and exclude tourism in spite of the hardships — in economic terms — which such an option would necessarily entail.

2.3 The Extension of Educational Provision

Of all social institutions other than the kinship s!stem, education more than any other tended, in all European countries, to remain most intimately associated with religion and the organization of the Church. Secular education has not got a very long history anywhere in the western world — perhaps longer in the United States than elsewhere — but in Malta it is of more recent provenance than in most parts of continental Europe. Religious education, however, has a considerable history, and until the middle of the sixteenth century this was provided by the various religious orders, primarily for those who intended to join their ranks. (Even so, those who wished and were able to pursue higher studies had need in those times to go to Sicily.) But all education remained essentially in the hands of the clergy until very recent times, and much of its content was directed to moral and religious ends. It is one of the crucial shifts in social organization from a religious to a secular basis which occurs when education — once left to religious institutions — is established at the public expense and under the direction of the secular agencies of the state. This change came late in Malta, and is itself an important indication of the recency of the secularizing tendencies that were at work much earlier elsewhere in Catholic Europe.

The beginning of systematized education in Malta, may be traced back to a Bull issued by Pope Pius IV in 1561, which permitted the degrees of M.Ph. and D.D. to be conferred. [25] With the collaboration of Grandmaster Verdala, this Jesuit-run Theological College was followed in 1592 by a lower college where grammar and the humanities were taught. [26] When the Jesuits were expelled by Grandmaster Pinto, in 1768, these two colleges and their endowments were appropriated by the Order and developed into a fully-fledged university and lyceum. The future of the two institutions was threatened during the short stay of the French between 1798 - 1800, but both were immediately reinstituted by the British when they established government on the island. During the first years of British control, however, mass education remained unsystematized, and Napoleon's plan for the introduction of primary education was abandoned to the extent that in 1836 the Royal Commissioners reported the existence of only three elementary schools and a 'Normal School' which had been established in 1819 as a purely private venture. [27]

In the late 19th century, suggestions for extensive reforms of the whole education system in Malta were made by Patrick Joseph Keenan [28] who had been invited to visit Malta after the 1870 Education Act in England. A number of Maltese intellectuals, foremost among whom was Dr Sigismondo Savona, did their best to eradicate mass illiteracy through a programme of teacher training and the use of the local language as the medium of instruction.[29] Education remained relatively little developed, however, in spite of the popular efforts by the Dimecchiani towards the end of the nineteenth and the beginning of the twentieth centuries.

The attempt to bring education more fully within reach of the entire population was launched by Dr A.V. Laferla, who became director of the Department of Education in 1920, and it was then that the attendance was enforced for children already on the school rolls. This was not yet compulsory education, of course, since not all children were on the rolls: the statutory minimum attendance to at least 75% of school hours by the children on the rolls, however, provided a certain amount of stability in the school population, and facilitated further planning. Proper teacher training could not be taken in hand, and efforts were made to improve teachers' pay, and to provide better school equipment and books.

Only after the war, in early 1946, were parents put under obligation to send their children to school, although there is some evidence that the Ordinance was, for the most part, merely a formalization of a situation that had already become normal. The war had made apparent the need for education, and in 1946 nearly 40,000 pupils were already attending schools voluntarily.

The early years following the 1946 Education Act were not without difficulties. Although the postwar increase in the birth rate had not yet started to affect the demand for education, by 1947 available facilities, teachers, classes and books, could not meet the increased demand generated by compulsory schooling. A uniform system of education was not yet possible and available resources had to be adapted to the new needs. Two systems of education were launched: one full-time, the other half-time. Classes run on the full-time system had thirty-five weekly hours of schooling — a daily average of five-and-a-half hours. Classes run on the half-time system had a total of twenty-four hours of schooling weekly.

In spite of the gradual increase in the number of classes and teachers available, this arrangement persisted until 1955 when all primary classes were re-organized into the full-time system. By then, the total number of students attending primary schools was 50,562, a net increase of nearly 12,000 over the 1950/51 figure. The abolition of part-time education, coupled with the net addition of more than 4,000 children, created increased demand for teachers, and 560 new teachers were enlisted in September 1955. Of these 560, only 90 had been specially trained in a training college.

Developments in the provision of primary education in Malta were heaviest up to the 1958/59 scholastic year, and tended to be less demanding in terms of accommodation and the provision of basic essentials thereafter. Table 2.3-1 illustrates how the postwar high natality rate affected the pro-

Table 2.3-1 *Developments in Education in Malta, 1952 - 1976*

	PRIMARY			SECONDARY		
Year	No. of Schools	Teachers	Students	No. of Schools	Teachers	Students
1952-53	112	1321	42,623	6	79	1,837
1955-56	109	1808	50,562	6	143	1,828
1960-61	114	2099	51,376	6	234	3,543
1965-66	113	2024	44,088	6	268	3,932
1970-71	109	1391	31,664	36	1114	14,122
1975-76	99	1397	24,842	38	909	21,904

	TECHNICAL			PRIVATE		
Year	No. of Schools	Teachers	Students	No. of Schools	Teachers	Students
1952-53	3	34	347	73	472	14,191
1955-56	3	35	297	92	761	16,223
1960-61	8	180	2,118	81	776	17,650
1965-66	8	365	4,249	81	810	17,053
1970-71	8	465	5,063	71	782	14,972
1975-76	17	409	4,128	78	920	18,157

vision of first-level education in Malta in the mid-fifties. Emigration and several other factors stabilized the population after the 1958 boom period for primary education, and no significant changes occured until 1970/71. The heavy drop, in October 1970, of 10,740 pupils receiving primary education was due to the re-organization of secondary schooling and the launching of a new scheme for free-for-all secondary schooling.

The basic institutions for secondary-level education had been in existence in Malta for some time, but there was for a long period no *system* of secondary-level formation, and the schools provided, in practice, for the fortunate few. The contribution of the Church in this area is too extensive and too prolonged in the history of education in Malta to be left unexamined. The religious orders in Malta were as a matter of fact already providing second-level instruction as far back as the thirteenth century; but their institutions were primarily intended to train recruits for their respective orders. *Table 2.3-2* gives details of Church-run private schools in Malta in 1972.

Thanks to the modest but pioneering efforts of the Church, the basic essentials of secondary schooling did exist in Malta, and at least provided the minimum requirements for the country to produce a number of indigenously trained persons for the professions. The effects of a good education were self-evident; and increasingly people became aware that social advancement could only be attained if they acquired the rudiments of culture and learning, and if, in some way or other, they balanced their inherited productive techniques by selective thought processes that are the fruits of a good education. Wartime experience made the demand for achievement almost universal. The new demand for education was not without difficulties since Malta could not hope to equip so suddenly an extensive educational system; and by 1947 people had begun to admit that before any effective planning for secondary-level education could be taken in hand, the efforts started on the primary level had to be consolidated. This was what, as we have seen, effectively took place between 1947 and 1955; but this itself did not prevent people from thinking hard on which paths should be followed to achieve an overall amelioration in educational standards despite the rapid growth of demand, and Malta's relatively poor — because limited — initial credentials. By 1948, in fact, a special committee set up to study primary education had already submitted practical suggestions on the best form of follow-up for primary education. The committee expressed themselves

> strongly in favour of the bifurcation system and decided that the most opportune time for introducing it was between the age of 11 and 12. [30]

Table 2.3-2   *Church-run Private Schools in Malta, 1972*

Name of Order	Nursery & Infants	Boys Prim.	Boys Sec.	Girls Prim.	Girls Sec.
Daughters of Sacred Heart	7	—	—	—	—
Sisters of Charity	7	—	—	2	2
Dominican Sisters	3	—	—	—	—
Franciscan Missionaries of Egypt	3	—	—	2	2
St Dorothy's	1	—	—	2	—
Dominicans (Gozo)	4	—	—	—	—
Augustinian Sisters	8	—	—	4	3
Franciscan Missionaries of Mary	1	—	—	—	1
Sacred Heart Sisters	—	—	—	—	1
Jesus of Nazareth Sisters	—	—	—	—	1
De La Salle Brothers	—	2	2	—	—
Augustinian Fathers	—	—	2	—	—
Dominican Fathers	—	1	1	—	—
Sisters of St Joseph	4	4*	—	—	3
Franciscan Sisters of Malta	21	—	—	4*	3
Ursuline Sisters	6	—	—	—	—
Society of Jesus	—	—	1	—	—
Carmelite Fathers	—	—	1	—	—
Seminary (Malta)	—	—	1	—	—
(Gozo)	—	—	1	—	1
Others	3	1	2	1	1
Total	69	8	11	15	18

* These schools are *mixed.*

They had earlier explained that

> the idea behind bifurcation was that boys and girls should follow a uniform course between the ages of 6 and 12 and then shortly before the age of 12 an attempt be made to introduce a branching off in the curriculum as a result of which those children showing the necessary aptitudes and abilities should be directed to the Lyceum and other Grammar Schools, and to the Technical Schools while those who remained on in the Primary Schools would receive such training as would constitute for them some preparation for after school life... [31]

The same views were expressed more than eight years later by D. Crichton Miller in his report on education in Malta. When he was in Malta, the old Preparatory Schools had been closed and since primary education had by then been well organized, the need for developments on the secondary level — both in the grammar as well as in the technical fields — had become more urgent. In the 1952/53 scholastic year, there had been only 1,837 students receiving secondary instruction in the 71 classes of the lyceum and grammar schools, and only 347 boys in the three small technical schools then in existence. By 1956/57 the number of grammar school pupils had become 2,547, whilst that of students in technical schools was still 403. Crichton Miller in fact summarized the situation in the following manner:

> The general idea is that provision should be made for about 5,000 pupils in two grammar schools (the Lyceum and the Girls' School for which new buildings are certainly urgently required), a 'clerical' secondary school, technical schools (senior and junior) and possibly a girls' 'clerical' college. [32]

He accepted the suggested developments as his own, and in his report emphasized the importance of greater provision for technical crafts. [33] Since 1948, grammar school population figures have maintained a gradual expansion, while the intake of technical schools has soared from 403 students in 1956/57 to 5,063 in 1970/71. The tiny seed sown half a century previously by Professor W.F. Nixon during his extended stay in Malta between 1905 and 1934 finally found fertile soil. Several technical schools had been established and training centres were set up in 1956. The Technical Institute was started in 1960 and, with the encouragement and money received from UNESCO and from the British Government, a Polytechnic, known as the Malta College of Arts, Science and Technology, was erected and affiliated to the University in 1961. The more recent creation of 'Trade Schools' complements already existing facilities in technical education, and provides an additional training for the craftsmen needed by Malta's planned industrial expansion. [34]

Developments in primary and secondary-level education could not but be followed by developments in tertiary-level education. As has already been indicated, Malta had for a long time possessed a university, but university education had for a long time been restricted to relatively few, and socio-economic conditions frequently made the University appear a mysterious place, and admission to it unattianable to all but those who already had family connections with the professions, or, more commonly, to those who wanted to enter the priesthood. The popularization of university education in Malta is a very recent phenomenon: the expansion witnessed in that sector — from 228 students in 1949 to 1,332 in 1972 — is perhaps one stark reminder of the alacrity with which the Maltese mind responds to new opportunities for advancement when the possibilities become known to it.

In 1947, the University was still a limited endeavour. Ifor L. Evans, in his report on Higher Education in Malta, immediately recognized the limitations imposed on the University by its limited size, and also by the scale of the community which it served; but insisted that it should be

something much more than a training ground for the chosen professionally-minded few: its ultimate *raison d'etre* is the enlightenment of the many... [35]

Relying extensively on the recommendations of the then recent Asquith Commission report, [36] Evans harshly criticized the 'very meagre financial provisions made to an institution which is undertaking instruction in six faculties'; [37] demanded that the library be extended as soon as war damage problems were settled; suggested a reform of the constitutional set-up that would bring the University to a level of full equality in the academic community of British universities; and even made concrete proposals for the re-organization of the Arts and Science faculties so that they might eventually meet the increased demands on them he was already envisaging. [38]

In spite of Evans' proposals, the University did not seem to be able to keep abreast of developments in the wider society; and in 1957 was still almost completely unequipped to meet demands that had by then become more urgent, the resources at its disposal still being 'insufficient to meet its present commitments'. [39] In 1957, as again in 1974, the autonomy of the University was being discussed in political circles, and after putting into perspective the exact meaning of a university's autonomy, [40] the Commissioners affirmed the need for a developing country like Malta to have a university of its own:

That Malta has some need of the service of a University is certain. Like every other community, it must have competently staffed professions: and professional education is part of the function of a University... [41]

In 1957 the Commissioners rejected the idea that such a demand could best be met by the use of the services of a foreign university. Echoing almost verbatim the earlier report by Evans, they maintained that the University's objectives should be the pursuance of

fundamental knowledge and fundamental criticism in a fashion which sets it somehow apart from and may even at times set it, or some of its members, in opposition to the prevailing disposition of the community to which it belongs. [42]

Within this perspective, far-reaching reforms, notably in the general administration, and in the provision of the central services, were suggested. The triennial entry system then in existence was also criticized, and was eventually changed. The earlier suggestion by Evans for the creation of a permanent commission as a link between the government and the University was repeated in 1957, and the now even more urgent expansion of the science departments insisted upon. Instead of being a threat to a possible closing down of the University, the Commission's report stimulated the establishment of the University as 'an important intellectual centre of the Southern Mediterranean'. [43]

From 1957, the University sustained a stable expansionory trend. A new site was chosen in the early sixties, and with the financial assistance extended by the British government it became possible for the University to move into a more spacious complex at Tal-Qroqq, where, for the first time in its history, the different departments could be comfortably housed, and facilities for the physical and cultural education of university students became available. In 1970, too, university education began to be offered free to anyone qualified to receive it. From a mere 228 students in 1949, the number of regular students had risen to 1,332 by 1972, and the number of the teaching staff had gone up from a mere 58 in 1950/51 to 179 in 1971. [44] The increase in the number of students occurred primarily within the Arts faculty; expansion within the Science faculty fell below the planned level and the increase registered there since 1949 has been only 73.1%. Law faculty enrolments increased by 375% over the period; Medicine and Theology had 272% and 110% increases respectively. Arts students increased by 477%. University expansion — like expansion in other sectors of Maltese education — included women as well as men: female emancipiation in Maltese society in general was also reflected at the University with an increase in the female population from a mere 23 in 1949 to 237 in 1973 when women students totalled a third of the student population. The implications of such a change are clear: women are competing on terms increasingly approaching equality with men for a variety of social roles. The development of a 'modern' society in Malta is made evident in these changes: in nothing was tradition so firm as in the division of male and female roles for the vast majority of the ordinary people. The dominance of the family as the primary unit of social structure, in which the differences in those roles was integrated, gives place, or some place, to the individual as the basic unit of society — an individual whose sex becomes in many spheres of activity a matter of increasing indifference.

In 1974, Malta's educational system was due for an important re-shuffle. Over the previous few years, educational structures had undergone considerable alteration, [45] and it was considered that unless all sectors were properly co-ordinated and programmed to cater for the increasing and specialized needs of a young nation just embarking on the road to self-sufficiency, the whole system might end up by becoming a white elephant: an instrument whereby the aspirations of the community could be raised beyond the level of possible satisfaction. The declared object of the 1974 Education Bill was in fact to 'replace the various laws concerning education by a comprehensive law based on modern exigencies in the educational field'. The Act also provides for the 'establishment of the necessary machinery for the progressive development of the educational service from the primary to the university level'. [46] The various sections of the Act were accordingly intended to bring education within the scope of national development, and although not inclusive of all institutions (the M.C.A.S.T. and the Colleges of Education were not covered), the Act covered and integrated substantial segments of education in Malta. During the extensive debate on the Bill in the press and in Parliament, the attempt to centralise education was severely criticized. In particular, the new structures and concepts introduced by the Bill on the running of the University were bitterly attacked by members of the Opposition, and it was repeatedly alleged that the Act, rather than extending the pursuit of knowledge, would in practice curb it. The University itself opposed the Bill primarily on three counts: (a) the new method of making academic appointments; (b) the spheres of teaching and research; and (c) the procedures for making regulations and bye-laws on academic matters. It was further alleged by the University that the new provisions that all major policy decisions should effectively require Government approval would curb the autonomy of the University, and, would, in practice, reduce the highest institute of learning to another government department. [47] Under the new Act, the selection board set up to make academic appointments would not have a majority of academics on it; [48] research fields for the various departments were to be set by Government in accordance with what the government assessed to be the needs of the country; [49] and the enactment of regulations and bye-laws would be made more complicated, and specifically, the power previously enjoyed by Senate to make bye-laws without the previous approval of Council was to be removed.[50] Widespread opposition through the media and in Parliament was not of much avail, and Mintoff did not hesitate to affirm — against what even the other members of his own party were saying — that he never intended to give full autonomy to the University,[51] which, being financed out of public funds, should be ready to make its plans conform to the needs of the nation. He insisted, too, that he was in no way obliged to accept all the recommendations of the University Commission set up earlier on by his Government under the chairmanship of R. Dahrendorf. The first part of the commission's report, though suggestive of various important structural changes in the general running of the University so that more dialogue between Government and University could be ascertained, had been publicly accepted by both institutions, but eventually it did not prove to be the exclusive source of ideas on which the section on the University in the new Education Bill had been drafted.[52] The second part of the report, presented a year later, eventually consolidated the University's position by relating the other institutions of tertiary education to Malta's needs, and by provisions for the University to move more into the social sciences.

The University of Malta was well set, even if not without difficulty, on the implementation of the Dahrendorf recommendations. But the second half of 1977 and throughout 1978 the tertiary sector of education in Malta again came to the fore of public debate. A protracted industrial dispute between the Government and Maltese medical practitioners sparked off a radical restructuring of University provision on the island. The stated aims of the reforms, as eventually embodied in amendments to the 1974 Education Act, were to introduce the worker-student concept in tertiary education; to provide financial assistance to students in the form of 'payment for work done'; and effectively to promote functional courses and phase out degrees (particularly B.A.s and B.Sc.s) that are not directly linked to particular professions or semi-professions.[53]

The implementation of such reforms created widespread dissent in Malta and abroad even among the Government's own advisors such as Ralf Dahrendorf and John Horlock who resigned from the Commission of Higher Education[54] and who publicly disavowed any link with Government action. The way changes were introduced could hardly have been forecast a year before they received statutory status by a simple majority in Parliament. A set of recommendations for reforms prepared by the University staff following a meeting with the Prime Minister were never officially discussed, although their drafters insisted that they incorporated the main policy orientations indicated by the Maltese Government.[55] Instead, by Act No XXI of 1978, the Maltese Parliament set up a 'New

University' to whom teaching in the following branches of learning was assigned: accountancy, administration, business management, engineering, medicine, surgery, dentistry, pharmacy and education. The University of Malta, now somewhat mockingly renamed 'Old University', was left with a provision to teach the sciences, humanities and laws. Theology was also assigned to the 'Old University' which could thenceforth award degrees but was specifically precluded from providing teaching or instruction facilities. This effectively resulted in a complete cleavage between theology teaching and the state-run tertiary sector in Malta.

The effects of these recent reforms cannot be properly discussed here. The existence of two universities in Malta has been acknowledged to be, of necessity, a provisional measure. Meantime, courses in arts and the sciences at the Old University are being dubbed 'capricious' by Government and, through direct Ministerial intervention as legitimated in the amendments to the Education Act, students have been made to pay high fees; many Maltese academics and students (particularly students of medicine) opted out of the system and found placement abroad; courses at the 'New University' (itself governed by a non-Maltese) are being taught by the staff of MCAST or by non-Maltese recruited primarily from Eastern Europe. [56]

But the 1978 reforms as such have only tangential relevance to the present discussion. The need felt in Malta for a comprehensive instrument of law on education is what is most relevant for our present discussion: it is itself a clear reflection of the dimension this institution was gradually assuming in Malta, and a clear indication of the extensive changes occurring in Maltese society over the last twenty-five years. As recently as 1946, Ifor L. Evans had lamented on the fact that transformation in economic life and social conditions in Malta, and the consequent changed outlook of the people as a whole, were being 'tempered by a corresponding advance in public education... Education provision is neglected, and illiteracy remains rife... [57] Later on in the same report, Evans felt it necessary to assert that

> even today it is estimated that over a quarter of the population are unable to read and write, though, as might be expected that it is probable that the larger proportion of these is found in the older age groups... [58]

By the period under study all this had changed. The number of complete illiterates had been reduced to an insignificant minority — now mostly in the higher age bracket — and the greater part of the existing population in Malta had a good enough grounding on at least the primary level. Many had also the opportunity to follow secondary-level education. No extensive social mobility studies have so far ever been carried out in Malta. One can clearly notice, however, that through education the old patterns of stratification are losing their importance. [59] Inherited titles are no longer associated with authority, and the patronage patterns of the past, though still a force within politics, are generally disintegrating as children help their parents to reverse the consequences of ignorance and illiteracy. The thrust of the political argument in both parties, in theory if not always in practice, is towards the creation of a meritocratic society; and the desire among the general population that this should come about as quickly as possible is, as a result of the general educational advancement, definitely present. Despite these unmistakable trends and aspirations, however, sceptics continue to believe that **the smallness of** Malta could never allow this to materialise fully. They believe that patterns of patronage — perhaps of a new type and directly linked with political allegiance — are bound to persist in Malta. The close-knit networks on which the political parties — especially the MLP — depend for their support, tend to support this view. Malta's economy, it has to be further recalled, cannot easily keep pace in the provision of employment opportunities with the mass of educated people emerging from the educational establishments. This process might offset the benefits accruing from education, and allows only those few with established contacts with influential people to achieve higher positions, or, as a result of the 1978 developments, the possibility of further training at University. This situation creates a deep sense of frustration, and alienation from life in general, among those who, because of their political colour or family traditions, cannot get the jobs they might otherwise have merited. Both the sense of satisfaction, and the undesirable feeling of alienation, now noticed to a much larger extent than a decade ago, are themselves an unmistakable effect of the process of rapid social change, of a sudden change in the aspirations and the values of the Maltese, brought about, not exclusively but to a considerable extent, by the diffusion of education.

2.4. Towards a More Open Society

The most significant change affecting Maltese society has clearly issued from the attainment of national independence. The British had not generally interfered with the customs and mores of the people, and certainly not with their religion, yet the activity of a vigorous occupying power, in Malta not for settlement certainly, but in pursuance of military goals of global magnitude, could not but affect the life of the island. That effect was filtered through a variety of channels, but was most significant in the provision of work of a kind which the island could never have evolved for itself, particularly in the docks and in service tasks for the military, and also in the political sphere. The Maltese economy was forged to the purposes of the occupying power, and while its concerns provided work and income, it also created a sense of dependence which was un-congenial politically and which — had anyone been prescient enough to see it — exposed the island's population to the likelihood of severe prob-lems in the event of changes in the world balance of power. Clearly, as long as the British regarded the island as of primary strategic importance, the political aspirations of the local population remained muted. Nor did the British regard their responsibilities in regard to education as in any sense equal to those which were assumed at home. In many ways, the long involvement of the Church in educational matters made it easier for the British governors to regard that domain as one in which they should not unduly interfere: unlike other colonies, Malta had no British mission-aries as such for long, and the superintendency of education by the Church (a Church which was not that of the British themselves) made it possible to ignore, or to give scant recognition to, the educational needs of the islanders. The relationship was not, of course, always or even predomin-antly contentious, and in some respects there was a clear coalition of the interests of the British and the Maltese people. For one thing the alternative was unimaginable: a people long occupied by one or another of powers immensely greater than themselves could not expect self-determination without some form of external guarantee of their inde-pendence. Only in the climate of the anti-colonial ethos disseminated through the United Nations after the Second World War, were the joint desiderata of independence and security conceivable.

Of course there were conflicts too; and the attempts to mobilize opposition took on the guise of a symbolic gesture — over the language question, or the vote for expenditure in education. At other times, as in the *sette giugno* riots in 1919, or the disturbances of April 1958, opposition crystallized more explicitly in acts of outright rebellion. As from 1947, when a limited form of self-government was re-introduced, the steps towards complete independence accelerated until its attainment in 1964.

The demand for political self-determination was reinforced by the assertion of Maltese national identity. When political independence came, there was an opportunity to do things 'the Maltese way', to look for an indigenous tradition of ordering public affairs, to assert Maltese style, and to restore, resuscitate, or re-create Maltese institutions. Foreign powers should now treat with Malta as an equal. Such a prospect was not without difficulties. Malta's social and public life had been dominated by foreign institutions; indigenous political consciousness had been affected and moulded by institutions imported from Britain; disparity in size and in economic viability between Malta and other independent states could not but affect her relations with them.

Increasingly it became apparent that to survive Malta needed to exploit her natural assets, and to sell herself as a tourist country. Conscious awareness of Malta's potential in this respect led to the attempt to project an image of the island for the tourist industry of the major nations. Tourism depends not only on climate, but on the appeal of the indigenous crafts and local cultural products, on the maintenance of folklore, and on the provision and maintenance of a wide variety of facilities. Inevitably, this development also brought new awareness of Malta's limitations in skills and technology, and the need for established economic, cultural, and diplomatic ties with other nations.

These developments led to a rapid intensification of contact with the outside world. Figures for the amount of air traffic to and from Malta, the volume of incoming and outgoing mail, and the increase in international telephonic communication indicate some of the dramatic changes occurring in Maltese life. When the overseas telephone service was introduced in 1952, there were, in that year, 497 incoming and 732 outgoing calls. Within ten years the number of calls had increased by more than one hundred-fold, and by 1976, there were more than 132,000 outgoing calls.

The shift from service to productive industry as a source of revenue entailed new processes of secondary socialization for a large number of people. Apart from the dockyard, which itself depended on the towns surrounding it for its labour supply and so was to a large extent an extension of the parochial way of the region, the increasing congregation of workers in factories was a new socio-psychological experience for many people, necessitating socialization to new conditions, a new adjustment between traditional mores and those developing within industries. The involvement of women in factory life — an entirely new phenomenon — was a virtually revolutionary circumstance.

From a dependence (in domestic service, for example) on an employer who was personally known, and with whom a long-standing relationship often evolved, work relations were now transformed into something much more impersonal (although given the size of Malta, far less impersonal than would be the case in an industrial economy), in which the cash-nexus assumed a larger role, and in which individual autonomy was a new possibility. As has been argued, 'what is most fundamental here is not the quantum of remuneration, but the fact that these young men and women have now obtained independent employment'.

Behind this extended socialization lay the positive strides forward in education. The postwar attempts to provide free and compulsory education were undoubtedly the greatest source of inspiration to the whole process. Not only did better education provide the tools for a quick cultural accommodation to tourists (whose numbers increased from about 4,004 in 1946 to 339,537 in 1976) and the skills required in the newly established industries, but it also dramatically changed the level, extent, and, most important of all, the quality of socialization. New types of knowledge at all levels broke the narrow focus of interests that had for so long directed the interaction and behaviour of the Maltese. Intelligent discussion of politics and world events no longer remained the prerogative of the village or town elite groups, the parish priest, the village doctor, and the village pharmacist. [60]

This new diffusion of interests and the increased awareness of new lifestyles created the demand for new media of socialization. The wartime introduction of Rediffusion, a piped sound system relayed on two networks for more than seventeen hours a day, had already started the process. To Rediffusion may be attributed an important if gradual process of the disruption of the traditional closeness of Maltese households. Increasingly it claimed a power previously enjoyed by a diffuse gossip system. Since 1946, Rediffusion has become a piece of household furniture, the number of its subscribers soaring from 6,176 in that year 48,443 in 1976. There has been no parallel increase in the number of wireless radio licences primarily because Malta had no Maltese language radio station in those years. The licence figures do not, however, reflect the widespread popularity of the transistor radio in Malta. In 1973, it was in fact estimated by an independent audience research survey that 68% of all Maltese households owned at least one radio set. [61] Television came into Malta soon after its introduction in Italy. Since 1962, Malta has also had its own television system, and together with the two Italian networks, which are also clearly received, Malta Television (now TVM) commands an audience comprising a substantial part of the local population. Television licences rose from 2,411 in 1957 when they were introduced to 32,284 in 1967 and to 62,898 in 1976. Radio Malta transmits over three channels, and since its introduction in 1974 has become an effective communication instrument in Malta.

Radio and television may be regarded as important new agencies of socialization for a society in transition from an essentially traditional, localized folk culture to a modern, industrial system. The speed of diffusion of these new media of communication has occurred more rapidly in Malta than in most developing countries, and the size of the country, which is small enough to leave no group or settlement unaffected, has ensured that their impact has been of more or less even incidence. To the increase of radio and television use must be added the widened demand for reading matter, and the availability of the telephone and the car.

The local press now comprises six daily newspapers, three published in English and three in Maltese, which altogether have an estimated readership of about half the total population. The contrast with 1946 is striking: then there were only two really diffused daily papers, one in each language, issued by the same printing house and providing only one view of affairs.

Telephone use within Malta has also grown considerably. In 1946, only 3,205 households or establishments had a telephone: in 1967, 17,923; in: 1976, 38,708. The number of local calls made in 1976 had risen to 38,000,000 from the 7,920,617 calls made in 1946!

In 1947, too, there were only 3,552 cars and 787 motor cycles on the road in Malta. In 1976 there were 53,372 cars and 4,665 motor cycles.

Changes in communications techniques are themselves indicative of changes in community organization. Developed modern means of communication enable individuals to transcend local community, and to take a much wider social entity as their reference group. Social procedures become more firmly oriented to the wider society; roles take on a more impersonal, more uniform specification; and values become more articulated in relation to the life and consciously envisaged needs of the whole society (evident, for example, in political exhortations for more responsive attitudes towards productive endeavour, tourism, exports, and so on).

Prior to the advent of universal education, of industry, of tourism, and of more extensive leisure opportunities, the basis of life in Malta was largely communal. Democratization at all levels has increased the associational aspects of life: Maltese society is gradually losing its *gemeinschaftlich* characteristics. Family control over the individual now diminishes as the individual reaches maturity; the village's grip over the family as a unit has now practically disappeared. [62] Socialization takes a wider reference, and hinges on a completely different set of fulcra. A multitude of interests, from sport and dancing to drama and sunbathing, now attract the young away from home. The time when emigration was the only way by which a determined son could sever his ties with his father's *luzzu*, or his family's *razzett*, are gone. Along with the loss of the *faldetta*, the child who always chaperoned two young lovers out for a walk has also gone.

Self-assertion and creativity are now positive values in the educational system: both represent an assault against the old kinship and community structure. In industry new patterns of association, focusing, at the extreme, on collective bargaining and strike-action, represent new conceptions of the in-group, demand new loyalties which conflict with older patterns of allegiance. The vote, and the demand for its responsible use, represents a radical democratic and ultimately individualistic perspective that stands in sharp contrast with the old community allegiances too. Conscious interests, consciously-formed associations, have not only caused the erosion but positively militated against the old 'natural' or 'given' social units, often to the bewilderment and shock of older generations.

3

The Response of the Maltese to Religion

Within the context of the changes in Maltese society that we have seen in their political, economic and educational aspects, the striking feature about religion is the way in which it is the complete incarnation of the local scene. Its vitality and expressive power, frequently attested to by foreign observers,[1] point to the extent to which the life of the Church is embedded in the life and activities of the islanders, and particularly to the success achieved by institutionalised religion in establishing itself as the unique superintending and legitimating agency of Maltese life.

Two basic questions immediately arise for the student of recent developments in religion in Malta: (a) to what extent has the Church[2] succeeded in coping with the process of rapid social change in Maltese life and culture, particularly since social change in the last century or more has everywhere throughout Europe challenged the erstwhile functions of institutional religion? and (b) to what extent was the Church passive in the process of change: had it any role in shaping the forces of change?

Quantitative data about religion in Malta is not available in equal degree over the whole period under study. Various monographic studies have been completed over the last fifteen years, however, and these, together with other data collected for the purposes of the present study, will be utilized in an attempt to provide answers to these two fundamental questions.

The relative scarcity of data militates against the adoption in this study — which is intended to focus primarily on the process of change — of the measurement techniques employed by researchers like Lenski,[3] Glock and Stark,[4] and, more recently, by Laeyendecker[5] in their studies of religion and religiosity. What is even more important is the fact that within the special context of Malta — where there is, in effect, only one Church; and where, as Towler[6] points out, not even problems of ecumenism and inter-church relations arise — both Luckmann's paradigm of 'invisible religion',[7] and Campbell's model of 'irreligious man'[8] are equally inapplicable: the phenomena they describe and analyze are as yet practically non-existent as *social* facts. Consequently, the criticism levied against the measurement techniques proposed by these researchers[9] can be considered irrelevant for the purposes of the present study. For similar reasons, Towler's paradigm [10] cannot be utilized and, since divergent religious orientations scarcely exist among the Maltese, this study addresses itself to the different levels of participation and sense of belonging in organized religion. As Luckmann himself suggested in his criticism of Laeyendecker's framework of research, [11] the analysis of this type of church-oriented religion calls for a completely different approach from the one to be used in an analysis of 'civic' and of 'invisible' religion. The Catholic Church in Malta is in a virtually monopolistic position. [12] No variant body exists to express a divergent perspective, and although — as in other Catholic countries — political anti-clericalism has been known in Malta for some time, anti-clericals like Dimech, Strickland, and more recently Mintoff, have always been emphatically 'Catholic anticlericals', in the sense that it is the Catholic Church specifically against which they protested, and which, in its pervasiveness, set the tone and even the issue of debate. As in Italy, as the most comparable major European country, Catholic practice, assumptions, institutions, and ideas, and a general Catholic feeling-tone, are part of the accepted circumstances of life. Local traditions are impregnated with religious meaning, and that religion, which has transmuted local custom, informed and permeated it, is Catholic.

The attempt to suggest answers to the two questions posited earlier can be approached in a variety of ways, of which two have been adopted in this book. This chapter limits itself to one of these, and intends to analyze the intrinsic aspects of religiosity, and to trace the vitality of *structured* religious expression in Malta. In Malta the expression of a person's religious orientation is structured more or less totally and completely within the Church institution itself; and the various degrees of involvement in the life of the institution may be regarded as indicators of the vitality of the response of the Maltese to religion. What is assumed here is that the extent of religious commitment may be measured by the degree of involvement in different aspects of religious life and in religious organizations. Thus, participation in organized movements of the lay apostolate (commonly known as *għaqdiet*) may be regarded as expressing a higher degree of religious commitment than mere participation in religious ritual. Of course, it might be argued that the religious movements are so deeply interwoven with everyday life in Malta that they perform certain social functions for which no other agencies are available, and that therefore involvement in these movements does not represent intensive religiosity as such. With some of the *għaqdiet* this may be true in some respects; and indeed, they are at times bitterly criticized for it; but especially over the last few years, the argument that no other agencies for sociability and the pursuit of 'secular' interests are available can — as has already been indicated in the preceding chapter — no longer be accepted. Other associations do exist, and the wine-shops and bars, the football and band clubs, and even the tailor's or barber's shop, so popular in Malta, have always provided alternative meeting places for people — mostly men, of course — who wanted to while away their free time in good company without getting involved in religious associations. The associations chosen are specifically church-sponsored; are specifically oriented towards active involvement in the apostolate; and some of them — especially that known as MUSEUM, about which more will be said below — impose quite strict rules of conduct and general deportment on their members. In turn, an individual's choice of the priesthood or the religious life points to an even more intensified commitment to the values propagated by religion than a choice to be an *għaqda* member; and the general trends in vocations in Malta will be taken up in our analysis as the 'third grade' of active response to the appeal of religion among the Maltese.

In the subsequent chapter, then, a second method of analyzing religion's grip on Maltese life will be followed. This will not be based on responses elicited by *individuals* about their individual religious behaviour. It will rather be an attempt to check the extent to which the Church, in some form or other, has sought to make itself present in seven dominant areas of social life in Malta.

3.1 Religious Practice

As elsewhere in Catholic Europe, the Church has for centuries involved itself as a vital agency in the celebration and interpretation of the individual's life-cycle, selecting the climactic moments of the individual's biological growth as the occasions for its solemnization of change. The functions of rites of passage are too well understood in the literature to require comment here, and the hold which these celebrations give to the Church over individuals is of great importance, particularly in a society where religious pluralism is virtually unknown. The religious activity associated with birth, puberty, marriage, and death is a powerful social cement in providing legitimations for claims to specific status; in assembling in solemn gatherings all those remotely associated with the individuals whose status is at risk; and in making public in the widest sense (for posterity, and, as the Church would have it, 'in the sight of God') just what is occurring. For the Church, of course, these activities are its claim to indispensability, and the idea is encouraged, and socially maintained, that men cannot properly (and at times properly may mean legally) do without its service. Inevitably, more is involved than a religious ceremony, and in Malta, as in other Catholic countries, there is a powerful interpenetration of religious functions and social festivities. The sociability of the occasion is possible, or so it seems, only because it is an occasion of the greatest religious significance: on the other hand, it is always clear, in folk practice, that the religious solemnization, whilst it legitimates secular celebration and jollification, does not exhaust or monopolize the importance of the occasion. The two occur, each inconceivable without each other. Even in countries where the separation has been forced, and where for example religious ceremonial has been eliminated or diminished, as in civil marriage ceremonies, what is generally noticeable is also the diminution of any sense of social bonding, of communal jollification, and of the legitimation of a traditional, but spontaneous, festivity. [13]

Baptism — and in Malta practically all the indigenous population is baptized — is not merely a perfunctory religious celebration. The initiation rite is always accompanied — even if increasingly at an interval of some days or possibly some weeks — by a reception held by the baby's parents for relatives and friends, and is therefore also an occasion for more sociability, and for the renewal — and the deepening — of social relationships. A mother anxiously looks forward to the occasion when — quite out of pattern with normal occurrence — a considerable number of well-wishers visit her home which is specially decorated for the occasion. [14]

Baptismal rites are extended into childhood and reach two new peaks on the days of first Holy Communion and of Confirmation. At the age of six or seven, all the children of a parish, after careful preparation by specially trained lay teachers — mostly għaqdiet members — receive Holy Communion for the first time. The Sunday when they do so is generally celebrated as a feast day for the whole parish. People throng to the streets through which the procession of white-clad boys and girls, accompanied by parents or guardians, is to pass. The streets themselves are often covered with green leaves and coloured flowers. The għaqdiet, or other lay association centres used for the preparation of the children, are festively decorated; and receptions to celebrate the new stage of Christian belonging are held not only for the children themselves in their respective għaqda, but, as with baptism, by their families at home. Friends and relatives visit the child's home, bringing presents, and their visit provides an occasion for the exchange of news and general gossip. Confirmation day is a similar occasion. As the child gets older, he starts to prepare himself for the day when one of the bishops comes purposely to the parish to confer on him, and on the other children of his age, the sacrament of confirmation. This sacrament is meant to conclude the initiation rites begun with baptism, and introduces the adolescent, now under the guidance of a specially chosen god-parent, into Christian adulthood. The 'at home' scenes of Holy Communion day are repeated, thus providing both a further occasion for sociability among adults, as well as an institutionalized way whereby the child's circle of friends is extended, and his socialization to adult life accelerated.

Up to the age of ten, then, and even during the early years of adolescence, each more important milestone of a child's life is, as a matter of fact if not as a matter of absolute necessity, associated with some kind of religious celebration. This is also the case for both the pre-nuptial engagement stage, and for marriage itself. The engagement party usually starts by the blessing of the rings and a very short instruction by a clergyman. Merrymaking, dancing, and gossip come later. Until the very recent introduction of civil marriage in Malta, [15] the Church used to exercise absolute monopoly over this very important social institution whenever one of the spouses was a Catholic; the relevant canons of *Codex Iuris Canonici* then regulated all the aspects of its valid contraction. The Church also plays an important role in times of grave sickness, when the first call in the event of imminent danger of death is often for a priest, and only afterwards for a doctor. Anionting of the Sick — which was always called that way in Malta, and never anything like 'Extreme Unction' — and the Viaticum are sacraments every Maltese would expect to receive before dying. The Church's influence, as would be expected, extends beyond the death-bed to the graveyard, and even beyond it. Church bells announce one's 'agony' as an appeal for prayer for the departing soul; the Viċi, or Vice-parish priest, is almost exclusively called to stand and pray by the bed-side of the dying. Funerals and burials are organized by Church officials. Most of the cemeteries themselves are Church-owned and maintained. The Addolorata cemetery, which is the biggest cemetery on the island, though state-owned, has a Capuchin friar permanently employed by government. [16]

An individual's life in Malta is therefore, almost necessarily, tied to some measure of Church allegiance. Belonging to the Church and practising its tenets cannot however be equated. Religious practice is very different from mere belonging and must therefore be tested at times and in circumstances as far as possible unconnected with social demands and pressures. When Francois Houtart surveyed the religious situation of Malta in 1958, he noted that there was no point in going out to count heads at Sunday Mass then, because practically everybody was in Church on Sundays: 'No large scale survey of mass attendance on Sundays has been necessary in Malta, for practically all attend mass on Sundays, and quite a high percentage on week-days as well.' [17] From a questionnaire he distributed to parish priests, Houtart discovered however that 'in every area, rural and urban, a number of people refrained from attending Sunday man'. In one village, with a population of 2,000, 10 did not attend mass.

Those not attending mass on Sundays, in some areas would be the same people who were not fulfilling their Easter duties [18] or who were leading a disorderly moral life. [19] But in several cases, those not fulfilling their Easter duties might even so attend Sunday mass. 'On the whole the number of those missing Mass is very low and at present creates no problem other than a personal one'. [20] When Houtart empirically checked his findings by carrying out a survey in three parishes in Malta, the parish priests were proved correct.

The overall impression emerging from the Houtart study had changed considerably by 17 December 1967 when the *Pastoral Research Services* (PRS) conducted a full-scale census of Sunday mass attendance in Malta. It was then discovered that

> 82% of the population who were bound by Church law to attend Sunday Mass went to Mass on census Sunday ... in numbers this meant that 198,150 had attended one of the 803 Masses celebrated between 4.00 a.m. and 8.00 p.m. of that day. It also meant that 43,753 failed to fulfil their Sunday duties ... [21]

A 6,000 sample from the questionnaire returned by each of those who had actually attended mass on census Sunday helped to define the profile of non-attendants. Men were found to be absent from mass more than women (22.7% as compared to 13.9% of the women). [22] It was further discovered that 'the percentage of Mass attendance decreased from the 82.3 of the 7-13 age group to 72.8 with the 30-34 age bracket. It then mounted again to 97.3 in the 50-54 age group, to dip again to 68.2 when it reaches the over 70s'. [23] In the prime of adulthood, people were found to be devoting less time to religious practices: Mass seemed to be 'more appealing to children and to the elderly'. Marital status, too, was found to affect religious practice: married people went to mass less often than those who were single. 'In fact the percentage of non-goers among the married was 21.8, or 3.7 more than the overall rate'. The most dramatic differences between these findings and those of Houtart concerned the practice of the different occupational groupings, the 1967 enquiry showing that religious practice was highest among manual workers who had an absentee rate as low as 6.2%. On the other hand, non-manual workers and self-employed categories had absentee rates of 32.2% and 38.2% respectively. [24]

Because of its essentially voluntary aspects, the frequency of reception of Holy Communion is a better indicator of religious practice than mere attendance for mass — with all its attendant socio-psychological pressures — could ever be deemed to be. Houtart himself noted that from a small Young Christian Workers' enquiry he carried out among 46 young workers, only 16 were found to be receiving Communion. In a further enquiry among a sample of secondary school adolescents — this time made by

Research Agency Malta (RAM) through a mail questionnaire — it was again discovered that reception of communion was less frequent than attendance to mass: 47.7% of the boys and 76.2% of the girls were daily communicants; a further 37.2% of the boys and 16.9% of the girls received Communion weekly; 13.0% of the boys and 5.6% of the girls received Communion only once a month. Of the boys 0.8%, of the girls 1.3% said they received Holy Communion only once annually. [25] Since 1961 no similar study has been conducted in Malta, and there is some reason to suppose that things may have changed in some measure. But the results of the 1961 survey are a good enough indication of the relative depth of religious allegiance among Maltese adolescents: the reception of Communion — a practice completely free of constraint — may be considered to be an indication of the acceptance of Church ideology rather than the result of any form of outside pressure.

Unconstrained religious practices are not however restricted to the attendance at Mass and the reception of Holy Communion; and the realization of the religious ideology into an accepted mode of behaviour can also be measured by the frequency of confession, by the extent of personal prayer, and by the participation in the general educative courses organized or sponsored by the Church. No quantitative data on the absolute frequency of confessions in Malta is available. It is often remarked by priests however that the practice is steadily on the decline. In 1959, Houtart reported that of the 46 members of the Young Christian Workers he questioned on religious practice, 20 used to go to confession regularly whilst 26 did not, and he noted that, 'the fact of having a regular confessor varied according to social status: the boys who have one for example are fewer among the workers and especially among the dockyard workers'. [26] The 1961 RAM survey on adolescents at school subsequently revealed that 35% of the boys and 25% of the girls had a regular confessor, but noted that 'girls seemed to find it more difficult to get one'. [27] Boys generally were found to establish contact with a regular confessor at school whilst girls did so at their parish church. Boys said they frequently used confession to discuss with a priest 'their knowledge about religion, girls and sins' (in this order), whilst girls preferred to discuss 'their boy-friends, the facts of life, and sex difficulties'. Marriage and the expectations of adolescents of either sex about life's prospects came up very frequently during their contacts with priests in the confessional.

In 1972, another survey among secondary-level adolescents was carried out by the Catechetical Commission. [28] 11.8% out of a total response of 415 boys and girls said they went to confession once every week; 19.2% did so once a fortnight; and 26.3% once every month. A further 9.8% said they went to confession every time they felt the need to do so. The difficulties noted in the 1961 survey regarding the availability of priest-confessors for the services of girls were once more noted in 1972: only 4.7% of the girls, as compared to 19.3% of the boys, said they went to confess every week. Girls however registered higher rates than boys for fortnightly and monthly confessions. The 1972 survey revealed several other important trends in the practice: as young men and women progressed in their educational attainments, they tended gradually to drop weekly confessions. Only 9.6% of class V students went to confession every week as compared to 13.4% of those in class III; and it is significant that this diminution appears to be primarily linked to class rather than to age. Traditional practices have been definitely changing, even though up to that time perhaps not drastically, and contact with the priest was maintained, and — with the exception of 1.0% of the boys who failed to reply to that question — each of them had at least a bi-monthly encounter with a priest.

Whether it takes the 'private' or the 'group' form, prayer is also a very important constraint-free indicator of religious practice. The Maltese bent for prayer has been amply documented over the years. De Domenico [29] mentioned several instances of the earnestness with which the islanders turned to God, to the Blessed Virgin, and to the saints for help and patronage. The daily recitation of the rosary, though again losing popularity, is still a rule for many families, and is normally recited in the evenings before retiring and, in the villages especially, often on the doorsteps during the cool summer evenings. Most houses are consecrated to the Sacred Heart, many bear the name of a saint, and one often finds a small carved representation of a saint placed on the facade of houses. [30] Statues of the saints throng the streets and fill every otherwise empty corner in the village squares. In Valletta itself, one finds a different statue at almost every corner, in a special niche overlooking the respective block of buildings.

Religious celebrations on the diocesan level, like that of Christ the King held in autumn, are usually well-attended. So are similar celebrations on the parish level. The frequent processions held in each town or village, especially those of Our Lady of Sorrows which is held in the week preceding Holy Week, of Corpus Christi, and of the Sacred Heart, both commonly held some time in June, seem to attract large numbers of people either to take part in them or at least to watch them go by.

The frequency and content of prayer in Malta has been studied several times as part of some larger sociological piece of research. Houtart's Young Christian Workers' enquiry showed that 'of a total of 46 young workers, 22 prayed regularly, 21 sometimes, and 3 never'. In yet another enquiry by interview carried out by Houtart, it was discovered that 'many people prayed in the daily circumstances of life like meals, morning and night, visits to church whilst a considerable number prayed on special occasions, especially when in some kind of difficulty'.[31] Similar results were forthcoming from the replies of the RAM survey among Schoolgoing Adolescents in 1961. It was then discovered that as many as 54.4% of the boys and 54.1% of the girls used to make a daily visit to the Blessed Sacrament.[32] The extent of religious practice within the family also became apparent from this last survey when it was noted that 63.2% of the boys and 66.2% of the girls reported that they generally recited the Rosary with the other members of their families.

The results of a 1968 PRS survey on the *Religious Attitudes and Behaviour of University Students in Malta* are perhaps more interesting. The respondents are all of age, and their university experience might be expected to have drawn them away from traditional practices enjoined by their families. Personal prayer was one of the areas specifically covered by the survey. To the open-ended question 'When do you feel you must pray?', 24% explicitly replied 'Always'. Only 5% declared that they 'never' or 'rarely' prayed. Most of the students (66%) prayed when they were in trouble. 20% felt they ought to pray in times of joy and out of gratitude. The report noted 'this general trend ran through all the faculties. But law and architecture students showed considerably higher percentages for praying in times of trouble, while, together with theology students, they recorded the lowest percentages for praying in times of joy and gratitude'. It is interesting to note that 15% of all students replied that they felt the need to pray before examinations, with 16.5% of the Arts faculty students, 21.3% from the Science faculty, and 19.5% of the medical students admitting that they normally did so. On the other hand, practically no student from the Law, Theology and Architecture faculties mentioned that he or she felt the special need for prayer on such occasions. The frequency of prayer also gives an indication of religious involvement, something which was then found to be quite intensive: 61% of students prayed to God daily, and only 4% declared that they never prayed to God at all. As was to be expected, the highest incidence of those who prayed daily to God, to Our Lady, and to saints came from the Theology faculty, even though none of the other faculties registered any marked deviation from the general rate. [33]

A similar survey held among students of the Junior College during 1973 showed that these tendencies still generally persisted among Malta's youngest generation of university students. Even though critical of the 'average' priest (27.3% of respondents considered him 'antiquated'), and of the ecclesiastical authorities (37% considering them 'good pastoral guides'; 48.1% describing them 'old fashioned'; 29.1% 'too money-minded';

and 44.2% describing them with other appellatives not arising from the questionnaire), many students were found to be 'helped by meditation' (47.5%), and by prayer (72.3%). Church functions, and the sacraments, though still generally made use of, were not always considered as helpful as expected, and the combination of negative attitudes to the Church and the institutions it patronizes, with a positive attitude to the need for God in the students' life, though not specifically commented upon by the compilers of the report, undoubtedly gives some intimation of the possibly new attitudes towards religion in general, and the Church in particular, which are being generated among Malta's up-and-coming intelligentsia. [34]

As already suggested, religious practice can also be measured by the extent to which people participate in the general educative courses organized by the Church. Different organizations within the Church, as will be evident from later sections, cater for the needs arising from different circumstances, but a typically Maltese institution within the Church has grown over the years as a sort of 'in-service training course' for all baptised: *lenten sermons.* Lent is a time when every Christian is bound to prepare himself for the re-enactment of the Paschal Mystery in his own life. *L-eżerċizzi,* or special courses of sermons, talks and discussions held in almost every church for different categories of people, attempt to remind those who participate in them of this great event, and help them prepare themselves for the Paschal renewal. Each course usually lasts for a whole week of daily meetings. Up to some years ago, five main streams of *eżerċizzi* used to be held: *tal-Irġiel* (the course for married males, *tan-Nisa* (for married females), *tal-Ġuvintur* (for unmarried males), *tax-Xebbiet* (for unmarried females), and *tat-Tfal* (the course specially prepared for children). Every parish, and very often every church, would organize each course independently of each other; would have its own promotion campaign; and would try to attract a large audience by selecting a good and popular preacher. Over the last few years, however, various other categories have been instituted, and since 1974 special courses have been organized for teenagers, for engagaed couples, for married couples, and for other social groupings both on the diocesan level as well as in some of the parishes. The places where these formative gatherings are now held have also changed, and are no longer strictly tied to a church: courses for teenagers are held in dance halls or theatres specially rented by the Church for the occasion; those for workers are often held during the mid-day break on the very shop floor of their factories or other place of work. Attendance at these courses — then still being held only in churches — was the subject of a PRS survey for two consecutive years, 1964 and 1965. In 1964 a 44% attendance rate was recorded among adults who, according to the PRS estimates, were 'supposed' to attend one of the courses. A year later a drop of 2% was noted.[35]

Religious practice in Malta is thus seen to be both extensive and comprehensive. It can be regarded as perhaps the most important manifestation of Maltese social life, patterned as it is on the dictates of only one creed. In consequence, the Church in Malta can claim extensive control over a vast area of human activity spread over the lifespan of every individual. All this, of course, is not in itself sufficient proof of an internal religious commitment, but it certainly provides a significant body of objective data of real importance in assessing religiosity.

3.2 Participation in the 'Għaqdiet' System

A second very important indicator of the vitality of Church religion in Malta is the spread of lay apostolate movements, known in Malta as *għaqdiet*. As already indicated, the quality of 'response' obtained in this area can itself be considered an 'intensification' of the response obtained in respect of religious practice: here participation entails not only the acceptance of norms and values, but also an avowal actively to promote them. Within the Maltese context, the lay association movement can be broadly divided into three streams. The first incorporates movements or associations to which the term *għaqdiet* specifically applies, and is made up of unts operating on a parochial level, but with diocesan co-ordination. Five major associations fall in this category: the various divisions of Maltese Catholic Action (*Azzjoni Kattolika Maltija*), the MUSEUM movement, the Marian Congregation (*Kongregazzjoni Marjana*), the Legion of Mary, and the Young Christian Workers (*Żgħażagħ Haddiema Nsara*). The second stream of lay apostolate movements is primarily composed of specialized associations which serve as facilitating agencies whereby the Church can bring its message to particular areas of human activity. The Cana Movement (*Moviment ta' Kana*) and the University Students Catholic Movement are just two examples of this type of association. The last stream would be composed of those other associations which, though very often replicated in different parishes, neither have any strict inter-parochial relationships nor call for any kind of particularized rituationzation of a person's behaviour in conformity with strict membership rules. Such are the Apostleship of Prayer (*l-Appostolat tat-Talb*), the Christian Mothers Association (*Ommijiet Insara*), *Ċenaklu* (groups of people interested in vocational recruitment), the Brotherhood of the Holy Name of God (*ix-Xirka tal-Isem Imqaddes t'Alla*), the Third Orders, and the various Confraternities.

Because of its spread and consequent impact, the *għaqdiet* (or first)

group is the most important in the present context; and what follows will
be limited to an examination of this type of lay apostolate movement.
Already in 1956, Houtart had noted that:

> the diocese has a good number of lay movements for the spiritual
> formation of members and the lay apostolate in various fields of
> activity ... They are playing an important role in the life of the Church
> ... the religious formation given by these movements in Malta is
> greatly needed and is one of the main sources, especially among the
> young, of the general religious education of the population.. [6]

Each *għaqda* has a specific elan, and its activities are found to be organized
in strict conformity to its rules. Most parishes have more than one *għaqda*,
and so an individual has a relatively wide option if he wants to join in
the lay apostolate movement. With the exception of MUSEUM, the *għaqdiet*
have all been imported from abroad: 'Catholic Action' follows the Italian
model, the 'Legion of Mary' the Irish pattern, the 'Young Christian
Workers' the Belgian and French systems, and the 'Marian Congregation'
the Jesuit style. MUSEUM, standing for 'Magister Utinam Sequatur Evan
gelium Universus Mundus', is one of the oldest societies of the lay apostolate on the island. As its official name 'Societas Doctrinae Christianae'
indicates, MUSEUM was founded with a specific aim in view: the training
of the laity for the spread of religious knowledge. As early as 1907, when
Dun Ġorġ Preca started the movement, the motto of its members
was *Nitgħallem biex ngħallem* — let me learn that I may then teach
In spite of difficulties at the time of its establishment, [7] extending even
to an order by Mgr Salv Grech, then Vicar General, for the closure of
the centres Dun Ġorġ had opened, MUSEUM is today very firmly established and plays an important role in the religious education of the
people of most of Malta's towns and villages.

The spiritual formation of MUSEUM members, be they male or female.
is imparted through a life of prayer and instruction. Members prepare
themselves for the daily catechism of children, a task now confided practically exclusively to them among the *għaqdiet*, by a daily hour spent
studying Scripture and Church doctrine. Penance and self-denial underlie
their whole life; they may not marry; they are not allowed to smoke;
as a rule males do not wear neckties or long hair, and females have to
wear a special oldfashioned black dress; they are forbidden to attend most.
sorts of public entertainment.

The spread of the various *għaqdiet* in Malta took place to a large
extent during the thirties and the forties, as evident from *Table 3.2-1*.
Socio-religious conditions, such as the increased educational attainment
of the people as a whole, facilitated their extensive spread. But it is
to important individual figures that the Maltese generally attribute the

Table 3.2-1   *Dates of Foundation by Decade and by Association of Ghaqdiet.*

	-1910	1910-19	1920-29	1930-39	1940-49	1950-54	1955-59	1960-64	1965-69	1970-72	TOTAL	N.A.
MALES												
CA MEN	—	—	—	1	13	2	1	2	1	1	21	1
CA GUV	—	—	—	5	3	2	1	—	1	1	13	3
KK. MM	—	—	—	—	—	1	—	1	1	—	3	—
LEGION	—	—	—	—	18	—	2	3	6	—	29	2
MUSEUM	5	9	4	10	4	5	—	3	1	—	41	—
YCW	—	—	—	—	1	1	1	2	1	—	6	3
TOTAL	5	9	4	16	39	11	5	11	11	2	113	9
FEMALES												
CA WMEN	—	—	—	1	9	6	6	7	3	1	33	3
CA XEB	—	—	—	11	8	4	—	—	3	1	25	7
KK.MM	6	4	2	1	3	1	—	6	2	—	25	2
LEGION	—	—	—	—	12	4	2	8	4	—	30	3
MUSEUM	1	9	4	12	6	1	—	2	2	—	37	4
YCW	—	—	—	—	—	1	3	9	—	—	13	—
TOTAL	7	13	6	25	38	17	11	32	12	2	163	19
GRAND TOTAL	12	22	10	41	77	28	16	43	23	4	276	28

Abbreviations:
CA MEN: Catholic Action Married Men Section; CA GUV: Catholic Action Unmarried Men; KK.MM: Marian Congregations; LEGION: Legion of Mary; YCW: Young Christian Workers; CA WMEN: Catholic Action Married Women; CA XEB: Catholic Action Unmarried Women; N.A.: No answer.
Source: C. Pace, *Maltese Lay Associations in Profile* (PRS, 1972), p.5.

sudden sprouting of these movements. In his early speeches as Archbishop of Malta in the early forties, Gonzi himself often demanded the spread and re-organization of Catholic Action. [38] Dun Ġorġ, too, despite his fame as a counsellor-cum-healer, retained his simplicity and eventually became an institution. People flocked to listen to his sermons and talks, to ask counsel from him, putting anything he said into practice without question. In return people were keen to assist him in the promotion of his *għaqda* whenever he wanted to open a new centre.

An attempt to make a complete census of *għaqdiet* membership by the Pastoral Research Services in 1972 was only partly successful. 78 out of the 374 groups then in existence in the diocese of Malta failed to return the questionnaire sent to them. In most cases it was later discovered that the non-respondent groups were actually the least active. In the report subsequently published by PRS, estimates based on the assumption 'that the membership per age group of a non-respondent group is equal to the average membership of respondent groups of the same association in the same region' [39] were produced, and published with the actual figures obtained from the returned questionnaires. For the purposes of the 1972 census, membership was taken to include even the children attending the catechism courses offered by the older members of the various associations. Overall membership was found naturally to be highest for the 5-8 age group since attendance for catechism in preparation for the reception of first Holy Communion is virtually compulsory. Membership figures tended to show a decline after confirmation when attendance for catechism classes is no longer mandatory. For all the age groups except for the 9 to 13 age bracket, membership was found to be higher among females. For the 14-year-old age group, a very sharp drop in membership was noticed. From this age onwards, as many as 80-90% of young men in Malta shed their direct links with the *għaqdiet*. Pace noted that the

> formation during these crucial years (i.e. over 14) depends more importantly on other institutions such as the school, the church liturgy, youth clubs, literature and mass-media generally, as well as on personal contact with priests and other influentials. [40]

Among the old-aged only 2% of males and 3-4% of all females were members of any of the five associations under study. *Table 3.2-2* spells out the details of the distribution by age group.

Despite the at times low figures in the membership levels, the enduring influence of the *għaqdiet* should not be underestimated. Contact with the *għaqdiet* system comes in the formative years of an individual's life, and as with any form of education the principles imparted then, are likely to be of great significance in moulding individual behaviour and character. A detailed study of *għaqdiet* membership by parish reveals that small villages

Table 3.2-2   *Għaqdiet Membership by Age*

Age Group	General Population		All Associations			
			Respondents		Estimates	
	Males	Females	Males	Females	Males	Females
5-8	9031	8534	2668	3819	3123	4264
			29.5%	44.8%	34.2%	50.0%
9-13	14008	13635	2697	2722	3270	3224
			19.3%	20.0%	23.5%	23.6%
14-19	17436	17264	1331	2722	1806	1392
			7.6%	6.6%	10.4%	8.1%
20-29	23834	26301	345	741	456	926
			1.4%	2.8%	1.9%	3.5%
30-49	29751	34122	341	1050	434	1331
			1.1%	3.1%	1.5%	3.9%
50-64	16851	18674	344	885	463	1113
			2.0%	4.7%	2.7%	6.0%
65+	10296	13434	190	304	305	380
			1.8%	2.3%	3.0%	2.8%
All Ages	121211	131960	7916	10652	9857	12630
			6.5%	8.1%	8.1%	9.6%

like Mġarr (18.1%), Marsaxlokk (13.5%) and Hal-Safi (14.8%) registered the highest percentages of participation. Medium-sized towns and villages like Siġġiewi (12.4%), Vittoriosa (10.3%), and Floriana (8.8%) also proved to have high membership rates. Differences may however be noticed in the more urbanized centres like Valletta (with St Paul's for example having a rate of only 5.9%), Sliema (with a 4.7% rate in St Gregory), and Senglea (3.6%).

When trends in membership were analyzed, it was discovered that the

> increase in membership is more frequent than decrease among children under 14 ... Attendance of children at *għaqdiet* centres [was] generally seen to increase ... Adult membership [was] seen generally to drop. Adolescent figures showed only narrow differences, the majority being on the side of increase for males, and with decrease on the female side ... [41]

When Pace analyzed the terminal education of a random sample of

Table 3.2-3 Terminal Education of Għaqdiet members compared with that of the General Population

| | MALES | | | | | | FEMALES | | | | | | MALES & FEMALES | |
| | 14 - 39 | | 40 + | | TOTAL | | 14 - 39 | | 40 + | | TOTAL | | GRAND TOTAL | |
	General Population %	Sample %	General Population %	Sample %	General Population %	Sample %	General Population %	Sample %	General Population %	Sample %	General Population %	Sample %	General Population %	Sample %
No School	3.3	2.2	27.5	2.9	16.2	2.5	3.3	2.1	8.8	9.2	16.5	5.6	6.3	4.9
First Level	64.4	22.5	52.0	60.0	57.8	58.9	72.7	59.0	59.8	75.0	66.2	70.1	42.2	61.
Second Level (General)	23.0	34.8	14.5	27.1	18.5	31.4	21.4	17.8	10.3	13.4	15.8	16.5	17.0	20.6
Second Level (Vocational)	6.8	33.7	2.2	7.1	4.3	22.1	1.2	2.5	0.4	0.5	7.9	1.6	2.4	6.8
Third Level	2.5	6.8	3.8	2.9	3.2	5.1	1.4	18.6	0.7	1.9	10.6	6.2	2.1	5.9
Total	100.0	100.0	100.0	100.0	100.0	100.0	100.0	100.0	100.0	100.0	100.0	100.0	100.0	100.0

Source: Based on Tables 28 & 29 of Ch. Pace Maltese Lay Associations in Profile, (Malta, PRS, 1972).

members, he discovered that 'the higher the education attainments of a section of the population, the greater the rate at which individuals belonging to
it join the *għaqdiet*'. [42] *Table 3.2-3*, composed from the data given by Pace,
demonstrates this clearly. Maltese who never attended school made up
between 25 and 30% of the over-40 section of the general population.
Association members with the same level of education account for 9.2%
of the females from the same age group, and for only 2.9% of the males.
The differences diminish as the level of education increases: even though
only 2.1% of the general population attained third-level terminal education,
7.5% of the total *għaqdiet* membership is recruited from this category.
Even though literacy can in no way be considered the only factor affecting
għaqdiet membership, some correlation between the two factors obviously
exists. Literacy generally creates the need for wider, and sustained, communication, and the *għaqdiet* system, especially in the 'old' Malta might
have provided an excellent — though, as has already been indicated, not
exclusive — opportunity where this could be affected. They may also
have provided a ready-made outlet for a greater measure of involvement
in social life, something which is itself generated by knowledge and the
acquisition of leadership techniques which result from it. If this is so —
and if this remains so in the coming years when more opportunities for
sociability will come into existence — the *għaqdiet* system, one would
have to admit, would have been providing a sort of service which is
typically their own. It could however be argued that illiterates are generally
less religious, and so feel the attraction to join one of the *għaqdiet* much
less than their 'more educated', and 'more religious' counterparts. Literacy
and religiousness, on the other hand, have been known to work against
each other rather than together. As things stand at present, most especially
at this critical stage of evolution of Maltese society and of the Church in
Malta, it is extremely difficult to determine how these factors are related.
It remains to be seen whether the extent to which the more educated
cleave to the *għaqdiet* has been a temporary phenomenon, resulting from
the relatively undeveloped state of leadership or quasi-leadership roles in
Maltese society, or whether, through some incidental process generated
by church activity, this will tend to be a constant, and so distinctive,
feature of religious life in Malta.

    The role the *għaqdiet* network has played over the last few decades
in the continued religious socialization of the Maltese has been vital in
many respects. Through the dedicated services of the many individuals
who wanted to take religion more seriously than the majority of the
population, religious doctrine has been diffused to the general population.
As was made evident by the 1966 *Christus Rex* survey on Maltese Catechists, they were instrumental — almost exclusively so — in the instruction

of the majority of the current population of Malta. [43] It is very difficult to assess the effect of the influence which these dedicated men and women have exercised; since contact with them comes in a person's formative stage in life, and hence is likely to affect him throughout life. More specifically, it still has to be seen whether a more widespread education will reinforce the *għaqdiet* system (as Pace would seem to imply), or whether this very same improvement in the population's educational standards will negatively affect the attractiveness of the *għaqdiet* system in favour of a less 'structuralized' response to a person's religious commitments. Such a phenomenon is already widespread in other countries, and could give rise to the eruption of a multitude of spontaneous groups where, with more flexibility than is possible in the *għaqdiet* as they have developed in Malta, the same urge for a pronounced religious commitment by the individual might still be expressed.

3.3 A Multitude of Vocations

A third and more telling indicator of the response of the Maltese to religion is the number of vocations in Malta. The abundance of priests in both dioceses gave rise in the past to the satirical comment quoted by Wignacourt that, 'Malta would have been a delightful place if every priest were a tree ...' [44] According to the figures produced by Forrestall, [45] and to those circulated officially by the Vatican Congregation for the Clergy in 1970, [46] Malta had a higher priest-people ratio than any other country. The total number of diocesan priests resident in Malta and Gozo on 31 December, 1972 was 599, 419 in Malta and 180 in Gozo. With an estimated population of 298,813 at the end of that year, Malta had a ratio of 3.4 priests for every 1000 population. It is not surprising therefore that foreign bishops consider the Maltese islands 'vocation islands', and frequently visit the two seminaries there in an attempt to invite seminarians to join them at least for a period. Maltese priests, both secular and religious, working beyond the confines of the islands, and scattered in dioceses spread over the five continents, run into several hundreds. *Table 3.3-1* demonstrates how Malta compares with other countries in the priest-people ratio.

As evident from *Table 3.3-2*, the total number of vocations to the priesthood in Malta since 1911 has tended to increase with the increase in the general population. The rate of priests per 1000 poplation in 1970 for the two dioceses was lower than what it had been in 1911, but not excessively so. Bigger differences can however be noted when figures for the diocesan clergy are analyzed separately from those for religious clergy. The absolute number of diocesan priests has fallen, and this fact, coupled with the natural increase in the population, has produced a more than

Table 3.3-1 *Priest-People Ratio for Europe*

	Catholic Population in thousands	Catholic Population Priests per 10,000
Malta	306	34.2
Holland	5,271	17.4
Switzerland (and Liechtenstein)	2,771	16.9
Luxembourg	319	16.5
U.K.	4,975	15.3
Belgium	8,901	14.8
Ireland	4,036	14.6
Italy	47,002	13.5
France	39,023	11.7
Spain	32,379	10.8
Austria	6,707	8.8
West Germany	30,706	8.8

Source: Vatican figures for 1969.

Table 3.3-2 *Diocesan Priests, 1911 - 1970*

	1911	1931	1963	1970
Malta				
Number	553	483	423	419
Rate per 1000 population	2.9	2.2	1.4	1.5
Ratio of priest to population	342	451	708	687
Gozo				
Number	181	160	155	154
Rate per 1000 poulation	7.9	6.7	5.7	5.9
Ratio of priest to population	125	149	173	168

Source: Maltese Priests 1911 - 1970 (PRS, 1970).

proportional fall in the priest-people ratio. Things were different with the religious orders, and one notices a more than proportionate increase in the number of vocations to the religious state than the actual increase in the population; a fact which results in a better 'religious' priest-people ratio in 1970 (1.5) than that of 1911 (1.1). [47] Gozo, too, must be dealt with separately: the smaller island proves itself to be considerably richer in vocations. In 1911, for example, the priest-people ratio in the sister island was that of one priest for every 125 persons, whilst that of Malta was one priest for every 342 persons. By 1970 the ratios of both dioceses had fallen, but the differences were still notable.

The number of priests, religious and secular, compares very favourably with the number of persons in the other professions within Malta itself, as evident from *Table 3.3-3*, which portrays the situation obtaining in 1967, when the last population census was taken.

There were as many as 347 Maltese priests (123 diocesan and 224 religious) working abroad, attracted either by the missionary ideal or by an earnestness to work with co-nationals in their new countries.

The abundance of vocations in Malta is not restricted to males; and a similarly large number of girls join one of the twenty-five different types of religious communities that thrive in the Maltese islands. In 1970, a study of Female Religious Vocations in the Maltese Ecclesiastical Province as from 1911 to 1966 was published by F. Mizzi. [48] The figures this study provided revealed that over the whole fifty-five year span, the overall ratio of nuns and sisters to every 1000 female population had gone up considerably. In 1911, there had been 5.93 nuns or sisters for every 1000 females; in 1966 the rate was 10.32 sisters per 1000 females. In the Archdiocese of Malta alone, absolute numbers went up from 591 in 1911 to 1437 in 1966, thus increasing the ratio of nuns and sisters to every 1000 females in the larger island from 6.3 in 1911 to 9.4 in 1966. As with male vocations, ratios in Gozo were always much higher than their Maltese equivalents: the rate of nuns and sisters for every 1000 females there had risen from 3.2 in 1911 to 20.0 in 1966. In 1966, therefore, there was a nun or sister for every 50 females in Gozo; in Malta the ratio was less than half, with a nun or sister for every 106 females. Comparative figures are presented in *Table 3.3-4.*

The relevance of trends in vocational recruitment as an indicator of the vitality of the response of the Maltese to religion is obvious. Continuous recruitment for leadership roles guarantees the perpetuation of ideologies and systems which could not otherwise hold together; but which, in the long run, would collapse or gradually disappear without the dedicated support of persons who have made their promotion and extension their own task in life. This is typically the case with the resilience evident

Table 3.3-3   *Professionals in Malta and Gozo, 1967*

| Occupation | Place of Residence | | | |
| | Maltese Islands | | Malta Only | |
	Male	Female	Male	Female
All occupations	73,779	20,588	68,491	19,153
Professional/Technical and Related	6,005	4,902	5,514	4,327
of which:				
Architects	70	—	68	—
General Practitioners	196	4	186	4
Specialists: Medical and Surgical and Pathologists	92	11	91	11
Dentists	27	4	27	4
Teachers: pre-first level	5	17	5	17
first level	1,051	1,654	887	1,457
secondary level	437	263	416	253
third level	97	24	97	24
PRIESTS	503	—	355	—
Monks and Nuns	824	1,778	783	1,500
Lawyers	114	2	113	2
Legal Procurators	18	1	15	1
Notaries	41	—	33	—
Judges, Magistrates	17	—	17	—
Economists/Statisticians	7	—	7	—

Source: Malta Census 1967, Report on Economic Activities (Malta, Dept of Statistics, undated), vol. I, Table E2.

Table 3.3-4   *Sisters in Malta and Gozo, 1911 - 1966*

	1911		1921		1931		1966	
	Malta	Gozo	Malta	Gozo	Malta	Gozo	Malta	Gozo
Number of Nuns and Sisters	591	37	761	105	849	145	1437	281
Rate of Nuns and Sisters per 1000 Population	2.3	3.2	7.8	8.8	7.6	12.5	9.4	20.0
Ratio of Nuns and Sisters to Female Population	159	312	128	114	131	80	106	—50

Sources: Mizzi, F.P., *Religious Vocations in the Maltese Ecclesiastical Province* (PRS, 1970); and *Census of Female Religious* (PRS, 1966).

in religion in Malta. Despite the periodic restrictions imposed upon the sometimes disdained life-styles of priests and sisters, the extent of influence exercised by the religious upon the secular aspects of Maltese social life, though diminishing, is still significant; and the Maltese social system generally still maintains this situation. Acceptance of, and admiration for, those who choose the religious life — apparent in the high status, prestige and confidence accorded to priests and nuns — is still widespread; and the indications are that if the incumbents of these roles consistently demonstrate that their choice has been motivated by an awareness to higher values, and a desire to commit themselves totally, it will remain so for the immediate, and perhaps even for the more distant future.

The overall picture of the quality and intensity of religious life in Malta, emerging from the preceding considerations of the three different levels of the involvement of the Maltese in the life of the Church, already starts to suggest answers to the two basic questions on the relationship between religion and social change as set out at the outset of this chapter. A more complete answer can only be obtained after more detailed consideration of the effort of the Church to maintain its presence in areas of Maltese social life, in addition to the response elicited in individuals in their relationships with God. It is this attempt of the Church to sustain its operation as widely as possible in social institutions that is our concern in the next chapter.

4

The Place of Religion in Maltese Societal Organization

In its attempt to select the climatic moments of the individual's biological and psychological growth as the occasion for solemnizing change, legitimizing social status and achievement, and eliciting personal response to its tenets, the Church, most especially in a non-pluralist society, has never restricted its interests to the private life of its individual members. Even in these intimate aspects of his life, the individual has been less its concern than the communities within which individuals participate. It is only in the atomized industrial societies of the West, perhaps, where the Church even appears to be primarily involved with individual well-being and personal identity. In more traditional societies, its function has been essentially social, and even its solemnization of the climactic moments of the individual's life-cycle have, in reality, had important consequences for the life of the community. It is in the community that the individual's status has been at issue, in the community that his claims, responsibilities, and social identity have had to be established and reinforced. Hence religious legitimations have always extended beyond the individual, and its reinforcement of the social order and of social arrangements have in themselves been the basis for the individual's own status in the community. By its very nature, the Church attempts, as Troeltsch put it, to 'become part of the existing social order',[1] to make itself an indispensable feature of existing social conditions, providing, very often, legitimation to existing social structure whilst promoting itself as the optimum integrative mechanism. Obviously, this is more easily achieved in comparatively simple, homogenous, and monolithically-organized societies, the very nature of which postulates the existence of heavy biases against any form of outside intervention in the areas of traditional beliefs, behaviour patterns, and in the ordering of social life generally. In situations — like Malta's — where the governing body already represented a distinctly foreign — even if at times welcome — power, this type of situation becomes even more articulated, and the Church, being the only indigenous institution with a longstanding heritage and claims of eternal usefulness, acquires added prominence, easily intertwines with social structure, and commonly acquires features which — if seen from a distance and out of their social context — may appear to be out of harmony with its own professed aims and practices. In reality, however, these features, accompanying functions, and secondary institutions are often found to be the response of a well-rooted and generally accepted agency to the practical needs arising out of the life of a community perturbed with the problems of cohesion and persistence. A number of the Church's present day functions in Malta may — because of the process of structural differentiation inevitable even in a small society as it undergoes modernization — be essentially temporary, but all the same indispensable at this particular moment in history. Meanwhile, they also serve as the basis for a further consolidation of the Church's claim to its own indispensability, and translate in understandable terms — a very useful thing when the population is just emerging from a state of mass illiteracy — the ideology at the basis of its universalistic claims.

Over the years, and even more so over the last few decades, the Church in Malta has had — primarily as a result of its unique standing in the island — ample scope to develop functions along the lines indicated. Recent social change, and the ensuing accentuated process of structural differentiation of Maltese social life, themselves provided new occasions for the Church to act in favour of the quality of life in the absence of 'secular' agencies to do the job; and in turn, in its attempt — whether consciously followed or not is another matter — to consolidate its position in a society no longer tied to traditional patterns of thought and behaviour, but of one caught in the cross-currents of technological and ideological advancement. Its presence in the educational, communal (whether village or town-based), political, economic, familial, migratory and touristic, and media sectors of the contemporary scene will now be analyzed. The data provided by such an excursus in the Church's activity in these vital area of social life in Malta, together with that already obtained from the preceding analysis of the Maltese individual's response to religion, will provide the framework for an overall appraisal of the involvement of the Church — conceived in its institutional aspects — in recent social change in Malta.

4.1 The Church's Role in the Provision of Education

The process of structural differentiation in Malta has already led to the considerable loss of control in education by the Church authorities. We have documented the growth of formal education in a foregoing chapter,[2] and the early process of growth was one in which the Church formalized an involvement with the socialization of the child which stemmed from the intimacy of religious involvement in social life and everyday affairs. The Church made the beginning in education, first for its own professionals and then for a wider public; it was to the Church that the task of providing instruction fell when the educational system itself was enlarged; [3] it was to clergy that recourse had to be made when primary education was made obligatory by legislation, [4] although this could hardly have been the intention of the political authorities at the time. Apart from this steady formalization of involvement, it was also the case that traditionally it was to the priest to whom parents looked for the moral, spiritual, and social development of their children — and, if intellectual development was itself at all at issue, that too fell to the clergy or to a section of the clergy. The process of social change has, however, been a process in which the easy association of the very words 'education' and 'religion', or 'upbringing' and 'morality', has diminished. [5] Whereas once the very stuff of education was 'true religion' or religious knowledge, the demands of a more technically advanced society are that the educated man should be the technically or professionally accomplished man, the able role-performer rather than the cultivated individual.

Not only has religion ceased to be so important an element in the school curriculum, but the religious implications of other subjects — literature, history, and even the knowledge of natural phenomena — have also declined. The content of education has itself been purged of much of its religious content, and the affinities which once seemed so apparent, between an understanding of nature and an understanding of God's creation, or a knowledge of history and an apprehension of God's wider purposes, are no longer self-evident, and may indeed be completely obscure. When Malta was still relatively untouched by the outside world, except for the somewhat insulated occupying forces, the continuities of religion and education were more readily seen: education was for a man's life, and since the life-chances were (emigration apart, and that never as a well-envisaged, purposed goal from early life) relatively circumscribed, so the function of education was to make sense of life as it was lived in a relatively static cultural environment. It was a perfect context for religion as it existed in pre-war Malta. The main elements of change were those affecting the individual's life cycle, as they affected him and impinged on his family and kinsfolk, and to lesser degree, his neighbours and fellow-villagers. These processes of change were sanctified by religious rituals. The meaning which religion provided for the individual's life cycle was intimately associated with the kind of knowledge acquired from whatever formal education he had. As long as these events, these regular, calculable items, and the incidental deviations associated with them, were the major incidents of life, religion had a well institutionalized set of generally satisfactory, and satisfying, procedures with which to provide them. Education was concerned with self-control, social control, the realization of a meaningful universe, and the satisfaction of legitimated rewards and statuses in this world, and the prospect of their continuance in the next. Now all these continuities have been disrupted. New knowledge has been required for economic ends, as these have steadily changed. New prospects of 'salvation', and in particular recourse to planning, conscious social organization, economic calculation, and the competitive search for status-enhancing roles and relationships, have made the old regular religious procedures less adequate. The Church, too, has changed in an attempt to cope with the situation — a situation more radically changed in continental Europe than in Malta, of course. Just as its once essentially localized, piecemeal operations — which may often have depended somewhat on the personal temperament and willingness, energy and enthusiasm of particular priests — have given way to more formal structures, as in the Cana Movement, [6] so in education new goals have been accepted, and new bodies of secular knowledge have steadily been incorporated into the acceptable body of educational matter. The curriculum has expanded, even in a sense exploded, both for the teaching of priests themselves — who can no longer be satisfied with a narrow scholastic approach — and for the general public of young people. As teaching has passed from the hands of religious to the hands of secular teachers, once these became available — even if not without the enormous contribution of the Church which had organized teacher training for so long — and as this continues, [7] so religion is likely to become increasingly a compartment of knowledge, rather than its constant underpinning philosophical base. That religion will continue to be accepted as important, and perhaps even as essential in some aspects in Maltese education, may be expected, at least for the foreseeable future, primarily because of still strong pressures accruing from the Maltese family and its traditions. But that its place and influence has visibly diminished in the course of the last three decades seems indisputable.

4.2 The Church's Presence in Village and Town Life

The relevance of religion in Maltese village life has been studied in some depth over the 1960s by J.F. Boissevain. Both *Saints and Fireworks* [8] and *Hal-Farruġ* [9] can be described as 'an attempt at tracing the extent and mode of the Church's influence in Maltese rural society'. Hal-Farruġ is a pseudonym for a particular village which Boissevain studied. From his studies, the Church emerges as an institution exercising a high level of social control in all spheres of the villagers' life. Boissevain summarizes his findings:

> Religion is part of their daily life. They make, in their own minds, little separation between the religious field and the secular, between Church and State. Religion is not a specialized activity. As a priest

remarked to me, life in Malta is not like *Time* magazine, where sections dealing with politics, education, religion and so on are neatly compartmentalized... [10]
The Church and all its activities, the belief system and the accompanying ritual that it endorses, were found to be so intertwined that any deviant behaviour soon became the object of 'correcting' social forces.

The dominance of the Church in Maltese social life is graphically portrayed even by the geographical layout of Malta's villages: houses are generally built as if in concentric circles around the big church which towers conspicuously over the one-, or at most two-storey, dwellings. In turn, all the village streets radiate from the *misraħ*, or central square, that is always to be found in front of the church. The *zuntier*, a Church-owned decorated platform that projects from the church into the *misraħ*, is the place for much post-ceremony gossip, and in a way symbolizes the way in which, in Maltese thinking, Church affairs project themselves into 'secular' life.

Parish and village are often synonymous in Malta. Religion permeated the organization of the village studied by Boissevain to such an extent that he could not easily classify the other existing institutions as either secular or religious. Even such apparently secular organizations as the local band and football clubs were found to be deeply entrenched in one or other of the *partiti* subcultures that to some extent divided *Farruġ*. A village in fact is not an easily defined entity in secular terms: it possesses no land or property; it has no political standing of its own. The venues of communication for a large number of government announcements tends to be the church and the parish priest. The inhabitants in no way have to bother about whom they should elect as their next 'mayor' since no mayor or similar political head exists. National security interests are represented only by the locally-recruited police whose main task is to deal with anyone who disobeys either the civil or criminal laws, and to keep official records of births and deaths. As a religious congregation, however, villages, or parishes as they are more aptly called, have an officially designated head, il-*Kappillan*, generally aided by a team of assistant priests. The older parishes own land and other immovable property, most of which has been bequeathed to the church by earlier parishioners as surety for prayer after their death. Parishioners also have a place where they can gather and worship in freedom: the village parish church which — with treasures gradually amassed by a people who are eager to outbid neighbouring villages in decorating their church — is considered as a jewel in which each individual can claim a share.

Specialized religious activities, spread over the whole year in accord with the liturgical seasons, often extend into social festivities that facilitate cohesion and continued participation in the village system. The village festa in honour of the village patron saint, and in several parishes that in honour of the secondary titular saint organized by the opposing *partit*, are in this respect the most important events of the year. Both the internal and external aspects of the feasts have to be prepared for months ahead to ensure that nothing goes wrong and spoils the status that a village traditionally enjoys in relation to the other surrounding villages.

Thus the value system of the villagers is necessarily related to, and based on, the norms proposed by the leaders of the dominant culture, which is religious culture. Boissevain's work, and that of Christopher Freudenberg and Adrian Langenger [1] in other villages, reinforced this conclusion. Loyalty to the Catholic Church and to the behaviour it enjoined was the dominant value of the inhabitants of the villages studied. This was expressed in their close attachment to the parish church, in the respect they showed towards their parish priest and his assistants, and in their fervent religious practice. Nor was assent merely notional: the quality of private and public morality indicated that the value system propounded by the Church had been to a great extent internalized and translated into behaviour. Boissevain explicitly attributed the rarity of adultery, theft, or violence, and the relatively low incidence of abuse of power not to the activity of the local police but to the villagers' high level of adherance to the projected principles of Christian morality.

The Christian code of ethics is acquired gradually but continuously by each individual as he passes from one stage of the socialization process to the other. First principles are transmitted to the child within the family itself. They are subsequently explained and learnt by heart at school as well as through the catechism network provided by the *għaqdiet*. Continuous reiteration and enforcement comes through Sunday homilies in church, through the confessional, and even through the influence of public opinion itself. Boissevain noted that 'there is a very tight fit between what should be and what is, between the teaching of the Church and the moral code of the people of *Farruġ*'. Even though this could be an over-simplification based on the essentially limited data that Boissevain could obtain from his 'surface' observation of public morality, there is no doubt that the social control exercised by the Church at least required a certain level of 'communal honesty', and that any lapse from accepted standards that may have existed among the villagers should be well concealed.

Despite this homogeneity and general attachment to religious traditions, areas of conflict do exist in Malta's villages. Reference has already been made to the '*partiti* subcultures that to some extent divided *Farruġ*', the village studied by Boissevain. Internal divisions within a village are mostly connected with the devotion to the principal patron saint of the village as compared with that due to the 'secondary' saint. In villages where more than one saint is honoured as patron, each villager is expected to profess his primary allegiance to either of the saints in question and to contribute to the persistence of his faction. Each *partit*, as these factions are called, usually runs its own band club, has its own festa decorations and, still more important, its own fireworks factory. Competition and exclusiveness between the members of the respective *partit* is not restricted to the colourful display of *murtali*, or to the quality of the decorations used to celebrate the cherished day, but extends throughout the year and appears as a subtle form of stratification in Maltese village society.

In the last few years, especially in the larger and more urbanized centres like Rabat and Vittoriosa, the old dissensions have tended to recede as people come to realize that religion is not intended to create divisions. Other events, public but more secular, may be alienating the interests and activity of the newer generations who tend to attribute to religion a more specialized role in social life. Such a development in practice means that the dissensions and differences that inevitably occur in village life are now no longer institutionalized as of religious consequence. This may be part of a process of structural differentiation of life even at the village level, and certainly at the level of the more urban centres. It can be interpreted by the Church as a gain, as a way in which the Church confines itself to more specifically 'spiritual' interests, but it must also mean a certain loss of intimacy with everyday concerns, and is therefore a measure of secularization. The younger clergy — as will become clear from subsequent chapters — are more inclined to see their mission in more specialized ways, and to seek legitimation as professional specialists, but they do so at the cost of the overall presidency which they, and more especially the Church institutionally, maintained over social life and civil affairs within the traditional ordering of village life. These new patterns have been emerging with different emphases and rapidity in different localities, and it is only in the smaller villages that the *partiti* linger on, their importance apparently inversely related to the relative parish size and to the educational achievements of the villagers themselves.

Over the last twenty years the extent of the influence of the Church in Malta was severely tested by the prolonged politico-religious dissension between the Church and the Malta Labour Party. During the sixties, Maltese villages became the 'arena' where the weightier questions of national politics were fought out. The traditional *partiti* often obtained added importance as the candidates of the different parties tried to infiltrate and act as patrons of the bands and football clubs all over the island. Frequent clashes between parish priests and interdicted members of the clubs dominated by Malta Labour Party supporters were often taken to court and worked havoc in practically every village. The traditional cohesion of village life was profoundly threatened as mounting social pressure forced individuals to take sides very often in opposition to those endorsed by friends and kin. Sometimes even family life appeared to be on the verge of collapse. With renewed friendly relations between the Church and the Malta Labour Party since 1969, these divisions have been gradually reduced and the unity of the villages restored. Though at times very depressing, the rivalries and divisions had not reached a point of no return. The deeper ties of family, kin, and friendship prevailed over the dangerous rifts that had taken place in the period of dispute.

At the same time, allegiance to the respective political parties was greatly strengthened throughout the Church-MLP dispute. Each party successfully sought to establish itself in the village structure by opening new political clubs and sponsoring other political activities. On the other hand, a wider spread of news media, coupled with increased educational attainments, led more people to discuss public affairs even when the fiercest politico-religious debates were being replaced by others of a more economic or political nature. Election time however reawakens the old political feuds, as candidates make their rounds, seeking votes, or at least second preferences. Supporters on their part woo their favoured candidate, sticking his photographs and posters on their walls in the hope that he, if victorious, might later earn his salt and provide good patronage when called upon.

In spite of the conscious attempt by the Church to disentangle itself from the sad experiences of the years when there was public dissension, it still exercises considerable influence in Maltese village life. Patronage and status, it is true, are no longer the sole prerogative of the relatively cultured parish priest. Even so, religious ideology and the values acquired from the Church's attitudes to the problems of life and death continue to dominate the distribution of their time, their value system and their social structures. The basic institutions such as marriage and family life are still essentially dominated by religious ideas and will probably remain so for a long time to come. The rhythm of village life is still regulated primarily by religious celebrations or activities: the *festa*; the baptism celebrations, first holy communion; the frequent processions; and the lingering rivalry between the members of the different *partiti*. It is in this latter area that the Church's presence remains as a paradox of some sort. As things stand, especially in some of the smaller villages, the Church and its festivities are the source of pique and at times of the ununderstandable rivalry between different groups of families living in the same village. Thus *pika* disrupts the cohesion of a few families living in a series of dwellings clustered around a dominating parish church. As one old man, who came from one of the smaller villages, put it to me however, 'the very fact that this *pika* is still evident among us, is itself an indication that religion still has a presence in our way of life!'

The Church's presence in Maltese town life reveals a number of striking contrasts. The old *partiti* feuds are — as already indicated — of diminishing importance in the bigger centres, and especially in the Sliema conurbation, village festas, the *partiti* system and the role of the Church in general are — no doubt because of the exposure of the population to foreign culture and values — quite differently regarded from the way they are viewed in the rural villages.

Perhaps the best way to bring out the divergent practice of contemporary Malta is to take an extreme case. An example is provided by a new town, constructed entirely over the last eighteen years on what was formerly agricultural land. [12] Although by no means typical, the new town brings out in high relief what may be the life style of the new generation of better-educated people, and reveals their expectations about their own involvement with the Church, and about its role in future Maltese society. Against this case, we may briefly contrast the traditional village of Farruġ as previously described.

The housing shortage which was to become so much more acute some years later was already being left during the 1955 - 58 Labour administration; and the construction was begun of a completely new town close to the new Marsa industrial estate. A dual-carriageway trunk road separated the old village from the new town. Two types of households were to be provided: several blocks of four-storey flats were to provide accommodation for a total of 204 families. The flats were to be virtually identical, and each adequate for a four-member family. Alternatively, government-owned land was to be leased and individuals could build houses on the leased land according to their own specifications. Unlike any other place in Malta, the plan of the new town, named *Santa Lucia* from a small country chapel near which it was built, provided a spacious pattern of residence, with front gardens everywhere. Each block of flats was to be surrounded by gardens, and people were encouraged, by means of competitions, to do their best to cultivate a park environment. The small streets were given the names of flowers, and for the first time Malta had a town where saints did not figure prominently on corners. Instead one met 'Gardenia Street', 'Tulip', 'Zinnia', 'Ivy Path', and 'Garden Drive'.

By 1964, the complex was almost ready and people had started to move in. (The very first family had taken up residence as early as March 1960.) The new residential town attracted primarily a particular category of people, mostly civil servants or skilled government employees, to live in flats; and, to live in their own houses, a number of higher civil servants. A small square in the middle of the new complex housed a number of shops and a police station. Children of primary school age were to attend a new school built to meet the needs of the nearby old village, just across the dual-carriage road, and to be reached by a subway opening into the school grounds. The only other service provided within the precincts of the new building complex was a playground intended to help parents provide some form of recreational activity for the large child population expected from the high incidence of newly-weds among the new residents. By 1974, Santa Lucia was no longer an agglomeration of about 500 independent family units, each living in a world of its own. A community of some sort was in the making; and one must ask what role the Church and religion played in the process.

Soon after the first families started to move in, on the initiative of an individual priest a daily religious service was provided in a big room which was temporarily converted into a chapel. When the number of people began to increase considerably and Sunday Mass attendance became too big for the temporary chapel, permission was granted by the government to make use of the large school hall for religious services on Sundays until an adequate place could be arranged. The presence of the Church in Santa Lucia was formally institutionalized in 1969 when the complex was constituted a parish and a full-time parish priest nominated. Meanwhile, a site for a parish church had been chosen and work on it started. People were encouraged to contribute but the building programme was speedily brought to an end by the provision by the Curia of loans at low rates of interest.

For a considerable time, concentration on the effort to secure a proper place of worship had been such that the clergy had been unable to indulge in any extensive form of organized pastoral activity. Contacts with people were common, but purposely kept as unofficial as possible. The Church in Santa Lucia was not to appear as a dominating monolitihic structure, concerned with restraint, but as a service agency. Processions and other public manifestations of worship were never held. Allegiance to *festa partiti* subcultures has not developed and remains unknown. The people coming to Santa Lucia, perhaps because of their educational backgrounds, generally appeared to have no interest in them. At most, anyone who felt ties to the *partit* or other traditions of the village from which he came had to go over to his old village on festa days. This was especially the case with people originating from the Senglea area. Otherwise, ecological factors prevented any form of transplantation of village traditions into the new setting.

For a relatively long time in the early years of the new urban development, in which people who had no previous acquaintance had now settled alongside each other, the Church was, even if in a very limited way, the only socializing agency. Social participation came primarily through the after-service gossip, but deeper ties were forged during the occasional dinner-dance organized by the clergy for the parishioners as an indirect way of fund raising for the expenditure on the church-building projects. The annual day-outings for all parishioners contributed to a sense of communal involvement. But the very temporary nature of these activities was insufficient to do more than provide a superficial sense of community relationships at Santa Lucia. The life style is still primarily *gesellschaftlich* rather than *gemeinschaftlich*. Since 1973, just at the time of the opening of the all-purpose church centre, things had started to change. Santa Lucia's Chess Club, boy scouts, and girl guides, were quite popular. 'Keep-fit' classes were well attended, too, but associations of any permanent or naturally self-perpetuating sort were as yet not clearly articulated.

The import of the factors at work in Santa Lucia thus become apparent. The presence of the Church there is completely different from that in Farrug. Unlike Farrug, Santa Lucia does not know of any crystallization of interests which result from deeply felt traditional allegiances. The occupational pattern of the population prevents the articulation of any political tendencies, a 'silence' which is sanctioned by law as no government employee is allowed to express his political viewpoints publicly. Life is centered around the family, and the home. Kinship is the dominant focus of the relationship network. The architecture and the whole ecological context itself facilitates this emphasis on primarily 'nuclear' relationships. The Church comes in to provide a service of a sort, not as the unique legitimating agency as at Farrug. Thus, for example, there are no social pressures of the type found at Farrug to exert corrective pressure in Santa Lucia in cases of illegal co-habitation. People are attracted by the religious services provided; show respect to priests; and appreciate their efforts to better the quality of relationships there. As a whole, however, the residents of Santa Lucia appear to be rather reticent to indulge in any large-scale efforts towards permanent forms of association. [13]

Unlike Farrug, the rhythm of life is in no way set primarily by the Church and by church activities. Private, familial, and vocational interests tend to take precedence over the communal. The privatization which is a common feature of western Europe, and which is particularly characteristic of new urban centres, is already evident in considerable measure in Santa Lucia. The presidency which the Church maintains over other life activities in the Maltese village has gone. Its service functions continue, of course, and there is perhaps no diminution in specific religious affiliation as a result of the new residence pattern, but the intimacy of involvement is no longer there, the penetration of other institutions, of life actitvities, leisure habits, social occasions, and community concern of Farrug are not part of the picture at Santa Lucia. Santa Lucia, it might be said in effect, is at the forefront of 'secularization' in Malta.

4.3 The Church in the Political Sphere

A brief reference to the role the Church played in politics during the 1960s has already been made in the preceding section. Theoretically, the Church regards politics as an area in which it should not interfere unless issues which affects its rights and freedom are at stake. The Regional Council of Malta, held in 1935, specifically ruled out the possibility of priests engaging in any form of political activity or standing as candidates at elections. [14] Serious sanctions were to be imposed on priests who disregarded these stipulations. In some respects this development shows some conformity with developments elsewhere, and certainly in England where the role of the priesthood was circumscribed in at least some respects in the political sphere. (Priests in England may not be candidates for Parliament, although bishops sit in the House of Lords, and the ban does not apply to Roman Catholics or Nonconfirmists.) But in Malta this emphatic restraint of priestly involvement in politics had other implications, based on a long history of the political activity of the Maltese clergy and their rights under the various constitutions which Malta had under British rule. [15] (In 1870, for example, the Letters Patent of 1857 disqualifying all ecclesiastics from membership in the Council, were revoked following the outcome of a referendum in which the great majority of the electors voted affirmatively to the question: 'Are ecclesiastics to be considered as eligible for the Council?') Priests were as a matter of fact the dominant group within the island intelligentsia, and, together with the small politically conscious elite, were an obvious focus for local patriotism against the occuping powers. Under the British, the priests — dispersed as they were in the various towns and villages — constituted the natural and almost exclusive leadership of the indigenous population. They were not only intellectuals and leaders themselves, but, because of the place ascribed to religion among the Maltese generally, the group who most influenced the formation of public opinion, and at the same time the representatives of the distinctive and divergent religious traditions of the islanders. Thus to preclude priests from active political involvement — and this time the preclusion would have been prescribed by the ecclesiastical authorities rather than by a foreign ruler — was at once a more significant step in Malta than it would have been in a homogenous and autonomous country.

In the past, a number of priests — including Monsignor Professor M. Gonzi, later Bishop Gonzi, himself — had played an active part in political elections before the 1935 Council rulings; some had even represented the political parties in the old Senate. Over the years, however, priest participation in the political field came to be recognized as a cause of unnecessary internal dissension. Matters had gone beyond control during the 1929 - 1931 politico-religious disputes when Strickland was involved with the Trade Unions and the Micallef cases. [16] The credibility of the clergy could be restored only by a complete ban, imposed by Church authorities, on participation in party politics by anyone in tonsure. During the 1960s, however, the drama of the earlier years were re-enacted. Mintoff's proposed policies and his alleged anti-clericalism appeared as a threat to Christian thought and life. If traditional standards of morality were to be safeguarded, and if the danger of Malta being 'made into another Cuba' was to be avoided, the Malta Labour Party was not to be given the chance to rule. Such were the thoughts of those connected with the Church. The test came in 1962 when, after heated protests to the British Government against what was considered an unacceptable Constitution, all the Maltese political parties agreed to participate in elections under the provisions of the Blood Report.

In many ways, the 1962 general election must be considered an extreme case. The stand taken by the Church in that election was a-typical, but it provides an interesting instance of the influence exercised by religion and the Church in the Maltese political subsystem. The degree and extent of mobilization of political forces for this election was unprecedented in Maltese history. Mintoff and his supporters were demanding immediate and full independence from the 'foreign masters who have fashioned them [our social, political, and economic institutions] to suit their own requirements ...', affirming the rights of the individual 'to fulfil his civic duties without pseudo-religious interference', urging the 'abolition of medieval priveleges', and declaring criminal any 'interference with the right of a democratically elected majority to implement the people's mandate'. Church property came under constant attack from the MLP leaders and was threatened by another ideological statement contained in the 1962 electoral manifesto of the same party: 'the state must exercise the positive function of preventing any individual or group of individuals from dominating the heights of the nation's economy and dictating living standards to their fellow citizens...' [17]

On the opposing side stood the Church. Sheltering under its 'umbrella', which then became a much used symbol, harboured the five loyal parties.

The historical importance of the 1962 elections is considerable: they were regarded as crucial for the future of religion in Malta and every attempt was made by the Church to mobilize forces against Mintoff and his supporters. The election resulted in thirty-four loyal candidates being returned to a fifty-member unicameral legislature. The result was received with great joy by the Church in Malta. [18]

Attempts by the Church to influence the turn of political events reached another climax in 1964 just before the final approval of the draft Independence Constitution by Westminster. Mintoff was still insisting on the principles on which he had fought the election campaign and wanted them to be included in the new constitution. Archbishop Gonzi himself flew to London and used his influence with Duncan Sandys, then Secretary of State, to reject the six points Mintoff had presented as amendments to the draft prepared by the Nationalists. [19] Since independence, the Church's official participation in political life has been purposely kept low. The 1966 general election came in the midst of peace discussions then being held by the Malta Labour Party with representatives of the Holy See. As yet no formal peace had been declared, and the position of the Church during that election seemed to be somewhat dubious. The 1966 elections were again lost by the Malta Labour Party and the Nationalist Party was again returned to power with twenty-eight candidates out of a fifty-member legislative assembly. The Malta Labour Party acquired twenty-two seats. The minor, middle parties were all eliminated.

A formal announcement of peace, resulting from protracted negotiations between Malta Labour Party leaders and Mgr Emmanuele Gerada, who had been called to Malta in 1967 to serve as Gonzi's auxiliary bishop, was announced on 4 April, 1969, Easter Sunday of that year. Article 76 of the Vatican decree on *The Church Today* (Gaudium et Spes) served as the basis of the long-waited agreement. The Church and the political community were thenceforth recognized by both parties to be 'mutually independent and self-governing, each with a particular mission in the service of man'. [20]

What then, has been the influence of the Church on the turn of political events in Malta over the period under study? How can the changes in the rhythm of involvement be interpreted? As a rule, the formal religious structure exerts only limited, indirect influence on the development of purely politico-economic events. When, however, the area of discussion is extended from the political to the socio-religious, or at least when the religious values are thought to be in danger because of some particular ideology, whether the danger is real or imaginary, the Church has exercised very considerable influence in the developments of political conflict. The value system of the Maltese was severely tested during the 1960s. Political allegiances run deep in the life of many Maltese, and the majority of those who rejected the directives of the religious leaders continued to claim to be Christians. Even so, the majority did give expression to religious values in their political behaviour, severely disrupting at times the erstwhile unbreakable family networks and allegiances. [21] The 1962 case study illustrates with quantified data the extent of the political influence which the Church in Malta has mustered, and possibly could still muster; it graphically demonstrates the intensity and extent of the conflict in which the Church was so directly involved less than sixteen years ago. In many ways, the development of Maltese political life since independence suggests that there may in fact be no further occasion for heated political disputation about religion. Rather than confront the Church on issues on which it is by no means certain of a majority, the Labour Party could possibly follow a policy that would make religious matters appear less and less relevant to political decisions. Occasionally, there might be issues, concerned with moral matters, perhaps particularly in respect of tourism — even though permissiveness and gambling now attract less attention than previously — on which the Church might disagree with public policy. Disagreement was clearly the case in 1978 when, as a result of the amendments to the Education Act, no further provision for the teaching of Theology was made at either of the two state Universities in Malta. A number of factors militate against open confrontation: (a) the Church's new leader, Archbishop Mercieca who succeeded Gonzi in 1976, clearly intends to avoid disputes even on issues that had been central to the debates of the sixties; (b) it has become much more difficult to rally popular support — especially against a party in Government — because of the widening interests of the Maltese on the one hand, and the extended presence of Government in the daily life of the people on the other; and (c) within the context of an emphasized theology of religious fredom, now more openly endorsed by a larger number of clergy, it is the more uncertain whether such points of disagreement could now or in future become real political issues. The wealth of the Church might in the future be another issue on which the Labour Party might be concerned, but given the present changes in the Church — especially the new awareness that the Church's wealth should be put to better use as soon as possible — it is possible, and indeed highly probable, that as long as the Church's freedom to teach and instruct its members is safeguarded, even on matters of this kind, direct political confrontation with the Church would be avoided.

4.4. The Church as an Economic Force

The involvement of the Church in Malta's economic life has often been one of the most heated issues of Maltese politics. As a result of the people's trust in the Church, a vast amount of land and money was bequeathed to it as surety for prayer after death, or for the maintenance of pious traditions or other charitable purposes. Until very recently, details of the Church's assets, and of its returns and obligations, were never made public; and this, added to the fact that the Church was always exempted from paying taxes on its capital gains, made it easy to suggest that the Church was engaged in something like capitalist activities. When, as in the case in 1893, the Church's administration of the Marriage Legacies was being questioned by the colonial government, anyone who challenged the Church's right to own and administer wealth was likely to be attacked as enemies of the 'Church and its privileges'. [22]

The Church's administration of property came under fierce attack during the late fifties and the early sixties. The Malta Labour Party leaders repeatedly insisted that the Church opposed the political plans of their party because it felt that its privileges could be better safe-guarded under colonial rule. In a report to the Socialist International in 1961, this belief was explicitly put forward by Dom Mintoff:

> Unfortunately for us, the British Government have found in the Catholic clergy and hierarchy the most astute allies and collaborators. Since the advent of the British rule, the priests and bishops have had their material interests and privileges rigidly protected by the Colonialist power and during the past hundred and sixty years the Catholic Church has become materially wealthy and powerful. To the Church, Maltese independence spells swift social changes and the absence of a foreign power to uphold the *status quo*. They felt it in their interests to prolong colonial rule indefinitely ... [23]

Even though integration had been abandoned by the Malta Labour Party as the constitutional solution to Malta's economic ills, and even though other factors were eventually accepted as having been influential in the change of the party's policy, as late as 1961 Mintoff was still claiming that, had the demands for written guarantees asked for by the Church during the Integration campaign been acceded to, they 'would have prevented future Maltese generations from reducing or increasing the present material and social privileges of the Catholic Hierarchy'. [24] The Church's wealth was again one of the main issues of the debated 1962 election:

> Why don't they [the clergy] give heed to Christ's words, give everything to the poor, and get rid of their Mercedes and all other things

they have ... (shouts of approval and heavy clapping) ... and go for some time in the glare of the African desert where they could really start defending Religion [by converting the Mohammedans]? ... [25] Again, a week later, the MLP leader returned to the same theme:

We insist that laws should not be discriminatory ... and if anybody asks us 'is it true that if you pass a law that everybody should pay [taxes] the Bishops too would have to pay?' we would reply: 'yes, why not? Aren't they too with us? If they make use of a street, wouldn't we still be obliged to maintain it for everybody? What has all this to do with Religion?' ... [26]

The fear that was developing in ecclesiastical circles was increased by the inclusion in the 1962 MLP electoral manifesto of a clause entitled 'Equal opportunities for all citizens', which stipulated that:

whilst the right to private ownership is by no means denied, the State must exercise the positive function of preventing any individual or group of individuals from dominating the heights of the nation's economy and dictating living standards to their fellow citizens. [27]

Although the Labour Party lost the 1962 elections, the polemic continued with fierce discussions, in public meetings and in the press, on the right of the State to intervene in the administration of the Church property. [28]

In ecclesiastical circles, the wealth issue was becoming an embarrassment. Church leaders sought to explain what the Church did with the income from investments, particularly in the field of social welfare. Besides running the country's orphanages and many schools, it was pointed out that the Church had of its own accord built flats for the lower income groups and that lately it had done its best to put its land on the market so that people could be able to build their own homes. Returns from the Church's capital assets, it was repeatedly pointed out, were relatively small, and the figures suggested by MLP leaders greatly inflated. [29] Priests and other Church employees were among the worst paid workers on the island.

An important report circulated to a limited number of people under a 'confidential' label by the Pastoral Research Services in 1967 was the first step towards long-term reform. [30] Four of its paragraphs succinctly presented the situation obtaining at the time:

69. The aim of ecclesiastical property is the help of the poor and the maintenance of the Church. This traditional function, confirmed by Vatican II, must be redefined according to the exigencies of each historical period. Today, it is realised that help to the poor is best administered by helping them to help themselves, and the maintenance

of the Church is best secured by making provisions for new pastoral needs.

70. Now, if this redefinition is not made, it may occur that property, instead of serving the Church, might hinder it in fulfilling its mission. Might this be the case in Malta? Perhaps it might, especially after Vatican II. The Council has in fact presented the Church as the server of the world. Theologically, it should continue Christ's mission, showing collectively its role as the poor servant of the world. In Malta the opposite is happening. It is said that the Church is very rich. The impression is given that the Church is always collecting rents, ground rents, interests, laudemia, and gifts; whilst on the other hand nobody knows how much it spends. It is only known that the Church does not remunerate its priests and employees sufficiently, and that it does not pay certain taxes. The Church therefore risks projecting the image of a capitalist institution, always looking for more money.

71. Besides, the Church is projecting its image as a poor administrative agency. Everybody knows that ecclesiastical property has been transferred at ridiculous prices; that a 'ricorso' [application] to the Curia runs the risk of getting lost, or worse, of finding itself in the hands of competitors; that its funds are not well invested and serve only to provide the banks with big profits; that those responsible are always the same people and are never replaced. Church property is administered by dozens of procurators rarely qualified to do the job, and without an up-to-date central inventory.

72. The need for action to change this situation is therefore urgent. We believe that the best way to proceed is to embark on two interdependent projects. The first is the creation and up-dating of an inventory of Church property: this first stage is necessary to develop intervention on the levels of re-organization in book-keeping and financial accountancy ...

The actual analysis of the Church's wealth was undertaken as a joint project carried out by McKinsey and Company Inc. and the Pastoral Research Services in 1969-70. On Archbishop Gonzi's suggestion, the Vatican's permanent representative with the Food and Agricultural Organization (FAO), Mgr Luigi Ligutti, was appointed Apostolic Visitor and started to investigate the financial structure of the Church in Malta. He soon decided that the complexity of the job called for a professional approach, and with Gonzi's approval invoked the aid of the McKinsey Company, whose proposals have, in the past, helped to streamline organizations like Shell, ICI, the BBC and British Rail. In their report, worked out on the basis of the inventory then being compiled by the PRS under Ligutti's instructions, McKinsey pointed to the over-complex administrative structure that had accumulated over the centuries; and pointed out the direction for reform.

The striking feature about the Church's financial set-up was not its vastness, but its diffuse and fragmented administrative machinery. The reforms proposed by McKinsey were accepted by the Maltese hierarchy, but the Ligutti mission was terminated in strange circumstances even before the McKinsey report had been made public. Developments since 1972 have been very slow; and although measures of reform have been taken and rationalization of resources undertaken, the specific social relevance of the Church's policies is not yet evident. The lack of clear and published information has merely prolonged the negative image inherited by the Church from its earlier practice, and has perpetuated the widely diffused impression that the Church is unduly preoccupied with money matters and money-making.

4.5 The Church and the Perpetuation of Maltese Family Ideals

To a large extent the prevailing system of family solidarity may be said to originate in and be reinforced by the involvement of the Church in family life in Malta.[31] The focus of all village-based Church activity was until recently essentially the family. In turn, the rhythms of each family's life were for a long time set to the varying tone of the liturgical cycle. As social conditions started to change, however, as new opportunities for work encouraged people to move away from the parental farm or trade in search of a better way of life, as the lure of tourism and the complexities of industry began to be felt, and, more especially, as Maltese women started to leave their sheltered kitchens in search of gainful employment away from home, family organization began to change too — from the patriachal and extended type to the nuclear, self contained. In this period of dramatic social change, the Church's influence declined, and its presence in family life, if it was to survive the changes, had to become geared to, and adequately cater for, previously non-existent demands.

The present involvement of the Church in Maltese family life differs considerably even from the period immediately following the war: today its presence is not limited to the traditional village occasions, or to the encounter of its members with the priest primarily in the confessional, but is effected especially through a para-ecclesiastical agency, specifically catering for the new family needs, and known as the *Cana Movement*.

The initial activities of the new form of organized family apostolate, which was started in 1953, were quite modest. From the very start, the objectives of the Cana Movement were described as being:

'1. to guide and motivate the laity in living the vocation of Christian marriage, and

2. to instruct couples "on the sanctity of the sacrament of Matrimony, the mutual obligations of husband and wife, and the duties of parents and their children" (Can 1033)...' [32]

As such, Cana's primary interest was the projection of an idealized family life, solidly based on Christian principles. Its programme of activities, which includes specialized courses and conferences for engaged and newly-married couples, is backed by an efficiently-run counselling service that, for the first time in Malta, made use of non-ecclesiastical specializations, such as psychiatry and medicine, for the nurturing of a sound family set-up.

As a result of its direct involvement with Malta's engaged and married couples, the Cana Movement tried to keep abreast of socio-economic events affecting family life, and to make itself heard when necessary. During the economic boom of the late 1960s, for example, Cana campaigned loudly on the rights of the engaged and especially of the married to a decent house. The artificial building boom then made it impossible for an ordinary Maltese couple to compete for a flat or a small house with the enormous sums of money then being offered to property managers by retired people from Britain and other parts of the old Empire who were taking up residence in Malta.

Over the years, the initiative of one young priest had gathered momentum. Only a year after its official launching, Archbishop Gonzi confessed:

Last year I inaugurated the Cana Movement, with fear, for it was a new thing and some said we did not need it. But I judge them from their fruits and after having seen the fruits of this first year, I say that this is a *providential movement for Malta.* [33]

With its continuous programme or educational activities, built upon the support and exchange of ideas received from well-developed contacts with similar movements in other larger conutries, Cana has acquired an 'indispensable' role (Archbishop Gonzi in 1971, Cana General Meeting) in the Maltese ecclesiastical set-up not merely because, 'it is a constructive response to a crisis of change within the family itself', but, in the words of Philosophy Professor Peter Serracino Inglott, 'because it also provides a mirror in which our most crying needs for basic social reform are reflected most clearly'. [34]

Attention has been paid to the work of the Cana movement because it is itself a specialized, well-articulated, and recent development of the Church's involvement in family life in Malta. It would be wrong to give the impression that this was in any sense the only facet of the Church's concern with the family. As will be evident from other sections of this book, the very institution of confession is an agency that brings the individual into the closest contact with religious regulation of his personal and sexual affairs. The problems of families are problems that are frequently mentioned in the confessional; the priest is often consulted in a much less formal and regulated way than is the case when couples consult the Cana authorities; and the affairs of many families are themselves often known in great detail by the *kappillan*. In a religion which has always maintained the sanctity of family life, which has always been concerned with regularity and order, and in which the 'legitimacy principle' has been of paramount concern, such informal, as may be said virtually 'natural', involvement with courtship and kinship issues continues. What has happened in the Cana Movement has been the development of much more explicit counselling services, and medical advice in the context of moral and spiritual guidance under the sponsorship of the Church. The services that Cana provides are often the services provided by various state agencies in other countries, and in particular this is the case in a country like Britain, with its marriage guidance councils, maternity clinics, family planning agencies, and venereal disease clinics. Although the process of specialization has occurred in regard to the Church's involvement with the family in Malta to a considerable extent, it has occurred without the transfer of these functions to secular agencies, and this is one area in which the process of secularization has been resisted — almost self-consciously within the Church.

4.6. *The Church's Participation in the Migration and Tourist Movements*

Emigration and tourism may appear to be unusual items to include in a discussion of the involvement of the Church in the life of the people, but, as has already been indicated, emigration has been of considerable importance in recent Maltese history, and has been referred to as 'one of the safety-valves used by the planners in Malta in their attempt to contain the disproportionate postwar demographic growth and the consequent inability of the economy to absorb the emerging manpower.' The Church's attitude towards emigration, and its provision of assistance to would-be migrants, are necessarily both more formalized and institutionalized than has been its involvement, say, with education or family life, in which religion is inextricably concerned. Emigration, as a pattern of personally chosen activity, might have remained of little or no concern to the Church. A migrating Maltese, it might have been argued, would necessarily seek out fellow countrymen in his new country, and the reassertion of Maltese cultural activities would have led him, very quickly, to the Church of his ancestors, even if that Church were locally controlled and serviced by priests of foreign origin (although in practice the emigration of Maltese priests often suggested that the Church, or some of her servants, had migrated with their kinsmen). Perhaps because of the frequency of clerical duty overseas, the Maltese Church took relatively early cognizance of the importance of migration, and from 1950 the Church in Malta has played a key role in the emigration movement through a special commission. Tourism, on the other hand, seems to be even more unrelated to Church activity than emigration. Tourists normally leave their country of residence in search of relaxation and an acceptable way of enjoying themselves in an atmosphere free from the restraints of their day-to-day lives. In so doing, however, they (especially those who are Catholic) nonetheless create special needs both for themselves — more especially so now that the liturgy is no longer held in the same language everywhere — and for the host population, most especially for the people directly involved in the tourist industry. Tourism is a recent phenomenon in Malta, and the Church has so far only partially directed its attention to the problems and special contexts it creates. The little done so far however deserves mention; but the more important — and older — migratory movement claims first attention.

From the Minutes taken during the early stages of the commission entrusted to look after prospective migrants, and from published reports of what happened in *Il-Ħuġġieġa*,[25] one can follow the birth pangs of what, in 1978 is a very important section of ecclesiastical structure in Malta. The 'Malta Emigrants' Commission' was in fact born during a meeting held by Fr Albert Brincat O.P., founder of the Malta Catholic Guild in London, with the directors of the Malta Catholic Action. During this meeting, attended also by the then Labour Minister for Emigration, John Cole, it was proposed to set up a special diocesan commission specifically intended to be of assistance to prospective emigrants from Malta.

In less than two decades, church interests in the migration movement had developed from the limited, ill-organized activities of a determined group of people into a fully-fledged para-ecclesiastical agency with precise aims and specific means to attain them, providing services to potential emigrants from the time when the intending emigrant first thinks of emigrating to the time when he either returns to Malta or dies in his adopted country. Preparation for acculturation is provided by courses dealing with the social mores, by language courses, and by the constant assistance rendered to people as they try to find their way through the often complicated paperwork necessary prior to departure. Contact with Malta is easily maintained through the extensive use made of the cheap charter flights which are regularly arranged by the commission to the major Maltese colonies abroad. The well-developed network of priests and other lay people spread all over the world helps the commission to remain in continuous touch with problems emigrants have to face, and to provide remedial help when necessary. This gives rise of course to a heavy load of casework: during the period 1958-1978, over 13,683 new cases were dealt with. Problems vary with different individuals, of course, but range from lack of immediate acculturation, through doubts about the fortunes of kin left behind in Malta, to severe marital troubles developing in the more open milieux of coutries much larger than Malta. *Table 4.6.-1* gives some indication of the vastness of the commission's caseload, even though lack of research so far militates against more detailed analysis of the variety of problems involved.

Table 4.6-1 *Malta Emigrants' Commission — Case Work, 1958 - 1972*

	Australia	Canada/USA	United Kingdom	Total
1958—66	3,055	551	1,753	5,359
66—67	551	190	266	1,007
67—68	369	213	243	825
68—69	329	186	243	758
69—70	274	157	213	644
70—71	211	141	241	593
71—72	602	216	280	1,098
72—73	610	209	222	1,041
73—74	515	303	283	1,101
74—75	597	193	190	980
75—76	232	197	350	779
76—77	214	200	143	557
77—78	240	178	170	598

Source: Annual Reports of the Commission.

The practical relevance of the commission came clearly into focus during the 1969 Maltese Emigrants' Convention held in Malta on the initiative of the commission. During early August, about 9,000 emigrants were in Malta, and most of them participated in one or more of the twenty-nine activities specially organized for them. Their leaders used the occasion to deepen their insights into the problems of migrants, and to share their views on possible remedial action. The discussions emphasized the need for a 'uniting agency' which, it was urged, should be free of political restraint, but which should emphasize the deeply-embedded cultural heritage of the Maltese. Ethnic unity was envisaged as a source of valuable support for the settlement of migrants in countries new to them, provided it did not hinder gradual acculturation. The persistence of this ethno-cultural unity, the participants themselves acknowledged, had provided the greatest psychological assistance in times of difficulties, most especially during the first few years, and was generally considered a welcome cushion for those who found adaptation to a foreign culture too difficult.

Through the enterprise of the men running the Emigrants' Commission, the Church has clearly been rendering a service which, in other countries, people would generally expect the State to provide. In Malta, however, the government's assistance to prospective migrants through its emigration department, though extensive, does not normally enter into the affective and intimate areas entered into by the commission's social workers; nor could the officials of a numerically restricted civil service, more concerned with administrative procedures than with social work as such, be expected to give the attention normally due to people who often need a listening ear more than they need practical advice. It is therefore only natural that within the special Maltese context, the Church should take the initiative and, though in full harmony and cooperation with government departments, plans, and policies, help to remove the deficiencies endemic in a service provided by non-vocational bureaucrats. To many Maltese as well, it seems natural that the Church should do so; in it they have always found attention and personal care for their most intimate problems, even when these did not arise out of their strictly personal relationship with their God. Whether this will continue to be so in future remains to be seen; but so far things have worked, and the presence of the Church in emigration, and to a lesser extent in touristic development, is not regarded as excessive involvement by the Church in areas which are not, strictly speaking, its concern. It is rather a welcome service which in many ways reinforces the identification, particularly in a foreign context, of ethnicity and religious affiliation, and the enthusiastic participation by emigrants and their relatives in activities sponsored by the commission, and the increasing use made of its service, makes this apparent.

4.7 The Church's Involvement in the Modern Media

The diffusion of news and opinions through mechanical means, in spite of the relatively uncultured general level of education and of the smallness of the Maltese population, has a long history on the island. From the time of the establishment of the first printing press in 1642 by Mario Vellari, [36] the relationship between the literate minority and the illiterate majority must have undergone significant changes, at first accentuating the differences between the two groups until eventually, with universal education, reversing the proportions as the island moved towards a completely literate public. The importance of the printed media has grown particularly in this century, followed by the .liffusion of radio and television. There is no thorough study of the role of the media in the development of a societal consciousness (as distinct from a community consciousness) in Malta, but the profusion of the media on the island is a conspicuous fact, and their influence on social life must be estimated to be considerable. Not only have the media been the agents of disseminating and intensifying the sense of Maltese identity, but they have also given Maltese an enhanced dignity as a language read and spoken by everyone, whilst at the same time the prevalance of English has linked Maltese life to that of a wider world.

As elsewhere, the Church's virtual monopoly of communication, its role as the agency providing integration throughout society, particularly in moral matters and in the more personal and immediate aspects of social control, has been eroded by the growth of the media. But initially it was churchmen who, because of their positions as the literati of the country, used and promoted the new means of communication. Already in 1840, when censorship laws were relaxed by the British Government, Maltese churchmen had started their own newspaper. [37] The early press was heavily influenced by religious concerns. Anti-Catholic papers were quite common in the nineteenth century, and the printing press was also used to disseminate Protestant propaganda, stimulated by the British colonizers under the patronage of the Church Missionary Society, who sought to emphasize — in contrast to the tenets of Catholicism — the authority of the Bible (over the Church) and the possibility of experiencing a direct personal relationship with God (without the mediation of the Church). [38] Such papers, which for all intents and purposes were considered to be 'anti-religious' by the local leaders, were immediately followed by others specifically intended to rebut the ideological traits promoted by these foreign editors and their local sympathizers. These early publications did not persist for long: the circumstances which created the need for them and the relatively small circle of readers militated against the establishment of journalism in the modern sense.

Journals and magazines, with a variety of names a catalogue of which itself provides a clear indication of their purpose, followed each other in quick sequence throughout the nineteenth century. Most of the anti-Catholic attacks on these papers were directed against the Jesuits, and it was the members of this Order who sought to establish a newspaper of their own to rebut the attacks of the *Malta Mail and United Services Journal, The Friend of Religion, The Illumination and Il Cattolico Cristiano—Giornale Religioso* and others; most of these papers tried to attract a wide readership by adopting names evocative of notions within Catholicism itself. The polemical contents of these journals by the two sides is very marked, and even though because of widespread illiteracy discussion was limited to a small group of literate foreigners and, very probably, to an even more limited circle of educated Maltese, the publications of nineteenth century Malta are a clear indication that the island's isolation did not exempt Malta from the experience of problems which had — albeit at earlier dates — affected other Catholic countries in Europe.

The first real attempt to popularize the Church's point of view through the printed medium came in 1928, when the Church-run paper *Il-Habib* (The Friend) was replaced by *Leħen is-Sewwa* (The Voice of the Truth). [39] Throughout the seventeen years of its existence, *Il-Habib* [40] had attempted to make the ever increasing circle of literate people aware of the presence of the Church in a new way. In 1928, the 'Commissione Diocesana Stampa' took over the task of Catholic journalism on the island. In the first issue of the new weekly paper, *Leħen is-Sewwa*, a congratulatory message from *Il-Habib* made sure of a peaceful transition. Since its foundation, *Leħen is-Sewwa* has undergone several developments, its impact and relevance to current events rising and falling with the urgency felt within the Maltese Church to make optimum use of the printed medium for the diffusion of its stand to the population at large. During the thirties, when the paper's directorship was transferred to the then flourishing *Azzjoni Kattolika Maltija* (Maltese Catholic Action), it was the Church's main platform during its dispute with Strickland in the 1930s, and again in the sixties, it served as the link between the Church's authority and the 'action leaders' engaged in the bitter struggle against Mintoff and the Malta Labour Party. In the post-World War II period, too, *il-Leħen* became actively engaged in the 'national campaign for the spiritual and moral reconstruction of our conutrymen' following on 'the moral and material havoc caused by the war'. [41] During the most hectic periods of the two major politico-religious disputes in the thirties and in the sixties, *il-Leħen* was issued daily, a measure which itself called for an expansion of the Church's own printing presses. Throughout its history, *il-Leħen* was assisted by other weekly papers, the most important of which in the more recent period were *il-Haddiem* (The Worker: initially the organ of the Young Christian Workers, but which attracted a wide readership in the early sixties as a weekly paper, until it was developed into a daily paper in 1964), and *The Maltese Observer*, an English language weekly, aimed at projecting the Church's viewpoint to foreign readers and at stimulating intelligent discussions on the more relevant issues among the Maltese intelligentsia. [42]

By 1968, this fragmented participation in an ever-increasingly competitive market became something of a burden on the Maltese Church. The Church now had three relatively well-established papers (the thrice-weekly *Leħen is-Sewwa*, the daily il-*Haddiem*, and weekly *The Maltese Observer*), but there was no co-ordination among thm until 1970 when il-*Haddiem* was dropped and replaced by *Il-Hajja*. [43]

The Church's involvement in the media has too long a history to be exhaustively dealt with in the present discussion. Its participation remains extensive and, especially in printing, considerable sums of money have been invested. Through this investment, the Maltese Church undoubtedly contributed substantially to the process of education in Malta, and, especially at a time when the most important presses were either Church-run or Church-owned, this contribution to the diffusion of knowledge cannot be disregarded. In spite of such extensive involvement, however, the Church competes increasingly unsuccessfully for influence in the media — indeed its role is diminishing rapidly. Its papers face increasing competition in a market with a limited readership, for which an increasing quantity of printed material is produced, and for which much is imported from abroad. The attempt by the Church press to keep out of party politics makes it even less competitive; so does some of the religious or quasi-religious material which it has to include. The absence of a *direct* cash-nexus between a radio or a television programme with its consumers (in contrast with the press, when a person opts to buy the 'religious' or 'Church-run' item rather than its competitor) makes the Church much more competitive in these media. The effort to improve religious programmes has increased their popularity, most especially that of *Djalogu*, the weekly television programme. The absence of the Church and of religion from two of the three radio stations does, however, greatly reduce the Church's potential, and contributes to a process of gradual 'alienation' from religious attachment among the Maltese generally since secular entertainment competes with religious programmes being screened simultaneously on television or relayed by one of the radio stations.

The third and, from some points of view, perhaps most disquieting feature of the Church's current involvement in the sphere of mass communication is the lack of a united front. The Church's involvement both in the press and in radio and television is bedevilled with dissention. Disagreement in both spheres has now become public, and in many ways runs the risk of being caught up in the tussle of political argument. From all this the Church can only lose: in a world where the communications media form the opinions of humanity, the Maltese Church is incapable of presenting a clear message. In part this development arises from the past dependence on efforts of individuals to develop a public — itself not a threat as long as religious ideology was unified, or as long as religious and hierarchical authority remained unchallenged. Recent ecclesiastical history in Malta has been one of divisions and of political machinations, and although these are not new in Church life, the media themselves, and the new spirit of public inquisitiveness which they have encouraged, have brought such divisions into the open. For this reason, events in this area of the Church's involvement cannot be studied in isolation, but rather integrated in developments in other sectors of the Church's life and organizational set-up. It is precisely to such a synthesis that our discussion now leads.

4.8 A Complex Mechanism in Search of a Delicate Balance

The foregoing analysis points to two different levels at which the Church's involvement with the process of social change can be evaluated: the national and the local. The distinction between village and nation (or, more precisely, between parish and diocese) is necessary in spite of Malta's small size because the factors promoting social change, although deeply related to the needs and aspirations of all inhabitants, were primarily national, or at least supra-village in nature. They did not arise out of a novel Church-inspired ethos, nor as a result of a *Spirit of Hermes* syndrome, [44] but out of Malta's necessity to survive the Empire on which its vitality and prosperity had for so long depended. [45]

On the village level, although the Church's *direct* [46] permeation of social life was, and remains, thorough, its involvement in the process of social change was minimal, and to a large extent negative. The new needs created by extended socialization and protracted education, as well as the new opportunities created beyond the precincts of the traditionally self-contained village or town, presented themselves as a potential threat to the harmony resulting from the tight cohesion of the old community and its traditions. Before the coming of the new media of communication and of transport, inhabitants in one parish frequently lived in complete isolation from those living in the next. Mobility was restricted to urgent needs, and only the more cultured few could look towards the commerce of Valletta for their daily living. In spite of the wider contacts with foreigners and world events, even townspeople — or people who had to move out of their place of residence for their work — tended to draw most of their values from their family and local networks, and to build their community life on the village model, with religion and the Church usually patronizing the most important aspects of social life. In this context, only special occasions like the village festa provided opportunities for people to leave their homes to attend the celebration of other nearby parishes, and then mostly in order to see the decorations, or to spy on the secrets of the latest *taħlita tal-kulur* so that they could subsequently attempt to improve on it, and put on a better, if noisier, show when their turn arrived. [47]

The forces of change gradually destroyed the barriers between the different communities, and diluted the level of internal cohesion that for so long had characterized this type of society. The nature of these changes, as well as the pace by which they transformed the fibre of Maltese society, did not allow the Church to exert any large-scale corrective action. [48] The only stance it could adopt was initial disapproval of the ways by which the traditional patterns of life were being disrupted by the carriers of the new social ethos; by fashion trends; in the restructuring of the timetable of the normal family by television; and by the provocative ideas emerging from developments in education and politics. Subsequently the Church has had to accommodate itself to them. [49]

It took a long time for parochial church structure to follow developments in parallel structures outside the Church, and particularly to adapt themselves to the emerging patterns of widespread democracy. Even when — largely as a result of the painful dissemination from Vatican II of concepts of co-responsibility — new ideas began to spread even at the grassroots, and parish councils sprang up everywhere, it was to be noticed that the old ideas of monolitihic authority nonetheless persisted, hidden behind the statutes drafted by the Council of Parish Priests. [50]

In the same way, the emancipation of women on the parish level was not effected without considerable difficulty. According to the conventional wisdom — traceable to the Manichean influences on Augustine — women were to be considered 'weak' creatures, secondary to men, and, due to their 'periodic incontinence', to a large extent 'unholy'. A woman's place was in the home, and Church-legitimized social pressures came into action whenever women departed from their traditional roles in dress or behaviour. It used to be considered quite improper for a married woman to seek employment outside the family concern. Male and female activities were — and still are in many places — strictly separate. Even in Church today, male and female segregation has often remained the rule —

especially in rural areas — and in some instances husband and wife, upon entering the church for the same Mass, are still 'supposed' to go to different parts of the church. [51]

The inability of the Church on the local level to adapt itself to change — clearly reflecting the mentality of parish priests who had remained immobile in the same parish for decades — did not prevent very different reactions at the diocesan level, where the supra-village forces promoting change were putting new challenges to the Church. The new needs created by increased educational standards, by the impact of emigration, and by the quest for a national identity itself, could not be catered for by the techniques and instruments that the Church traditionally had at its disposal. At the same time, the Church had direct interests to safeguard if it wished to retain its social relevance. Just at this time, in the 1950s, a number of new initiatives did occur within the Church, arising usually from the inspiration of particular priests, who, in spite of the lack of professional training in social work, took upon themselves the task of mobilizing people to deal with specific social issues. In this manner, the tentative efforts made by Fr Charles Vella to conserve and reinforce the traditional health of Maltese family life grew up into the Cana Movement. Similarly, Fr Philip Calleja took up and developed pastoral assistance to prospective emigrants and their families; Fr Fortunato Mizzi founded the Social Action Movement; [52] and Fr Maurice Grech started to coordinate the Church's diocesan orphanages. [53] This tendency continued into the sixties and extended the Church's involvement in catechetics with a new commission headed by Frs J. Pace and J. Borg Micallef; [54] in youth activity with the work of Fr M. Mifsud; [55] in the field of the media through the *Il-Hajja* complex; [56] and, with the work of Fr Ch. Vella and his team, in radio and TV broadcasting. More specifically ecclesiastical interests, such as liturgical reform, the re-organization of seminary training and discipline, and vocational recruitment, also found energetic men to deal with them in the persons of Mgr J. Lupi and Fr V. Grech respectively. Other attempts to meet new social needs, particularly the housing shortage, were not always fully successful. [57]

The striking feature of this kind of departure from the traditional form of pastoral activity as prescribed in Canon Law — some of which has been analyzed in some detail in preceding sections — was its spontaneity and the absence of a specific mandate from the heads of the institutional Church. This is not to say that Church authorities disapproved of the new initiatives, or that they actively withheld support for them, but simply to note that the authorities themselves did not start them. These initiatives sprang less from planned, rational analysis of new needs, and of planned and concerted action to meet them, than from the vigorous concern of individuals who saw the need for completely new forms of enterprise. As institutions gradually took shape around their 'founders', the process became legitimized through public pronouncements on their relevance and utility by the Bishops, who did not however in any way intrude directly in their internal organization or violate other aspects of their newly acquired autonomy. [58]

Cutting across the birth and gradual institutionalization of new patterns of pastoral activity, the Church in Malta underwent the traumatic experience of its dispute with the Malta Labour Party. The tendencies Mintoff had shown as early as 1939 [59] gradually evolved into a clear programme for the effective secularization of Maltese life, and for the planned diminution of the Church's superintendency of social affairs. The extent of conflict has already been discussed. On this level, the Church's effort to keep Mintoff out of power before a peace agreement was reached, and its attempts to fight the secularizing trends to which he was committed, could be interpreted as an attempt to retard social change. At the same time, it is also very important to note that the whole experience, paradoxically enough, greatly facilitated the rise of a national ethos. In spite of the disruption it occasioned, the politico-religious dispute contributed to the replacement of old parochial mentalities by a new politicized consciousness of national involvement — a process begun during the war with the big *refuġjati* movements.

By the mid-sixties, the Church in Malta manifested very mixed responses to the demands for change that were already current both within the Catholic Church at large, and in Maltese society. At the Vatican Council, there had been a call endorsed by many bishops, for dialogue with the wider society, for more freedom of conscience, for deeper social awareness, and in Malta the Church had already a number of new initiatives to its credit, some of which had already achieved a considerable degree of institutionalization. On the other hand, these agencies often lacked adequate channels of communication and coordination with each other. The internal administration of the Church, particularly in financial affairs, remained antiquated and unreformed, and was a source of continuing concern to many in the priesthood. The dispute with the Labour Party had left the Church in a somewhat ambiguous position in relation to one of the most powerful and effective agencies of social change. The development of the new organizations for social welfare operated in a context of religious life which appeared to be resistant to many of the externally-induced forces of change operating in Maltese society.

There were, however, already demands, formulated in a rudimentary way by François Houtart as early as 1958, for more active planning, conscious formulation of policy adapted to local needs. *Pastoral Research*

Services was an agency first established as a department of a marketing research operation *(Research Agency Malta)* set up in 1960 by a young priest who had returned from a period of training and apprenticeship in the flourishing school of sociology of religion in Lueven, Belgium. In 1963, this agency was formally separated from RAM and established as part of the institutional church. Its purpose, delineated in the Statute given to Fr Benjamin Tonna by Archbishop Gonzi, was 'to discover, promote, and apply modern techniques and scientific informational resources for practical use in a coordinated and effective approach to the social and religious mission of the Church in the modern world'. [60] Its functions were intended to include (a) research; (b) cooperation among institutions; (c) projection and planning; and (d) education. In conception this was, then, itself a radical departure from traditional procedure. The Church intended to examine its own operation and to promote measures to make this operation more effective. Instead of depending on the age-old and apparently 'natural' coordination of religious activity in the life of each settled community, the Church was now concerned at the centre with a conscious, rational strategy to promote its mission. Such a development itself indicates perhaps one facet of a secularization process, in which reliance shifts from unspecified dependence on traditional ritual procedures and the provision of received teaching and practice for a settled immobile population, to a future-oriented, well-articulated, and coordinated operation in which manpower was to be more effectively deployed for a range of specified tasks. It is perhaps not altogether surprising that the implementation of the plan was more difficult than its originators conceived. [61]

Initial research up to 1966 prepared the way for the launching of the draft pastoral plan for the Maltese diocese. The plan was formally announced by the Archbishop in his Pentecost homily that year as an 'instrument whereby the Church could play a more effective and meaningful role in society'. In 1974, eight years after the first draft of the Pastoral Plan, priests and people in Malta were still talking about the need for the Church to adopt pastoral planning. [62] Two different commissions subsequently attempted to revise the drift and present a final document; but both failed. The steering committee of yet another commission was expected to present a draft plan by June 1974. The replacement of Archbishop Gonzi by Archbishop Mercieca in 1976 put back the activities undertaken by the newly established pastoral secritariate. [63] In 1978 the Maltese Church was still without a pastoral plan.

Since the first draft of a pastoral plan was submitted at Christmas 1966, much has happened in Malta. Many of the structural changes — mostly concerning the instruments of co-responsibility — envisaged in the first draft, have been realized. The politico-religious dispute was settled in 1969; the financial reform began; a bishop co-adjutor, at one time expected to succeed Gonzi as Archbishop, came and went.

The overall image of the Church that emerges from this web of intricate relationships, initiatives, and practices, is primarily one of an over-complex mechanism constantly in search of a delicate balance. The complex relationships among its members, changing as they do from day to day, and the areas of conflict among the many interest groups, prohibit direct answers to questions concerning the exact role of the Church in the process of recent social change. On some levels, and in certain areas, the Church has certainly facilitated and legitimized change. In others, however, and at particular times, its global effort was designed to restrain it. As yet, the Maltese Church — perhaps to a large extent in reflection of the character and world-view of its 'leaders' — has repeatedly escaped the development of a unified pattern of behaviour. Clashes of personality, each with a particular history and vision, still prevent the adaptation of a unitary plan, and hence of a unitary vision towards the future. The evident paradoxes in the Church's stance in contemporary Malta can therefore be attributed to a combination of factors, and to the acceptance of new theological trends — primarily in the fields of ecclesiology, moral theology and liturgy — alongside the old. These paradoxes and apparent contradictions necessarily severely affect all levels of participation in Church life, but most significantly the life-patterns and role-sets of its professional ideology carriers: the diocesan clergy. It is to the unsettled conditions in which contemporary priests have lived in recent decades, and especially to their apprehension of them, that our discussion now leads.

5

The Diocesan Clergy

Priests, as the traditional intellectual stratum widely diffused throughout Maltese society, have always tended to be conscious of the patterns of social life and its changes. Change in the past was principally in the regular cycle of birth, emigration, marriage and death — very much the sequence of change allowed for, for example, by Talcott Parsons in the penultimate chapter on social change in *The Social System*. [1] On to this sequential pattern were imposed the broader fluctuations of the island's political and economic life, as discussed in foregoing chapters. The more adventitious processes of change were of course evident to all, but, in the traditional society, priests alone were likely to have had any well-formulated analytical understanding of the nature of events, except perhaps for a small stratum of politically and socially conscious people around Valletta. Today, though education has extended the horizons of many people on the island, and the process of politicization and democratization has meant that social and economic changes are reported in the newspapers and on radio and television, and are discussed with considerable *savoir faire* by a much larger section of the opulation, the priest is still — by virtue of his work, his considerable prestige, and his general intellectual training — likely to be among the more acutely aware members of Maltese society. Priests are, in a sense, the custodians of morality and consequently have to register, reflect upon, and seek to explain the changes which they cannot fail to perceive in their daily work.

What follows now is a closer examination of the persons whose task is to perpetuate religion in Malta. Knowledge of the particular life-styles of the 419 persons who are the professional carriers of the religious ideology of the community is essential to an understanding of how the institution of which they form part — the priesthood — affects, and is in turn affected by, the social forces at work in Maltese society at large. As in the preceding sections of this book, the theoretical reflection on current patterns will be preceded by a presentation of basic data. This chapter limits itself to a depiction of a blueprint of the life-styles of Maltese priests as it emerged from a complete census of the 419 diocesan priests resident in Malta on 31 December, 1972. [2] In this section, their place of origin, residence, age, educational backgrounds and achievements, experience abroad and deployment — that is to say, the social structure of the priesthood — will be analysed in turn. The ideas, attitudes, and aspirations of the clergy will be dealt with more specifically in the subsequent chapter.

5.1 Origin and Residence [3]

As evident from *Table 5.1-1*, all but six of the diocesan priests resident in Malta on 31 December, 1972 were born in the Maltese islands. Twelve (2.4%) had been born in the sister island of Gozo; whilst the six priests born outside Malta bear Maltese surnames, and can therefore be presumed to be sons of Maltese nationals.

No significant differences are traceable between the rates of vocations originating from rural as compared to urban parishes. Vocations tend to originate both from the big urban parishes as well as from the rural ones: nonetheless, some parishes (both urban and rural) have conspicuously high rates of vocations whilst others have conspicuously low rates of vocations per 1000 population. No details of the social origin of Maltese clergymen were forthcoming from the census returns, but *Table 5.1-2* may give some indication of what might be the case with Maltese priests, as compared with their counterparts elsewhere.

5.2 Age

As a rule, priests cannot be ordained before they are twenty-four years old. The three who, in *Table 5.2-1*, appear to be under twenty-four on census day had obtained special permission for early Ordination, and were both in the first post-ordination year. The same table shows that Malta has an ageing priesthood. Even though only eleven priests (2.6%) were over eighty when the census was taken, 272 (62.8%) were already over forty-five years old as compared to 147 (7.2%) under 45. Again, as evident from *Table 5.2-2*, a considerable number of priests — 259 or 61.8% — had already given the Church over twenty years of service as against 160 or 38.2% who had served less long.

These figures point to the fact that although priest-people ratios in Malta in 1972 were still as a whole higher than those of other countries, they cannot be expected to remain so for very long.

Table 5.1-1 *Priest-People Ration in Malta (by Parish)*

Name of Parish	Population	Priests Originating	Priests Resident	Inhabitants per Priest
ATTARD	2,571	2	4	642
BALZAN	3,301	3	10	330
B'KARA S.H.	15,000 E	27	29	517
B'KARA S.J.	4,200 E	—	7	600
B'BUGIA	4,876	3	6	812
COSPICUA	9,123	23	12	760
DINGLI	1,793	2	3	597
FGURA	2,723	—	—	—
FLORIANA	4,944	10	12	412
GHARGHUR	1,770	6	4	442
GHAXAQ	2,866	3	3	955
GUDJA	1,728	3	5	345
G'MANGIA	3,600 E	—	—	—
GZIRA	9,576	6	7	1,368
HAMRUN S.G.	10,500 E	15	12	875
HAMRUN I.C.	6,058	—	2	3,029
KALKARA	1,946	4	4	486
KIRKOP	1,225	1	2	612
LIJA	2,135	10	11	194
LUQA	5,413	3	4	1,353
MARSA T.	8,000 E	8	1	8,000
O.L. OF AEARS	7,000 E	—	—	—
M'SCALA	877	—	1	877
M'XLOKK	1,462	2	2	731
MDINA	988	1	6	164
MELLIEHA	4,279	3	3	1,426
MGARR	2,117	2	3	705
MOSTA	8,335	19	20	416
MQABBA	2,119	6	4	529
MSIDA	11,424	7	12	952
NAXXAR	4,642	10	9	515
PAOLA	11,796	17	15	786
QORMI S.G.,	8,896 E	22	20	444
QORMI S.B.	8,000 E	3	5	1,600
QRENDI	2,094	3	3	698
RABAT	12,242	13	18	680
SAFI	784	2	3	261
SAN ĠWANN	2,123	—	—	—
ST. JULIAN'S	7,395	3	6	1,232
ST. PAUL'S BAY	2,789	1	2	1,394
STA. BENERA	6,135	1	7	876
SENGLEA	4,749	24	8	593
SIGGIEWI	4,971	14	15	331
SLIEMA S.H.	11,000 E	4	4	2,750
SLIEMA S.G.	8,000 E	4	12	666
SLIEMA S.M.	9,300 E	15	13	715
STA. LUCIA	1,800	—	2	900
TARXIEN	7,992	6	7	1,141
VALLETTA S.A.	4,500 E	3	7	642
VALLETTA S.P.	5,800 E	3	16	362
VALLETTA S.D.	5,500 E	19	4	1,375
VITTORIOSA	4,014	8	7	573
ZABBAR	10,165	13	10	1,016
ZEBBUG	8,133	10	13	625
ZEJTUN	10,443	14	16	652
ZURRIEQ	6,751	18	7	964
		4		

E = Estimated population.

Table 5.1-2 *Father's Occupation of Students for the Priesthood*

	Gregorian (76) %	Italy (44) %	Paris (34) %	Malta 1964 (16) %	Malta 1972 (64) %
Farmer, not Proprietor	9.2	15.9	—	6.7	—
Farmer, owner of own fields	19.7	22.7	2.9	6.7	10.9
Entrepreneur, commerce management	27.6	9.1	41.2	6.7	23.4
Military	3.9	4.6	8.8	6.7	—
Services	11.8	15.9	8.8	6.7	28.2
White Collar Employees	14.5	9.1	17.6	33.3	12.5
Manual Worker	5.3	20.5	2.9	26.7	23.4
Liberal Profession	7.9	2.3	17.7	6.7	1.6
Total	100%	100%	100%	100%	100%

Source: H. Carrier S.J., *La Vocation — Dynamisme Psycho-sociologiques* (Rome, Presses de l'Université Gregorienne, 1966), p. 31. For 1972: the Malta Seminary.

Table 5.2-1 *Age of Maltese Priests*

Age	Frequency	Percentage
under 24 (1948)	3	0.7
25—29 yrs (1943 - 47)	26	6.2
30—34 yrs (1938 - 42)	34	8.1
35—39 yrs (1933 - 37)	36	8.6
40—44 yrs (1928 - 32)	46	11.0
45—49 yrs (1923 - 27)	59	14.1
50—54 yrs (1918 - 22)	64	15.3
55—59 yrs (1913 - 17)	37	8.9
60—64 yrs (1908 - 12)	46	11.0
65—69 yrs (1903 - 07)	26	6.2
70—74 yrs (1898 - 1902)	18	4.2
75—79 yrs (1893 - 97)	13	3.1
80+yrs (— 1892)	11	2.6
Total	419	100

Table 5.2-2 *Years of Service since Ordination*

Years of Service	Frequency	Percentage
Up to 5 yrs (after '68)	39	9.3
6—10 yrs (1963 - 67)	24	5.7
11—15 yrs (1958 - 62)	45	10.7
16—20 yrs (1953 - 57)	52	12.9
21—25 yrs (1948 - 52)	58	13.8
26—30 yrs (1943 - 47)	63	15.0
31—40 yrs (1933 - 42)	78	18.6
41—50 yrs (1923 - 32)	35	8.4
over 50 yrs (up to 1922)	25	6.0
Total	419	100

5.3 Educational Backgrounds and Achievements

Before being ordained a priest, a young man must have followed from seven to eight years of seminary training. Entrance to the Major Seminary comes only after a full course of primary and secondary education. Two hundred (48.1%) of all Maltese priests had all their secondary schooling at the Minor Seminary and another forty-five finished it there. The Minor Seminary has been traditionally considered to be the appropriate place for a boy to go to if, from an early age, he intends to become a priest. It was also considered as the place in which prospective candidates and students might be attracted to the ministry, and where they would receive special vocational guidance. Furthermore, the survey showed that the Government-run Lyceum was also very important as a source for candidates to the priesthood.

Major Seminary training runs concurrently with training in Philosophy and Theology which is provided by the Faculty of Theology, in 1972 still part of the University of Malta, for those students who satisfy standard University entry requirements. Of the 419 priests in Malta, only 29.4% and 29.2% were regular students of the University during their philosophical and theological studies respectively. Those who did not meet the University's entry requirements were looked after by the Malta Seminary. These latter students attended the lectures in the theology faculty as 'occasional' students; but instead of being examined by the University, submitted to examinations set by the Seminary authorities. In this way, the Malta Seminary catered for the philosophical preparation of 47.8% of all Maltese priests and for the theological preparation of 47.4% The Gozo diocese has its own Seminary and runs its own philosophy and theology courses. Forty-four priests currently serving in Malta had their philosophical, and 46 their theological, training in that institution. Some Maltese priests chose a foreign university for both their philosophy and their theology. Eighteen in fact studied philosophy, and 26 studied theology abroad. The Gregorian University (with 14 students for philosophy and 16 for theology) was the most popular in this respect.

Membership of the Faculty of theology implies the acquisition of an academic degree. 279 (66.6%) of the Maltese clergy held no such degrees. Of the 140 who had a degree in Theology, 32 were awarded a B.D. (Bachelorship in Divinities) after a five-year course in Philosophy and Theology. A further 72 were awarded a Lic.D. (Licentiate in Divinity) after an additional two years of Theology and a research project. Another 36 earned a Doctorate in Divinity in recognition of an original piece of research and a thesis. Specific degrees in Philosophy are earned by priests only if they further their philosophical training abroad after ordination, and are therefore less common. Only 19 priests have degrees specifically in Philosophy. Of these, 4 hold a Bachelorship (Ph.B.), 5 a Licentiate (Ph.L.), and 10 a Doctorate (Ph.D.). Several priests had followed their 'general practitioner courses' at the Royal University of Malta and the Seminary by postgraduate studies at foreign universities, thus extending their theological studies. Sacred Scripture, Canon Law, and Ecclesiastical History were the most popular fields in this respect: 21 priests (9.4%) specialized in one of these disciplines. Doctorates had been conferred on one priest in the field of Sacred Scripture (S.S.D.), on two in Ecclesiastical History (H.E.D.), and on ten in Canon Law (J.C.D. and J.U.D.). Licentiates had been conferred on one priest in Sacred Scripture (Lic.S.S.), on two in Ecclesiastical History (H.E.L.). Bachelorships in Canon Law (J.C.B.) were conferred on four priests by a foreign university.

Non-ecclesiastical university specialisations were also very common among the Maltese clergy. The most common was the Malta university B.A. because, up to 1968, students following the theology course could, by lengthening their whole span of studies by one year, join the general course of arts within the Arts Faculty, and read for a B.A. in three subjects — one of which was normally Philosophy — over a four-year period. Fifty-four priests actually read for this degree, one had an M.A.

degree, and two held a Ph.D. in Arts subjects; five read and acquired diplomas in the Social Sciences and/or Banking; one was a Doctor of Laws (L.L.D.); six had a diploma in education; ten a music specialization; two a youth leadership diploma; ten had followed some foreign language course abroad, and another two a course in journalism. Only eight priests had a second specialization in a non-ecclesiastical field.

Various other members of the Maltese diocesan clergy had followed courses in foreign countries in fields related to their specialized ministry, and in fact twenty people specialized in fields like Sacred Art, Bibliotechonomy, Sociology of Religion, Spirituality, Liturgy, Catechetics, and Pedagogy. This group made up 4.7% of all the clergy.

5.4 Present Deployment

Because of the diversity of tasks being done by the Maltese clergy — most of the 419 priests had taken up tasks as they came their way — it is very difficult to group them according to the type of service in which they were engaged. This was all the more so when — as until recently — seminarians were ordained in the final year of their seminary training and then left to find their own way into the system. Only the more important jobs, such as that of parish priest or vice-parish priest, were stable roles. To the question 'How was the workload distributed among the clergy in 1947?' put to Archbishop Gonzi, he replied: 'Some stable offices existed: parish priest, vice-parish priests, canons, procurators etc. Others used to exercise their ministry without any ties to a particular office. They used to do merely what they were asked to do.' Despite this lack of a rationalized organization and ranking system, six broad occupational categories may be constructed on the basis of the 1972 census of the diocesan clergy.

(a) Parish Priest

Each of the fifty-five parishes is looked after by a parish priest.[4] According to Canon Law, any priest may be called by the bishop to move into a parish as his representative there. Until quite recently, vacant posts used to be filled by selection following an open call for applications and a subsequent one-day examination in moral theology. This has ceased to be the case, and though legally the bishop is still free to ask any priest whether he would like to become a parish priest, the first call is now normally for a priest who has had some experience in the running of a parish, primarily as vice-parish priest; and, generally, no nomination is affected unless prior consultation with the clergy of the receiving parish had shown that the person the bishop has in mind would be acceptable to them. Small parishes are often the training ground for the larger parishes; and many of the larger parishes in Malta had at their head somebody with previous experience as parish priest in one of Malta's smaller villages. Parishes like Kirkop, Qrendi, and Għargħur, have in fact a much higher average turnover than larger parishes such as Rabat, Siġġiewi, Żabbar and Ħamrun. [5] The mobility of parish priests in the larger parishes is often minimal, and the appointment tends to be for life. Priests nominated to take over a large parish might — if not previously occupying a parish priesthood in one of the smaller parishes — have been doing some special kind of work on the diocesan level.

There is no set age for a priest to be considered for appointment as a parish priest. Quite recently — after the 1972 census was taken — a candidate was nominated as parish priest of a sizeable rural village only a year after his ordination, even though a man three years his senior is said to have expressed his desire to get the appointment himself. The absence of a regular system whereby an individual priest is noticed, selected, and advanced, makes it very difficult to establish the qualifications which make a priest eligible for such a promotion. When the post in any one parish is vacant, one often hears, even reads in newspapers, of delegations to the bishop from groups of parishioners; and the influence of pressure-groups, especially in parishes where the *partiti* factions are still alive, should not be underestimated. Even though one can never establish the truth of it all, during the period before and just after the nomination of a new parish priest, gossip in clerical circles often abounds with allegations of 'nepotism' and 'favouritism'; and it is frequently alleged that influential members of the clergy — and of the college of parish priests — like to make 'humble submissions' to the authorities, and, on the presumption that the standards of their ranks should be kept high, to comment on the qualities, or lack of them, of any individual who is known to be in the running.

Once nominated, the terms of reference of the parish priest within the territorial limits of his parish are very extensive. He is considered by the people to be the bishop's representative and, within the framework of the older conceptualization of the Church as 'the perfect society', subject to no one but him. The parish priest is responsible for the day-to-day running of the parish, and for the provision and organization of all religious services. In virtue of Canon Law, he and the bishop alone have the right to celebrate some of the more important sacraments in a person's life. Without his permission, a baptism celebrated within his parochial limits would be illicit, and marriage invalid. [6] It is the parish priest's duty to look after the parish archives and to keep proper records of all deaths, births, marriages and confirmations. One of the most important tasks for most parish priests is the preparation and organization of the annual village festa. Responsibility in this regard is — as of recently — often shared with an *ad hoc* committee which he nominates for this purpose.

The Maltese word for parish priest is *il-kappillan*, a derivative of the Italian *cappellano* (Latin *caput*) which clearly portrays the role of the parish priest in the parish community. He is the 'head that rules the parish'; his word is often regarded as sacred and, in the smaller villages especially, deviant behaviour is likely to be subjected to the scorn of others in the tightly-knit community the values of which he is both custodian and guardian. [7] The dominating position of *il-kappillan* often leads him to take on substitute roles that are not strictly an essential feature of his ministry. When illiteracy was still a common feature of Maltese society, he used to be frequently consulted by his parishioners on all kinds of problems, ranging from advice on which doctor to call as consultant, to advice about business deals. He often had to act as the writer of letters to kinsfolk who had emigrated, and commonly served as a link between his parishioners and important personages outside the village. This type of patronage, though greatly diminished by the increased levels of literacy and educational attainments of parishioners, is still evident, and is rarely limited to purely religious matters. As a matter of fact, the parish priest's contact with his parishioners is in no way restricted to official occasions such as baptisms, marriages and deaths. *Il-kappillan* normally visits each family at least twice a year. The visit most eagerly awaited is the one immediately following Easter when housewives make sure they put up their best curtains for the big occasion when the parish priest comes to bless the house. Informal contacts between parish priest and parishioners occur on occasion when a parishioner needs a birth certificate or, even if less frequently nowadays, a good reference. In Maltese society, the office of parish priest is most important. The number of years which most parish priests spend in one parish, as evident from *Tables 5.4-1* and *5.4-2*, turns them into an institution; and analysis

Table 5.4-1 *Ages of Parish Priests*

30—34 (1938 - 42)	3	(6.1%)
35—44 (1928 - 37)	23	(46.9%)
45—59 (1913 - 27)	18	(36.7%)
over 60 (before 1912)	5	(10.3%)
Total	49	(100%)

Table 5.4-2   *Duration of Term of Office as Parish Priets*
(As in October 1974) *

	First Appointment	Last Appointment
under 1 year	5 (10.6%)	7 (14.9%)
1—5 years	8 (17.1%)	13 (27.6%)
6—10 years	12 (25.5%)	12 (25.5%)
10—20 years	15 (31.9%)	13 (27.6%)
over 20 years	7 (14.9%)	2 (4.4%)

* This table is not inclusive of two diocesan priests who, on 31 December 1972, were the *kappillani* of the National Chaplaincies, and who are included in other tables.

of the belief-content and behaviour patterns of parishioners frequently shows a high correlation between what they think and the ideology and mode of behaviour of *il-kappillan*, even though recent social change is reducing the correlation. In many ways, however, the activities of the parish priest are still the linch-pin of parish life; and the man and his office make of themselves an institution in terms of which all is measured, and by reference to which all events and activities are either applauded or completely rejected. [8]

On census day, there were forty-nine diocesan priests who were serving as *kappillani* in the Malta diocese; those of the remaining parishes came from Religious Orders.

(b) Vice-Parish Priest

The Viċi, as the vice-parish priest is called in Malta, is a familiar figure of everyday parish life. Like that of the parish priest, his work duties extend as far as the parish limits extend; and he is expected to dedicate himself exclusively to the parochial ministry under the direction of the *kappillan*. His primary duties are related to the needs of the sick and the dying. Unlike the parish priest, who has more liberty of movement outside the territorial limits of his parish, the *Viċi* is *tal-għassa* (on guard) twenty-four hours a day. He can never refuse a call for assistance or refer it to some other priest, even if it comes in the middle of a cold wintry night.

The *Viċi's* ministry to the sick demands that he makes regular confessional and communion rounds. Their frequency depends on the size of the parish, the number of sick people, and their own desire for frequent communion. There are, therefore, quite unexpected disparities between one parish and another; and even variations within the same parish: some people ask for Holy Communion at home twice a week, others only once a month. When someone is in imminent danger of death, the *Viċi* must not only administer to him the rites of passage, but stay near him as long as possible. People in Malta still expect their dying to die in the presence of a priest, and are often very concerned if this does not occur. To cater for this, a special room is sometimes provided in case the *Viċi* has to stay with a dying person all through the night. In instances when two or more people are on the verge of death at the same time, the *Viċi* has to go from one house to the other, giving as much attention to each as he can manage. He is often expected to preside during burial services.

The *Viċi* is the parish priest's right-hand man in the affairs of the parish; he is expected to help in the administration of the sacraments in church; to have fixed times for the celebration of Mass, and occasionally to run any associations that operate in the parish. The *viċijiet* frequently preside over the evening eucharistic service held before or after evening Mass. Parishioners too have become accustomed to the many occasions when the *Viċi* assists the parish priest in organizinz collections especially during Sunday Masses.

The ministry exercised by the *Viċi* necessarily brings him into close contact with the people. His work, much more than that of the parish priest, is at the grassroots level of the parish. His long and frequent visits to the sick and dying, and the help he gives whenever called upon, gives him a deep and intimate knowledge of most parishioners' lives; and he is usually trusted and loved. In a hidden, unofficial way, the *Viċi* comes to share the social status and esteem formally given to the parish priest. People go to him with less formality than they would go to the parish priest, and the advice he gives on family affairs, which might range from the imminent announcement of an engagement in the family to an assurance that the money confided to his care by an elderly couple will be used for prayer after their death, is usually scrupulously followed. [9]

Although the *Viċi's* standing is very high among the people as a whole, he has much less standing among the clergy themselves. The *Viċi's* ties with one particular parish, especially when he is alone in a big parish, the continuous strain imposed by inconsiderate parishioners, and the often stringent demands made by parish priests, all make the *Viċi's* type of work undesirable. [10] In a survey of the activity of the *Viċijiet* conducted in 1970, the image of the *Viċi* emerged as that of 'a solitary

worker, ever ready to fill holes left unfilled by others, but unable to get
a good grip of reality ...' [11] Tension among the *Vičijiet* themselves was
located under four headings:

(a) the individual Viči's sense of 'suffocation';
(b) the sense of a need for closer collaboration among the *Vičijiet*
themselves and between them and other priests on the parochial
level;
(c) their aspiration for greater respect for the work they did — an
aspiration crystallized in the unexpressed but continuously noticeable desire for wider participation in the actual running of the
parish — both in the decision-making and the decision-taking
processes, at all levels and in all aspects of parish pastoral life; and
(d) their 'neutral' reaction to both personal and situational rapports,
evident from the respondents' mixed feelings towards their various
activities and especially in their constant concern with financial
amelioration ... [12]

In larger parishes, the *Viči's* workload is often shared between two
vice-parish priests, dividing the load in one of three different ways:
(a) *territorial division:* two *vičijiet* divide the parish into sectors; and each
exercises rights and duties in the area allotted to him;
(b) the *shift* basis, in which each *Viči* has the care of the whole parish
during his working hours, although he would usually be living outside
the parish when not on duty; and
(c) the *functional* basis when two *vičijiet* parcel out specific duties between
them.

Table 5.4-3 gives more details on the ages of the *vičijiet:*

Table 5.4-3   *Ages of the Vičijiet*

Under 29 (after 1943)	10	(17.9%)
30—34 (1938 - 42)	15	(26.8%)
35—44 (1928 - 37)	10	(17.9%)
45—59 (1913 - 27)	16	(28.5%)
over 60 (before 1912)	5	(8.9%)
Total	56	

Table 5.4-4 gives further details on the distribution of the *Vičijiet* in relation to the number of parishioners in the respective parishes. This table is not all-inclusive as it was based on the replies of the 33 *vičijiet* to the questionnaire circulated by the *Kulleġġ tal-Vičijiet* in 1970 (response had been only 58.9%), but it does give an idea of the imbalances in the distribution of work which has already been referred to above.

Table 5.4-4 *Distribution of Vičijiet in Parishes according to Population*

No. of Parishioners (000)	One Vičí	Two Vičijiet
1	1 *	—
2	1	—
2	2	—
4	2	—
5	3	2
6	4	2
7	1	—
8	—	3
9	—	2
10	—	1
11	—	—
12	—	1
13	1	2
14—17	—	—
18	—	2
No answer	—	1
Total	17	16

* Numbers refer to no. of parishes.

Source: M. Vassallo, *The Work of Malta's Vice-Parish Priests.*

On 31 December 1972, the day when the census of the diocesan clergy was taken, fifty-six priests enjoyed the office of *Vičí* in the parishes not manned by the religious orders. Of the thirty-three *vičijiet* who had answered the 1970 questionnaire, sixteen were found to be working jointly with another *Viċi* in the same parish. Five of these shared their work on the territorial basis, seven on the shift basis, and three on the 'functional' basis. Twenty-seven out of the thirty-three respondents were working in the same parish in which they were born. Only six had then been assigned work outside their parish of residence.

(c) The Ecclesiastical Specialist

Some priests are engaged in activity of a more specialized nature than that of a parish priest or of a *viċi*, and usually operate not in one given parish but over the whole diocese. Activity on this level is generally connected with a particular service needed by the diocese as a whole: at the Archbishop's Seminary or in the Faculty of Theology, for example. Otherwise this type of activity would tend to be related to the specialized services provided by agencies designed to look after the needs of particular categories of people. Such would be the Cana Movement, the Catechetical Commission, and the Emigrants' Commission. [13] Now that these organizations and movements have gained ground, and have become part of the Maltese ecclesiastical structure, priests working in them are generally designated to do so by the Archbishop, but most of the priests currently working in them are their founders, people with initiative who started to do something when they noted that a particular field of activity was needed, and nobody else cared much about it. Such priests are generally found to have developed good relationships with those in parallel institutions in other countries. New recruits, on the other hand, often feel the need to prepare themselves for their taks by following a course of further study abroad.

The parochial ties of the 'specialist' are necessarily limited. Most of his time is taken up by his specialized duties, and he cannot offer much more than marginal services to a parish community. Some of these priests were recognized — for the purposes of a small sum they receive from the Curia once a year — as 'parish auxiliaries' if they say Mass in a parish at fixed times, and undertake a limited number of hours in the confessional. It is not infrequent to find one of these priests acting as a director of, or as spiritual assistant to, one of the *għaqdiet* of the parish in which he resides. On 31 December 1972, as many as one hundred priests could — in one way or another — be put in this category since their main duty was related to a diocesan office. *Table 5.4-5* gives further details.

As many as twenty priests had director staus; twelve had assistant director status; ten served as secretaries to diocesan commissions; twenty-five were engaged in some kind of clerical work at the Curia or in some other diocesan office; [14] eleven had a diocesan office with liturgical

Table 5.4-5 *Ecclesiastical Specialists*

Director Level	20
Assistant Director Level	12
Secretary to a Commission	10
Journalistic Affinities	6
Clerical Jobs	25
Ecclesiastical Tribunal	4
Liturgical Affinities	11
Director of Children's Homes	1
Pastoral Secretary	1
Others (e.g. TV advisor)	3
Theology Faculty	7
Total	**100**

affinities; six were engaged in work related to the Church's press. The professors and lecturers of the Faculty of Theology also fall into this category.

(d) Teacher-Priest

Lack of deployment opportunities in strictly ecclesiastical roles has led priests to seek other outlets for the exercise of their qualifications, the most attractive of which has been teaching. A teacher-priest is here considered as being one who had teaching — not necessarily restricted to a Church-run school, or to the teaching of religion — as his main day-time profession, and can be related to any of the primary, secondary, or tertiary levels of education with the sole exception of the faculty of theology. *Table 5.4-6* shows that on census day there were one hundred and one teacher-priests in Malta, of which only twenty taught at the Minor Seminary. The academic qualifications of these teacher-priests varied extensively, and were directly related to the type and level of teaching in which the individual priest was engaged. As with the *ecclesiastical specialist*, the parochial ties of the teacher-priest were found to be essentially limited, and generally restricted to the marginal services that can be provided before or after school hours, and over the weekend. Some of the parish auxiliaries already referred to also come from this group of teacher-priests.

Table 5.4-6   *Teacher Priests*

Minor Seminary	20	(19.8%)
Primary Schools	15	(14.8%)
Secondary Schools	60	(59.4%)
University/Junior College *	5	(5.0%)
M.C.A.S.T.	1	(1.0%)
Total	101	(100%)

* Later removed from the university's jurisdiction, and renamed 'upper secondary school' (see above, p. 105, n. 1), but still called Junior College when the census was taken.

(e) Parish Helper

A parish helper is a priest who best fits the description given by Arch-bishop Gonzi of those priests who do not have a stable office: 'one who is always ready to do what he is asked to do'. A number of priests have no strict ties with a parish, nor do they have any particular type of specialized work assigned to them. Their activties are thus not easily categorized. A parish helper's main task is the regular celebration of mass in the parish in which he lives; availability to hear confessions regularly, dis-tribution of Holy Communion during services; and, on special occasions, when the *Viċi* cannot reach everybody, to visit the sick in their own homes. Parish helpers might be found in charge of a secondary church where ancillary services are provided for the people living around it, and would in such a case be called its 'rector'.

No specific data was forthcoming on this group of priests from the 1972 census of Malta's secular clergy. These priests may, however, be put into two main groups: (i) the dwindling number who had been parish helpers throughout their lives; and (ii) those who, for reasons of age or health, have had to give up their previous commitments, and exercise this type of ministry for the remaining few years of their lifetime.

(f) Student Priests

The 1972 census returns pointed to a further — though very small — category of priests among Malta's secular clergy. The recently developed fields of specialized apostolate, as well as the demand for priests specialized in areas of theology in which they might become teachers, call for a preparation beyond the general-practitioner course at the Malta Seminary. Six priests, all ordained in the preceding few years, had left Malta to further their studies in institutions of higher studies abroad. This group of priests had no special standing in Malta, and, on returning to Malta for their vacations, were expected to give general assistance when required.

Even though methods of recruitment, selection, and professional socialization to the diocesan priesthood in Malta have for long been well-defined, and are articulated in easily identifiable and persisting institutions — primarily through the Seminary and the Faculty of Theology for centuries part of the University — and even though the clergy of Malta have had the same bishop as their leader and immediate source of inspiration and guidance for half a century, [15] the image of the individual priest emerging from the foregoing analysis of the census results can hardly be considered stereotyped in any respect. Patterns of similarity do exist — in, say, the great number of priests who joined the Major Seminary after finishing their secondary schooling at the Minor Seminary; and in the substantial number of ex-MUSEUM members within the clergy ranks — but these similarities are woven in a web of dissimilar tendencies and orientations that point to very varied life experiences. Not only are there marked divergencies in both social origin (in terms of urban versus non-urban and of parental occupation), and in the level of educational attainment (varying from degrees obtained from the best universities of Europe to the rather parochial style of pre-war philosophical and theological training imparted at the Gozo Seminary), but one can also notice extensive diversity and diffusiveness in the clergy's form of commitment. Though basically tied to the Church's sacramental activity, the exercise of the ministry in Malta, in terms of the clergy's principal day-time commitment, has developed into areas widely different from each other. It reaches into contrasting areas, ranging from work conditions at the dockyard or in one of the factories, through the hectic town life of parish work in Valletta, to the stable farming community atmosphere of *Manikata* or *Imġarr*.

Encapsulation of the experiences, and the expectations, of the incumbents, and of their diffused role-set, is therefore by no means an easy task. It is made even more difficult in our case by the rapid transformation occurring in almost every aspect of Maltese life and culture. And yet, an attempt at a thorough understanding of religion in such a transitional stage of societal development makes the portrayal of the changing priesthood — as seen by incumbents themselves — mandatory. This is the task we set ourselves in the following chapter.

6

The Worldview of Malta's Diocesan Priesthood in a Period of General Upheaval

The closeness of the patterns of interaction among Maltese clergy, the elements of secrecy endemic in a profession that has to deal almost exclusively with the realms of the occult and the affective, together with the diversity and diffusiveness in the specific role-sets in their day-to-day exercise of their priestly tasks, create difficulties for research. It was not felt that a catalogue of yes/no answers to a pre-set questionnaire would really penetrate the complexity of the situation, or reflect the subtlety of clerical attitudes to their role and to the changes occurring in Maltese society. A cluster of research techniques and approaches had to be devised therefore, in order to obtain an accurate intimation of the processes of thought, and the patterns of action, of the clergy. At the same time, research ought not to disturb their consciences, the way of life, or the mode of behaviour of the subjects, and care had to be taken to approach the clergy in ways acceptable to them without compromising the object of the study. A battery of four research techniques was adopted — all of them dependent on the cultivation of mutual respect between researcher and respondents, and on their confidence in him: [1]

(a) direct observation of what the members of Malta's diocesan clergy were doing in their day-to-day lives;

(b) frequent informal discussions on aspects of their work and on the problems that arise out of continuous interaction with other members of the clergy and with the laity as a whole;

(c) the analysis of Church reports and documents — most of which were of a confidential nature — and especially of the archives of the Pastoral Research Services which included all the letters and manuscripts from members of the clergy after an open call for suggestions in preparation for a Regional Council had been made by the Archbishop in 1966; and

(d) lengthy interviews with a 10% sample of the diocesan clergy currently engaged in the ministry.

The interviews — some of which extended to more than five hours and which frequently had to be divided into two sessions — were conducted on the basis of a questionnaire (Appendix C), which was not however intended to elicit 'yes' or 'no' answers to structured questions; but rather to provoke insights into the way the clergy envisaged the changes in

Malta, and the Church in Malta, were undergoing. Interviewees were randomly selected from the directory of diocesan clergy compiled for the purposes of the present study; and were divided into three broad groups, according to the years of service they had given the Church since ordination. Group A was made up of priests ordained in the preceding ten years, i.e. since Malta attained Independence, and since the start of Vatican II. Group B, the largest and most important of the three, was composed of priests ordained over a twenty-five year span, from 1938 to 1962. The choice of dates is relevant as 1938 marks the prelude to the war, and 1963 the prelude to Independence and to Vatican II. Priests ordained in 1937 or before constituted Group C. *Table 6.0*, which gives

Table 6.0-1   *Composition of Sample*

Group	Years of Service	Actual Population	Sample Taken
A	up to 10 yrs (since 1963)	63 (15.0%)	7 (17.1%)
B	11—35 yrs (1938 - 1962)	252 (60.2%)	25 (61.0%)
C	more than 36 yrs (before 1937)	104 (24.8%)	9 (21.9%)
Total		419	41

details of the composition of the sample, shows a bias in favour of the first two groups. This bias was deliberate since the study was designed to concern itself primarily with the way in which people in the middle group, who (unlike people in Group C, some of whom had retired from direct involvement) were all actively engaged in the ministry through the years of rapid social change affecting Malta, envisaged its effects on their unique way of life. In the selection of the interviewees, an attempt was made to include an over-representation of 'opinion formers' — those whose ideas tended to be influential in the Church and among their fellow-priests. [2]

The results obtained from the combination of these four approaches follow; and are presented in four sections. The priests' social consciousness comes first, followed by their awareness of themselves as individuals and as members of the larger society. Section three analyses their own apprehension of the daily chores of their ministry, and the concluding section deals with three selected areas where patterns of assent and dissent were evident, and specifically with the clergyman's views on (a) the nature of the Church, (b) ideal Church-State relationships, and (c) their vision of the priesthood.

6.1 The Priests and Social Awareness

Without a single exception, all the priests interviewed showed a deep sense of awareness of Malta's 'radically' changing features. The influence of education, of tourism, of more extensive participation in social life, of industrialization, and of a more developed social services system, were all repeatedly mentioned and to a large extent evaluated by the incumbents. Consensus on the actual effects of social change were summarized by one of the interviewees in the following manner: [3]

1. Levelling down of class differences: it used to be *professjonisti* [professionals] and *mhux professjonisti* [non-professionals];
2. Levelling down of topographical differences and distances: city, town and villages are practically one thing now;
3. Levelling down of insular mentality: what other nations can do, we can do, or we must do, or we shall do ... [C.20] [4]

Widespread education was generally considered to have been the main change-producing factor in Malta's recent developments. Frequently, however, concern was shown on the quality of education currently being imparted in Malta's schools. Comments like 'essential education, leading towards responsibility, is by and large still lacking' [C.14], 'even though *instruction* has become more general, the quality of education is still very poor in Malta' [D.24], and 'education [referring to general education not exclusively to 'moral' education], at present, is perhaps at its lowest level: lack of discipline, continuous changes, the tarnished image of teachers, big schools and classes etc.' [B.4] were not uncommon. One particular priest who had extensive contacts with school-children graphically described the situation:

I would argue the point whether there is a better education today. The education (culture, literature, languages, general knowledge, manners etc.) of the old *professjonisti* is absolutely missing from present day so-called 'education'. School is fast becoming that purgatory where you have to pass your life between early childhood and your first job — whether you like it or not. Too much education: if education is meant 'in depth', can never be a danger. What can be, and is a real danger, is a smattering of education so thinly spread out [C.20].

Due to Malta's small size, change can never be restricted to particular areas. This fact too was unanimously acknowledged by the diocesan clergy. The greater mobility of the population, following the coming of the motor car, the needs of an increasing number of people to travel away from their place of residence for work and leisure, coupled with the effects of television and the printed media, accelerated the trend towards 'homogeneity and standardization'. The rhythm of change, it was easily recognized, was greater in the villages where the 'slow tempo of rural life has been broken', but the village younger generations were generally considered as being incapable of 'tolerating any differences at all' between their mores and those of their town-bred contemporaries.

More extensive interaction did not spell the end of village particularities; and typically rural features still persist:

The older social patterns can still be noticed to persist to a larger extent in the villages, especially those based mainly on agriculture, fishing, or construction economy, than in the towns and villages where industrial expansion has occurred [C.11].

Townspeople were, because of their previous generally higher education and their higher level of sophistication, considered more able to take changes more easily in their stride.

More impressive than a catalogue of 'important changes' is the *way* priests of different ages expressed themselves about changing Malta. To the older group of priests, those who grew up and were trained to serve the old Malta, many aspects of social change appeared to present a threat, the occasion for the infiltration of values alien to Christian culture as they knew it in their boyhood. Neutral comments like 'girls, still in their teens, and unmarried women are, in increasing numbers, leaving domestic work and farming to work in the light industries', and the common assertion that Malta has gradually attained a 'higher standard of living', were often followed by disparaging comments on feminine fashion trends and the greater freedom of speech. Such feelings of uncertainty about the value of change occasionally took the form of total denunciation in expressions like:

for good or ill, tourism has brought the Maltese into closer contact with foreigners, non-Catholic included ...;

amusements hitherto unknown in Malta, such as the Casino and nightclubs, tend to spread a hedonistic idea of life; and

lax views on sexual morality are gaining ground, and the birth rate has gone down considerably ... [C.39].

These feelings were further amplified when the priests were specifically asked whether the changes they had mentioned earlier had any special kind of impact on the religious life of the Maltese people at large. Morality and traditional social mores, especially in relation to the previously all-important village festa, were seen to have been negatively affected by social change, which allegedly led to a 'lowering of moral standards, especially among the young' [E.46].

The replies of the middle-aged group of priests contrasted sharply with those of the older members of the diocesan clergy. Nostalgic feelings towards the irrevocable past were completely absent, and evaluative considerations were kept down to a minimum. Their long lists of changes in Maltese social life were often couched in either neutral or positive terminology, such as

> One notices greater national self-awareness, leading to political independence and gradual detachment from paternalistic-subservient attitudes; progressively wider education, especially higher education for all strata of society, leading to demands for more self-responsibility and self-determination and higher critical powers (gradually); secularization of public life; wider travel (tourism, migration, returned migrants); industrialization, greater opportunities for, and more varied forms of leisure; less closed societies even in villages, wider marriage selections [C.33].

To some priests, the questions provided them with the first occasion they had ever had for a specific evaluation of their life experience; several exclaimed that so much could happen — and in fact had happened — in twenty-five years. In general, too, the middle-aged members of the clergy proved themselves very sensitive to the overall impact of the process of change on the religious life of the Maltese. Downward trends were noted in the level of general religious practice and, with the exception of Holy Communion, in the number of participants in sacramental life. Social change generally had caused the Church to abandon, or even renunciate, its position as the unique legitimating agency in social life and of social order, and was fostering the gradual 'demythologizing of religious life'. In the process,

> many people suffered crises. Others, especially the young and a growing number of intellectuals, lost their faith, which no longer seemed capable of answering their problems and satisfying their aspirations ... [D.11].

The refusal 'to submit to clericalism' was seen to be widening. Again, the changing trends were rarely considered to be negative, but were considered to be conducive to 'a deeper, more committed attitude on the part of the really "faithful" ' [D.11]. The trend to small numbers in church ran parallel with deeper convictions among those who stayed on.

The lack of nostalgia for the old times was even more pronounced among the younger clergy. For them life and change were inseparable: they were conscious of the changing features of Malta; but rather than fostering a critical attitude towards the process of change (as the old priests did), or expressing feelings of gratitude for the achievements of their contemporaries in other spheres of social life (as the middle-aged priests did), the younger priests took change for granted, as part of their job, together with the challenge that it presented to religion. They saw their task primarily as being one of 'consolidating the positive aspects of our religious heritage and expression' [F.2], and of seeking new ways by which the Gospel message might be made more understandable and might be more fully internalized by the people they served.

6.2 The Priests' Self-Appreciation

Change in most sectors of life in Malta could not have left the clergy unaffected. This fact was readily appreciated by the priests interviewed. Two major areas of the priest's life were actually singled out by the incumbents themselves to demonstrate the new interpretation they give to themselves as individuals, and to the type of service they give to society.

6.21 The Discovery of an Identity

Wider democratization in society brought parallel democratization in the Church. Both the clergy and the laity increasingly recognized the importance of self-affirmation. Dialogue had gradually come to be substituted for the kind of blind obedience that previously prevailed in the priests' command-obedience relationships with their superiors. As is quite evident from a personal letter written in 1946 to Archbishop Gonzi by a *Viči* who had served his parish unstintingly for thirteen years at a salary of £8 per annum, [5] one then had to show considerable boldness and courage to insist on any form of dialogue. The graphic description this particular priest gave of his plight is best left in his own words:

> Hereby I humbly and confidently submit that I have been keeping up with the dignity in my parish the Office of vice-Parish priest for more than 13 years i.e. since January 1932. This administration, here, may be said to be a totalitarian one, as it comprises the administration of all baptisms, viaticums, extreme unctions, further assistance to the dying, transportation of all corpses either from the parish or from hospitals to our local or other cemeteries, daily eucharistic benediction, given at a quarter after sunset, communion to all sick on certain appointed days, singing of Vespers on Sundays, besides other activities

developed in common. As one may see, most of the burden, if not the worst lot, lies within the responsibility of the vice-Parish priest in a parish like mine.

Apart from the rest of all this role of undertakings, one cannot tell, perhaps for lack of experience, all the toil, anxiety and prostration the only resistance to the dying involves when it is singly conducted. Because of the uncertainty and all the keen earnest of the faithful, the vice-Parish priest, being the only person fetched for the purpose consequently to him falls the duty to keep up the watch most of the time nailed to his parish. Then for him a sick in the parish becomes something worse than a sick at home. In order not to shake the piety of the faithful or give source to idle gossip the vice-Parish priest has to surrender each time to all calls of the faithful which at times are so tiresome. And this surrender means something: it means patience, self-denial, endurance and utter prostration. It means sometimes to spend whole hours locked up in dirty and filthy rooms by the side of the dying which in most cases are sick-smelling, covered with lies [lice], ugly looking, horribly blood-bleeding (sometimes) in cases of casualties, and at times affected by infectious diseases, all of them groaning under pains of an agony, which only God knows when it will end. It means to be ever on the alert to answer with promptitude to all calls from whatever corner of the village they come, either by day or by night in summer or in winter, and at times are so rife, that you leave the bed of a sick only to receive a fresh call the next moment. To say, only in one month of January I have had more than 14 night calls!

What a nice thing it is to get out many a time in a hurry, on certain winter cold nights under a pouring rain splashing in water and mud either to spend long hours by the bed of the sick, or to find that your services are no longer required because of the slight recovery of the sick.

All this struggle is divinely sublime, but humanly speaking is truly agonizing. Self-humanity cannot be crushed at all even despite our own desire. During the war all this naturally grew worst, the population being swelled to several thousands spread in distant localities of the parish. Needless to tell that ... the more work for the vice-Parish priest which at times was carried out with an abnegation nearing heroism ... [6]

In the context of such difficult life, cooperation could be expected from other members of the clergy, the more so from the parish priest. And yet this same priest wrote on in the same letter:

Through my devotion to this my duty, my parish priest has ever practically been free and at ease, and indeed, he has been never hindered in his almost daily wanderings out of the parish during daylight ... Why the toil and prostration of a vice-parish priest should be so far ignored and exploited to such unbelieving bounds? ... Well all this may turn but to constitute to some degree an overlord and a slave in one and same parish, making out of the latter only an instrument of stark exploitation ...

When this same priest was interviewed for the purposes of this book more than eighteen years after writing the letter — to which, incidentally, he never received and sort of reply or acknowledgement — he could not but recall the enormous differences that had taken place since then. The life-style of the *Viċi*, though he was still involved in more or less the same duties, had improved considerably over the years. The *Viċijiet* had since then formed a 'College'; they had bargained for the recognition of an official set of duties, and for days off every week; regular channels of communication with their superiors had been established; and their salary had been increased considerably. The *Viċi*'s role in the 1970's is no longer one towards which seminarians and priests show a 'strong dislike' (as was the case in 1946, and for some time afterwards), but is the most attractive and popular among the newly-ordained; ten of the seventeen priests ordained in 1972 and sixteen of the twenty-four who were ordained in 1974 asked for and were actually assigned a *Viċi* job. The extent to which the *Viċijiet* have gradually affirmed themselves is evident from the forceful words they used in their declaration on 'the need for consultation' issued in November 1973 on the eve of a decision on who was to succeed Mgr Gerada, who had been earlier appointed Apostolic Nuncio to Guatemala and El Salvador, as Malta's auxiliary bishop:

Gathered in a special session, today, the 23 November [1973], we the vice-parish priests of Malta, in these difficult times, and particularly now, when the choice for a new bishop is being considered, would like to express our pastoral concern and explain our views on the consultation which we deem appropriate and necessary for a good choice, and on the qualities which we should like to see in the new bishop.

As regards consultation, we should like to recall that a document was published by the Holy See in March 1972 which recommended such consultation. We should therefore like to witness a real consultation in the sense that all the sectors of the Maltese clergy, and all the established groups of the laity, should be asked for their views; and that this consultation should be carried out with the urgency appropriate to the times and conditions prevalent in contemporary Malta.

This consultation is so much in line with the spirit of Vatican II, and is so necessary in practice, that we are certain that no priest would now accept the office of bishop unless he was certain that adequate consultation in the community in which he was to serve had taken place. Our church is a Collegial Church.

With regard to the qualities of the new bishop, we should like a man who understands the signs of the times, who has a large measure of sincerity, who really loves the clergy and the people of God in these islands, who has the courage to put into practice his evangelical convictions, who has already given testimony of pastoral experience, and who has already achieved success in his relationships with other people, in particular with the clergy. [7]

The stand taken by the *Viċijiet* is indicative of the new awareness of self-responsibility that the clergy have gradually built up. Other examples may be cited. On 29 August 1966, a call to all the clergy to 'send in observations for an interdiocesan council' was made. [8] An analysis of the returns — which run into some thousands of pages — suggests that bishop-priest relationships were then at a very low ebb. Priests repeatedly appealed to the bishops to come down to their level, and to communicate with them, and to show them more comprehension and love whenever they were guilty of faults. Strikingly enough, at least thirty-four priests then expressed criticism of the way the bishops of Malta and Gozo were exercising their authority, and of the antiquated way in which they condemned and punished members of the clergy who seemed to deviate from the established patterns of behaviour. [9] The frequent insistence that 'the accused priest should be given the right to defend himself before he is punished', and that punishments should always be given '*sapienter, prudenter et charitative*', suggest great disparities between the priests' expectations and their day-to-day experience. In the same year, 1966, the need for somebody to assist the Archbishop, his equally old Vicar General, and also Mgr Pace, then bishop of Gozo, or to replace them, was already experienced, particularly in view of the impasse in which the politico-religious crisis had resulted. No priest dared to express this in public, however, and the twelve priests who, in their replies, actually expressed themselves in favour of the immediate resignation of the two bishops in Malta and of the Bishop of Gozo did so anonymously, and in very polite and moderate terms. Another three expressed the need for a co-adjutor who could gradually take over the administration of the diocese. In no case was it suggested that consultations should take place about Gonzi's successor, and when the nomination of Mgr Gerada as Auxiliary, and eventually as co-adjutor with right of succession, came in 1967, it was a decision taken from above, and one which nobody questioned.

During the Ligutti affair, the clergy's courage in expressing themselves loudly and publicly, to demand explanations for sudden turns of events, exceeded anything previously experienced. Several priests wrote in the daily press, condemning 'holy alliances', and claiming that 'wounds cannot be medicated unless uncovered'. [10] 226 priests eventually signed a petition to the Pope in response to an *ad hoc* committee which had the courage to express itself openly in oppostion to the termination of the Ligutti mission. When, in late 1973, Mgr Gerada was called to rejoin the Vatican Diplomatic Corps, and the bishopric again became open, the daily papers carried signed articles and letters on the type of person who should be chosen to fill the vacancy.

The discovery of themselves, the priests who were interviewed admitted, did not restrict itself to a more accentuated call for dialogue. The way of life of every priest was greatly influenced by change. Increased affluence in Malta as a whole, and the relatively more lucrative salaries of the priests who had taken up teaching in government schools, accentuated the need for the Church to examine the distribution of its resources, and to secure a better way of life for its clergy. Even though a priest's income still fell far short of the income obtained by people with similar training and qualifications (a lawyer's university was cuorse of one year less duration than that of a diocesan priest; but his income would be at least five times as much), priests admitted they no longer had 'to count their farthings' as they had to do some years before, and could at least enjoy a decently modest living. [11]

6.22 Self-Appreciation in Society

Members of the secular clergy were found to be very much aware that their image among contemporary Maltese differed extensively from that previously enjoyed. The attention that priests as a group used to receive whenever they appeared in society has declined considerably, as if, as one particular priest put it, 'the advent of industry has alienated the people from us' [D.24]. Greater knowledge and learning among the people rendered superfluous several kinds of services previously supplied by the village clergy; and priests were conscious of the fact that the area of their activity was shrinking fast. In their replies, the older respondents expressed themselves in terms that indicate lack of understanding of what was actually happening to them in the process of rapid social change. Sometimes they even expressed doubts as to whether social change was forcing them to secularize themselves unduly, and in the process loosen their previously strong religious attachments and convictions.

Awareness of this changing standing of the priest in society was very much in evidence in the replies given to a question on whether people still respected priests as much as they used to do in 1947, and in 1955. The two years in question were chosen because of their relative importance in Malta's social history, the first being the year when self-government was re-introduced and when primary education became compulsory, and the second because it was the eve of the politico-religious crisis that began with the Integration issue. It was generally agreed among the interviewees that the years 1947—1955—1974 mark a three-stage development in priest-people relationships in Malta. As one priest put it,

> before 1947 they used to show 'reverence' to priests. Since 1955 they learned to criticise and to judge. Today they may not 'respect' the priestly caste but can show admiration and ask service of individual priests ... [C.11].

As a result of the changed status, one noticed signs of insecurity: ordination and the profession no longer provide status umbrellas, and each priest felt he had to establish success by his own merits. Several reasons for the shift in the general attitude of the population were suggested. The politico-religious dispute, several cases of drop-outs especially among the religious clergy, and internal discord among the clergy themselves — now no longer concealed in respect for the priestly office — were thought to have been the main reasons for the shift in the clergy's social standing.

In effect, two main tendencies were noted by the majority of the clergy. First, they noted that, as a result of increased exposure to the discoveries of science and technology, and to rationalistic values imported from alien cultures, Maltese society as a whole, and therefore the clergy, had become *more secular*. Several indicators of this change were mentioned: priests and people were becoming less narrow-minded, more tolerant; the emphasis in the apostolate had shifted from the traditional authoritarian position of the priesthood (one particular priest said that before 1955 'the people expected to be shouted at whenever they were in the wrong!' [C.13], to one where faith was presented as an invitation to be accepted or rejected in freedom. Secondly, the priests noticed that *the exercise of their ministry was becoming more specialized.* The increased awareness that some of the services previously provided by the clergy in the non-religious sphere were no longer demanded of them has already been noted. Its effect, the priests suggested, was to make them retreat to a more purely religious role, and become more 'ministers of the cult', rather than the natural leaders of the community in which they lived. More detailed analysis of this aspect of the clergy's life, as it unravels itself in their day-to-day tasks, will be dealt with in the following section.

6.3. The Priests and the Daily Exercise of their Ministry

The unplanned and unrationalized distribution of tasks and activity within Maltese clerical circles has already been described. The diffusiveness of the priest's role became even more evident in the preceding analysis of the present deployment of the diocesan clergy. An idea of the extent of this diffusiveness is reinforced by the replies obtained from priests to questions about the way they allocated their time. Several priests pointed out that until quite recently, specific full-time jobs were rarely assigned to those newly ordained. For the first few months, each newly-ordained priest had to make his way through the labyrinth of parochial and diocesan organizations in his own particular way, taking up odd jobs as the need arose. Strangely enough, this was found to be most common among priests who had extended their educational experience by following a course of studies abroad. Daily Mass and personal prayer — the latter presumably arising out of the obligations attached to the daily recitation of the breviary — and work in the *għaqdiet* were considered to have been the most important items in the daily programmes of all the priests in this group on their return to Malta, and of the rest of the clergy who had not taken up some form of teaching immediately after ordination. Consequently, few could say that in their first post-ordination year they had a very important 'weekly item' to look forward to, and most could not answer the question on the subject at all. Those who did answer suggested that weekend activities (Saturday confessions and Sunday Mass and homily) were perhaps the weekly event they had looked forward to most in those years. When asked about the existence in the past life of an important 'annual event', several priests suggested that they had, at that time, considered their annual retreat as having been most central. The annual village festa and lenten sermons ranked next in importance.

Priests were further asked whether they still attached the same importance to items or events they had mentioned as having been important when they were newly ordained. The majority replied in the negative and explained why. Most of them had since changed their job: parish assistants had become parish priests, student-priests had become teachers. The shift to a wider ministry brought about a change in the priests' activities, and consequently in the way they evaluated their day-to-day activities. Sunday Mass and homily however had remained the weekly event which attracted most of the clergy's attention.

Over the last decade, the liturgical reform within Catholicism put to a severe test the clergy's adaptability to new demands and needs. Before Vatican II, liturgical activity had been the object of minutely detailed rubrics and every gesture made by the celebrant or an assistant was fully controlled by red print. Knowledge of a set of rules, however complicated they might have appeared at first sight, made it possible for the individual priest to hide behind a facade of exact ceremonial. The language was Latin, about which priests did not really have to bother since for the most part texts had to be read in silence. Furthermore, all sacramental action was celebrated within the framework of an *ex opere operato* theology, and so the priest's physical presence was more important than the mode of his action. The promulgation of the decree *Sacrosanctum Concilium* by Vatican II on 4 December 1963, was the beginning of drastic changes. Rubricism and ritualism suddenly had to be replaced by more live and meaningful liturgical action; the vernacular was to be substituted for Latin; new texts, more appropriate to man's contemporary aspirations and with the new biblical scholarship, were to replace the traditionally sanctified readings. Church music too was to change: choir singing was no longer to enjoy absolute monopoly. The sonorous drum of classical polyphony, and the soft intonations of Gregorian chant, were to cede their place in favour of more participation by the congregation, however mediocre first attempts might be.

Increased emphasis on the theology of the Paschal Mystery, integrated within a new evaluation of the whole history of salvation, shifted the emphasis from merely devotional celebrations to the more central sacramental activity. This too was bound to affect the life pattern of the minister of cult. Devotions to the saints, to the Blessed Virgin, though not to be abolished, had to be re-evaluated — and in a measure devalued — and were henceforth to be seen as secondary to the main stages of the liturgical cycle. What then, was to become of the traditional village festa? What would be the reaction to the sudden shifts of emphasis in a society which had put its stake on the miraculous powers of *San Nikola* or *San Gejtanu*? What, above all, was to happen to the credibility of the village clergy, for so many years the patrons of the *partiti*, the promoters of the dominant ideology, and the staunch supporters of the 'only true and unchanging creed'?

The replies given by the respondents to questions related to these delicate aspects of their life are quite revealing. Not even the old priests declared that they had met insurmountable problems when conducting the liturgy in the vernacular. They all recognized that the major difficulties they had envisaged when the change first came about had, since then, been gradually overcome. 'All this is wonderful', a priest in his seventies explained, 'because the people can now understand what is happening, and not simply look at us whilst we "act" the Mass!' [E.46] [12] The only criticism which was levied against the introduction of Maltese was not directed against the use of the vernacular itself, but rather against the particular translations currently in use. Written Maltese is only about two generations old, and has not yet developed to the extent that allows fluidity of style when certain texts, especially those written by Paul, have to be translated. Elements of 'rigidity', resulting from the translators' attempt 'to steer an uneasy middle course between classical and colloquial Maltese' [E.20], were purported to be evident in the new liturgical texts. Preaching in Maltese, especially outside Mass, had been common long before the Vatican reform — even if the sermons and homilies delivered by the Bishop in the Cathedral were in Italian up to the Second World War — and the clergy said they had been accustomed to it. Again, it was only when concepts obtained from theological literature written in other languages had to be translated into a language which is not sufficiently rich to allow for a succinct expression of abstract concepts, that difficulties were normally met. A comment made by a young priest on this matter perhaps summarizes what normally happens in such cases:

> ideas which cannot be rightly expressed in Maltese are unununderstand-
> able to the Maltese — so I don't preach them at all ... [B.4]

One of the important aspects of the new liturgy is its added emphasis on community participation. Priests were questioned on their reactions to this, and asked to comment on the difficulties they encountered in their attempt to create an atmosphere of communitarian worship as envisaged in the new rites, and specifically on the extent to which the re-organization of the primary sacraments, and their inclusion in the celebration of the Eucharist, was acting beneficially to this effect. Their replies were very diverse and are not easily tabulated: each priest was obviously talking from his own particular experience which was often determined by factors beyond his control — the size of the church, its architecture, and the age distribution of the congregation for example. It was generally agreed however that Malta's big churches, and the big congregations that normally fill them, inhibited the expression of a real sense of community during Mass. Active participation by the laity, however extensive, could never involve more than a few people at a time, and most people were constrained to play a predominantly passive role during the liturgy. Liturgical action itself, despite the many variations incorporated in relation to the varying themes of the liturgical cycle, is essentially repetitive, and not very well adapted to anything resembling a 'crowd atmosphere'. Smaller congregations, it was frequently pointed out, were much easier to handle.

Despite the added complexity involved, the recent inclusion of the main sacraments (baptism, marriage and confirmation) in what have become known as 'ritual Masses' was condoned by a substantial majority. Careful planning by the parish priest was considered necessary, however, lest frequent repetition of the same ritual Mass in the same church at the same time for a number of successive Sundays became a nuisance, rather than a help, to the general atmosphere, increasing rather than reducing the boredom arising from repetition.

As already suggested, the drastic changes in the liturgy embodied in the Vatican decree were bound to clash with one of the most important institutions of Maltese parish life: the annual festa. The relevance of the festa for the village life, and for the individual's participation in it, has already been described. [13] Viewed as a liturgical act, with active participation in its liturgical aspects as the main value, the traditional celebration of the village festa, with the music used at its more important moments, did not easily fit with the new norms. Something had to be done to bring the people into active participation in its liturgical celebration, rather than to provide them with an occasion for a different (one time unique) kind of leisure and relaxation. In many ways, the village festa was bound to test the clergy's willingness to accept the principles put forward by the Council fathers. In the interviews for the present study, clergy reaction to the change were examined. The basic question on the subject was phrased in a way that elicited as clear a response as could have been hoped for, and ran something like: [14]

> Some people condemn the new liturgy because it is stealing from the people a tradition of grandeur and mystery, especially on special occasions like the village festa when traditional music used to have such a great importance attached to it. Others on the other hand are enthusiastic about the new liturgy because of its informality and what they see as its greater didactic content. What do you feel yourself?

In general, the clergy appear to have tried to give a balanced response. While accepting the principles on which the liturgical reform was based, they could not understand why the new developments had not somehow tried to retain the elements of grandeur and mystery which special occasions like the village festa used to carry. The older clergy were particularly reticent. One said,

> I do not condemn the new liturgy for the village festa, but on the other hand I do wish we could find ways and means of catching some of the grandeur of past years! [E.40]

Similar feelings were expressed by a prominent Monsignor:

> I am very fond indeed of Plain (Gregorian) chant and of Sacred Polyphony of the Palestrina-Pergolesi-Victoria-Perosi-Bartolucci etc. type. The organ is the only musical instrument I like in church. The new liturgy has done harm to this type of sacred music; but the Pope has just promised to reconsider the problem. Of course, I am not against the moderate use of popular songs in church, but only as an

addition to the devout and heavenly music just mentioned ... [C.39]

Observation of what actually happened in Malta's churches and in clerical circles since the promulgation of the Council decree on the Liturgy, closely reflects the views on the subject expressed by the middle-aged and younger members of the clergy. Informal discussions on the future of village festas often became heated as different groups of priests could not see how they could suddenly change tradition. It was not difficult for the newer parishes (like that of the Immaculate Conception in Hamrun, and that of St Pius X in Santa Luċija), or for the more urban ones (like St Gregory's in Sliema), where traditional feelings for the annual festa never ran deep, to adapt themselves to the new liturgical norms. Contrary to what a few progressive priests were saying, the existence of pressure groups, often based in the parish band clubs, and concern for the piety of the 'faithful', strongly militated against sudden reform in most towns and villages.

In an attempt to bring the different viewpoints together, an *ad hoc* commission under the auspices of the Liturgical Commission was set up in 1968 on the advice of the Senate of Priests. The report of the commission, which took the form of a draft directory for feasts, was eventually circulated but remained a dead letter. The special commission had suggested a clear distinction between the religious and the more secular aspects of feasts, and suggested that 'folklore elements', though to be conserved as part of Maltese national heritage, should be taken out of the liturgy and held within the framework of a different setting, preceding or following the strictly liturgical parts. [15] This, and the suppression of Latin (and consequently of traditional music) was too much for *il-Monsinjuri* and for *il-Kappillani* to accept. [16] Greater tolerance towards popular feeling, in its manifestation on such special occasions, should be shown, they argued, and any change which might be considered necessary in the long run was to be very gradually introduced.

In 1973, the feelings expressed in 1968 when the draft directory was circulated did not seem to have changed much. Two primary trends were in fact noted in the replies of the clergy: on the one hand a sizeable group was completely in favour of reform, but the majority was in favour of caution and more tolerance. Many priests explained their position in terms such as, 'I am for a dynamic liturgy!' [D.24], and 'what is more intelligible leaves better results' [B.10]. Others were more vociferous in their stand. One said,

> The answer is obvious: in favour of the second group of opinions not only for practical reasons and those adduced, but also because modern society tends to be distracted or even antagonized by a surfeit of pomp and grandeur ... [C.11]

Another's reaction ran:

> I don't think that the music played in Solemn High Masses in festas had anything traditional in it. In many instances it was just operatic music played very loudly and very badly. Certainly there was not much active participation but a lot of distraction (musicians talking, tuning their instruments etc. etc. ...) In festas more solemnity could be given to the liturgy by preparing choirs of parishioners ... [D.24]

The following comment is the most forceful one obtained on the issue and came from somebody who urged immediate and radical reform:

> That our festa had a tradition of grandeur is admitted; whether it did have a tradition of mystery, unless in a quasi-superstitious meaning, is debatable. What was mysterious in the 'old' liturgy was more due to a lack of understanding of its real mystery. The new liturgy brings this mystery within the people's grasp and has, certainly, greater didactic content since it is understood, at least literally, by the congregation ... [C.14]

Attitudes of tolerance for the people's desires and sentiments, however imperfect these might be, were more common than rigid stands in favour of abolishing the old forms. In the opinion of most, recent developments in the liturgy were specifically brought about by a more accentuated need for diversity and pluralism. As such, it was pointed out that recognition of the wish of the young to use the guitar during mass should not be interpreted as necessarily implying a replacement of the old, but rather as an affirmation that old and new could live side by side; and that liturgical celebrations could be adapted in a way that catered for the needs and desires of different social groups. Some examples of this stream of replies illustrates the point more clearly:

> The new liturgy is quite nice as long as you do not have to ram it down other people's unwilling throats ... [C.20]

> Much can be said on both sides. I am in favour of the liturgical renewal, but I cannot stomach those who use it as a means to despise and ridicule our traditional heritage ... [A.17]

> Individuals have the right for their opinions and a particular sensitivity by which they worship God and elevate their minds and hearts to God in prayer. I do not like to condemn any opinion ... it will be excellent if everyone has his share ... [A.11]

> I agree with the latter opinion. However, I do not feel that traditional festa customs should be disregarded, even pastorally, since they are popular ways of celebrating which should be at the basis of every liturgy. I also feel that the new experiments at new para-liturgical celebrations (pageants, biblical celebrations, etc.) are 'imported' ideas

and still do not have the merit of reaching the people at depth as the old traditional forms of celebration ... [D.11]
Perhaps the most considered opinion was the following:
I am for the very-new liturgy. BUT ... we must be reasonable, especially where groups of people are very touchy. Two principles, at least, should be kept in mind:
a) reforms should never create a vacuum (as if they were intended to give more free-time to the priest); and
b) liturgy which is attended by the general public should cater for general tastes, which are brevity and simplicity. But that which is normally attended by the 'traditional' kind of Christian only, *should* cater for their tastes. They have a right to it as much as have the young to folk masses ... [B.4]

Festas are a very important element in parish life, but they are only an annual occurence. The place where the priest comes closest, and most frequently, to his parishioners' life and problems is undoubtedly the confessional. Catholic sacramental theology insists that under normal conditions reconciliation with God and pardon for sins can be obtained only through an encounter with Christ in the sacrament of Penance. The 'penitent' is supposed to confide his innermost secrets and his spiritual problems to the confessor who is then expected to provide practical help on how the individual's way of life might be improved, and then to grant absolution. Because of its confidential nature, a great aura of secrecy and mutual trust between priest and penitent is involved in the practice. A priest could very easily lose his credit and esteem if he acted on knowledge acquired through the confessional, or if he went beyond the normally accepted limits in the questions he asked. Stiff censures against abuses of this kind are provided for in Canon Law; [17] and they act as powerful deterrents. In many ways the popularity of a priest-confessor is an indicator of an individual's rectitude and general acceptance by the people in his capacity as mediator between themselves and God.

In spite of the highly confidential nature of the sacrament, the majority of the clergy interviewed did not find much difficulty in sharing some of their *general* impressions of confessional practice with a fellow member of the profession. Questions had to be couched in general terms, but the answers elicited are conducive to an analysis of the areas where strain and tension do exist. Practically all the clergy agreed that the number of confessions was decreasing whilst the reception of Holy Communion was on the increase. In the views of the older members of the clergy, this was mainly attributable to increased laxity. 'Contemporary people have lost their *sensus peccati*' [E.46], one priest insisted. In most cases the decline was negatively viewed, and people were blamed for it. As one relatively old priest explained,

The main reasons why fewer people go to confession are:

1. some ultra-modern confessors, preachers and writers stupidly insist less on the great utility of frequent confession, even if one is not in the state of mortal sin;
2. lax views on sexual morality; and
3. the widespread rumour that the ecclesiastical law prescribing confession before receiving Holy Communion, if one commits mortal sin, is going to be replaced. [C.39]

The views of the middle-aged and younger clergy were more varied. The decline in the frequency of confession was attributed to many factors, and on the whole was not taken as necessarily pointing to a corresponding decline in religiosity. The majority of priests in this category considered the decline to be indicative of positive forces: 'At last our people are distinguishing between Confession and Holy Communion' [D.16]. It had previously been the prevalent idea in Malta that one could not go to Holy Communion if one had not prepared for it by confession, even if one had no mortal sins to confess. For a few years priests have been trying to correct this false impression; and the decline in the practice could thus signify acceptance of the new teaching. Many priests actually said this: 'people have learned that it is not necessary to go to confession before receiving Holy Communion'. 'It is quite true that we are having less confessions', another priest said, 'but I think that previously many came to confess just out of habit, without at times having anything to confess. The meaning of their confession is being brought out more clearly to our people. Reconciliation to God should be sought when there is a real need for it' [C.15]. Similar comments were frequent: 'People are going to confession when they really need it, not just out of devotion ...' [A.20]; 'People are often satisfied with fortnightly or monthly, instead of weekly, confession; and still go to communion regularly: they are perhaps showing a more mature attitude to life, to sin and to contrition ...' [C.10]; 'the decline is due to a higher sense of responsibility in that intelligent Catholics have realised that so many so-called "sinful acts" were not sins ...' [C.13]; 'they now have better knowledge of the gravity of their offences, and perhaps individual conscience is not so strict and scrupulous ...' [A.10]; 'today we have fewer confessions, but these are much better than the former habit of just going to "play the same old record" to the priest ...' [B.1].

Otherwise the general decline, and to some extent the process of maturation itself, tended to be attributed to social factors, and specifically to the general shifts evident in the pattern of village and parish life. It had previously been the custom that Saturday afternoon was to be reserved for confession. People often had to queue for hours to be attended to, but the slow rhythm of rural life permitted this, and in some way provided a structured occasion for people to prepare themselves for the important Sunday Mass and Communion. Things changed; and as one priest put it:

Life was not so fast in those days. If it took an hour to confess, it also took an hour to arrive home after your work. Time was no problem. One had enough of it. Suffice it to say that quite a lot of families used to have time to go to the village pump for water and queue up for it. Maybe it was a communitarian act. You met everybody while waiting for your turn. Today people are so rushed, they just cannot stand any waiting — for anything ... not even for confession. [C.20]

Confession as a 'Saturday evening "must" for most people is a thing of the past', another priest [D.20] declared.

Despite the decline in the strength of important factors that previously facilitated an almost rhythmic regularity in confession, it was agreed by all but a small minority of the priests interviewed that the Maltese generally still tend to go to confession on particular occasions, and in view of particular 'events' in which the social and the religious are closely intertwined. Two main groups of occasions were actually singled out. The traditional village festa, the feast of Our Lady of Sorrows, the feasts of Corpus Christi and of the Sacred Heart of Jesus, Christmas, Lent and Easter, All Souls' Day, and to certain exetent First Fridays, still attract people to the confessional; and form the first group. These are all red-letter days in the life of the ordinary Maltese Catholic and people are encouraged to do their best to participate fully in the eucharist. The practice of inviting guest confessors (konfessuri barranin) to every big church on the eve of such occasions has always made it easier for the people to conceal their identity, and thus more easily comply with the clergy's insistence.

The second group of occasions is not as institutionalized as the first. It has grown out of the increasing practice by the Church of integrating the major sacraments and rites of passage in a eucharistic celebration, and out of the repeated appeal that all people present for the service should participate fully by receiving communion. The celebration of baptism, marriage, funerals, and of confirmation has consequently been extended to include, in a more active way, the family, relatives, and guests of the person or persons who are actually receiving the sacrament. It has recently become the practice, for example, for a child who is to receive its first Holy Communion, to be accompanied in church by his parents or guardians, and then for them to receive communion with him. Invitations for the marriage celebration, too, nowadays frequently include the suggestion that guests ought to join the couple in the celebration of the eucharist, and to offer Holy Communion for the needs of the newly-weds. Most people comply with the new custom. Even if this occurs not strictly in a structured manner, it has to be appreciated that latent social forces (especially the psychological feeling that one should not be the odd man out) press the individual to seek a confessor. Priests acknowledge the possible short-comings resulting from this attempt at an authentic liturgical renewal, and during my interviews with them frequently talked of the new custom as a 'subtle form of post-Conciliar regimentation' [A.21].

People of different sexes, ages, and of different educational back-grounds, respondents agreed, had different ways of approaching confession. Not many differences on the acceptance of this fact were noticed in the replies given by priests in the various age categories, a fact that possibly indicates that a priest's popularity as a confessor is more related to his mentality and approach rather than to mere age. Respondents often talked about children's confessions with a smile: 'they have their own peculiar way of confessing their tiny sins', one priest [C.11] said. Children, it was said, very often repeated a list of petty faults rehearsed with their mother in preparation for the reception of the sacrament. Old people, on the other hand, seem to look at confession as a safety-valve for their problems, and often 'prefer to chat with the priest all about their daily chores' [B.3]. Although confession is meant to be a place where one's sins are forgiven, old people too seem to prefer to 'confess other people's sins rather than their own, excusing their "necessarily wicked" behaviour as they go along' [F.3]. Men were least frequently seen for routine confession. When they did go, 'they are the most difficult to deal with: they are guarded and shy. But they can open up to a careful approach' [D.10]. Normally, 'men are straightforward and brief' in the first part of confession, but then 'like to argue' about the advice given. Women were described by respon-dents to be 'highly reticent on sins against purity', 'generally timid', but 'can be very talkative when discussing family problems' [A.21]; sometimes 'they even cry, and tend to be more docile to the advice given to them by the priest' [E.20]. Young people, whether they are boys or girls, were held not to differ much in their approach to the sacrament. Their confessions were more spread out, but once they did go, 'sometimes they feel awkward, but are always sincere'; 'they are more articulate and relevant in their confession and questions'; 'they eagerly accept good and convincing advice'; and they preferred to make use of confession as if it were a counselling session, during which they could 'discuss their life-problems, expectatons, and their attitudes to religion in general'.

Because of the strict rules safeguarding the secrecy of the sacrament of Penance, questions on the 'contents' of people's confessions were purposely left vague and general. The different interpretations open to the question 'What do people show most anxiety about in general in the confessional?' were consciously retained as a safeguard against possible abortive reactions from incumbents. In effect, the way the above question was phrased allowed the more 'scrupulous' members of the clergy to suggest answers like 'the integrity of their confession', and 'accessibility to Holy Communion'. Most replies, however, did point to areas of human activity that were the most common objects of people's confession. Almost universal consensus was obtained that the greatest preoccupation among penitents was related to their sexual behaviour. Priests were very reticent to go into details in this particular area. General replies like 'problems related to *de sexto* and *de nono*' [E.39] and 'the way in which to control their sexual instincts in whatever stage in life they might be' [A.21] were frequent. These answers suggest that sexual activity presented men and women with the greatest problem in their attempts to lead holy lives, both before and after marriage. Masturbation, and 'impure thoughts', were mentioned as being the most common problems with the young and the old. Middle-aged married penitents tended to relate their guilt in this area to their use of the marriage act, and especially to problems of birth-control. Relationships with other members of the family often gave rise to serious, and repeated, problems, and many of the priests interviewed suggested that this area too frequently became the subject matter of people's confessions. When further questioned about the truth of the statement that 'one rarely hears a mention of sins against charity, faith, other people's property, etc.', the general feeling was that although sex was often the primary preoccupation of those who went to confess, sins related to language (swearing, lying and idle gossip) were also very common. In their replies most priests heavily qualified the 'rarely' in the question, and comments such as the following were repeatedly offered by the clergy: 'people often confess sins against faith and charity' [C.10]; 'people are learning to examine themselves on the ten commandments and not on one only'; 'it is true that they emphasize faults against the sixth commandment. But they feel guilty of detraction, lack of trust in God's providence, thefts, and so many other things as well ...' [A.21].

6.4 The Beliefs and Opinions of the Clergy: Patterns of Assent and Dissent in Selected Areas

The attitudes of the individual priest to the daily exercise of his ministry cannot be divorced from his overall evaluation of his profession, or from his evaluation of the Church in which he exercises that ministry.

In an attempt to integrate these two aspects of the priest's life, analytically distinguishable even if closely intertwined in practice, three areas were chosen for closer study: (a) the nature of the Church; (b) Church-State relationships; and (c) their vision on the future of the priesthood itself.

6.41 The Nature of the Church

What is the image of the Maltese Church like in the minds of the Maltese clergy? In particular, how do they evaluate its internal dissensions and problems? (Respondents were asked to speak frankly on any particular area of clerical life which, during the last few years, they considered as having given cause for concern.) Although no question was specifically directed to the question of communication within the Church, the subject arose spontaneously from many interviews, and this reflects the concern about this matter that had been aired in a number of different places during the previous decade. Clearly, communication itself is intimately related to the authority structure of the Church and the hierarchical organization of the clergy, and is in itself a delicate and difficult issue. To provide some indication of the climate of opinion on this subject, it is perhaps necessary to indicate some of the comments that had been expressed in a variety of places. These provide a prelude to the comments elicited to the more general questions included in the interviews. Respondents tended to concentrate on the lack of proper channels of communication within the Church, and on the gradual evolution of patterns of dissent and of a general feeling of apathy among the clergy. Among earlier comments, the following give some idea of the depth and range of clerical concern with this issue.

When Tonna analyzed the work and remuneration of the diocesan clergy in 1964, no specific mention of the existence of large-scale dissension was made in the report. Occasional hints in it did, however, indicate that a basic lack of communication, and a consequent disunity, existed even then:

> The socialization process [for priests] takes the form of an eight year, residential course at the Floriana Major Seminary ... [where] a stratification process gets under way. Candidates are ranked — both by superiors and by their peers — according to mental ability, personality, and spirituality ... [After ordination] the inner group of their [priests'] friends is recruited from these [their parents' or relatives'] homes. While bringing in the additional advantage of coming in close touch with the realities of everyday life, these groups also conceal the risk of adulterating the purity of the pastoral spirit cultivated in the Seminary ... if occasionally cut off from their fellow Priests (and

Superiors) Diocesan priests are never far off from the people ... [18]

In response to a call, in 1966, for suggestions in preparation for the Regional Council, several criticized existing relationships between parish priests and other priests in the parishes. One priest said parish priests should stop 'playing the dictators and the bosses of their parishes', [19] and another pointed out that.

> The parish priest should govern the parish together with all the other members of the clergy. There should be *real* consultation, and not merely a fake one, carried out when everything is already planned, very often with the help of laymen rather than priests ... [02]

A specific question on what people thought on the correctness of priests' behaviour towards fellow priests and towards their bishops had also been put to all those who had participated in the August 1967 survey on the Image of the Priests in Malta. The results reported that:

> 60% approved the behaviour of priests towards their fellow priests. Only 13% were not pleased with relations among priests. 26% expressed no opinion ... 67% of the respondents thought that priests had good relations with their immediate superiors. But 27% had no opinion to offer and 6% thought the contrary... 77% of the sample considered the behaviour of priests *vis-à-vis* the bishops to be correct. 3% affirmed the contrary while 20% offered no opinion. [21]

A later comment affirmed that,

> the low percentage of people mentioned above who consider relations among priests to be good, constitutes a warning: priests should sincerely cultivate and project a brighter image of mutual love among themselves ... [22]

In 1970 the report on Malta's *Viċijiet* noted the existence of lack of unity in pastoral effort in the following words:

> the tension is apparent ... in [their] aspiration for a greater respect for the dignity of the work being done [by them] — an aspiration crystallised in the unexpressed but continuously noticeable desire for wider participation in the actual running of the parish ... [23]

A year later, the heated discussions on the suspension of the Ligutti mission [24] added a further dimension to the rift, and eventually brought dissension on a much wider scale. In an interview given to the Church-owned paper *Il-Hajja* on 19 August 1971, Bishop Co-adjutor Mgr E. Gerada condemned the attempt by an *ad hoc* committee to collect signatures from fellow priests in favour of the reform in the following terms:

> the fact that this call for signatures has been made under the pretext that the report has been suspended ... appears to me to be at least inopportune ... Events of this kind create only sensationalism and dissensions among the clergy ... [25]

A few days later, on 31 March, Bishop Gerada criticized the attitude taken by the clergy in a declaration he read to the Senate of Priests. In his declaration, he condemned rumours that even Major seminarians had formulated some form of protest:

> the same newspaper [*The Bulletin*] said also that the seminarians had protested. If this is so, one cannot but be disturbed, because such an attitude leads only to anarchy, and I do not think that it is in accordance with the spirit of the Church, and the loyalty that each one of us holds towards the Holy See ... [26]

A prominent layman, and former leader of the then defunct Democratic Nationalist Party, Dr H. Ganado, vehemently attacked 'revolutionary priests' on 26 May, in *Il-Hajja*:

> it is sad to note that during the last few months various members of the clergy seem to have lost their heads and think that, since the Council, they can go down to the squares and from there accuse, criticise, badly portray, give inexact information and consequently detract the respect due to the Bishops ... [27]

In a subsequent reply by Fr J. Felice Pace, whose previous letter had been referred to by Dr Ganado, the latter's criticisms were forcefully rebutted:

> Our revolution goes beyond that of a simple protest, however just it could be. We are not revolutionaries because we simply like protesting. No! We are revolutionaries because we understand — and time will prove us right — that nothing less than a radical transformation is necessary so that we could attain the ideals set to us by Christ ... [28]

The extent to which the rift gradually widened as it came more into the open called for some sort of remedial action; and a suggestion that a Vicar for the Clergy should be appointed found general approval among the clergy. By June 1972, the suggestion had been taken up by the bishops, and Mgr J. Sapiano, a retired Philosophy Professor, informed the clergy of his nomination as the Pastoral Secretary and Vicar for the Clergy of the Malta diocese. [29] In its subsequent issue, the clergy review *Pastor* [30] welcomed the news in an editorial; and, in an attempt to instil trust in the new office and its incumbent, bypassed the discussions then current in clerical circles on the choice of the person for the task. A motion brought before the Priests' Senate in July 1972 for the separation of the office of Vicar of the Clergy from that of Pastoral Secretary was defeated by a majority of one with one abstention.

In the meantime, a second attempt was being made for the establishment of better channels of communication between members of the clergy on the parish level. In June 1972, the Archbishop announced to the members of the Senate that he had presented a draft statute for the erection of the 'Parish Presbyterium' in every parish to the College of

Parish Priests for their comments. Discussions of the draft statute took several months; the final draft was approved on 20 February 1973; and became effective in the following April. The aim of the new instrument was to foster a more collegial sharing of duties, and to serve as means whereby co-responsibility on the parish level could be brought about. Several criticisms were directed to the final draft, most especially to the underlying principle that made the new body merely consultative. [31]

The 'Parish Presbyterium' had been functioning officially only for a few months when incumbents were interviewed for the purposes of the present study. Questions on relationships between parish priests and priests therefore drew on the longer term experience of priests rather than specifically on their impressions of the effectiveness of recent changes. Priests in different age-groups did not differ markedly in their remarks, and changes for the better were mentioned as frequently as the lack of any change. The effectiveness of the nominated Vicar for the Clergy was not apparent to all respondents, and one contemporary of Mgr Sapiano, himself a Monsignor and at the same time also a member of the Priests' Senate, even suggested that such a post should be created:

> I see no change at all. What we need is a Vicar for the Clergy who would visit the various parishes, hear the problems of individual priests, and try to solve them ... [E.39]

On the other hand, the changes for the better over the years which were mentioned were generally attributed only to the characteristics and openness of individual priests. Again, a small selection of the comments elicited from the clergy interviewed on his point demonstrates the trend:

> Some changes have occurred in some parishes, none in many parishes, and a lot of change towards the ideal of brotherhood and teamwork in only a few: the showing on the whole, despite the *Presbiterio Parrocchiale*, is disappointing. The reason: mutual distrust, authority seen as power ... [C.11]
> There has been a little improvement in the way of sharing responsibility — but there has been no radical impulse towards true communitarianism ... [D.11]
> Changes for the better ... younger priests are more exigent and vociferous about their rights and parish priests have to oblige ... [D.24]
> The parish priest — priest relationship depends very much on the character of the persons concerned. However, they have generally come closer together because many parish priests have come down from the high pedestal on which they used to stand. They are learning to consult their priests and share responsibility ... [D.17]
> Hardly any significant change (in my parish). Co-responsibility has

not taken root. A section of Maltese priests are not sensitive enough to the signs of the times ... [C.21]

In spite of the general feeling of discontent with relationships among the clergy, and with the general relevance of Church activity, most of the priests interviewed did not entertain a pessimistic view of the Church's future. A question aimed to test the way priests looked at the institution in which they had to exercise their priestly tasks was purposely framed in forceful words, and ran something like:

The end of the MLP — Church dispute has at least put an end to an organized form of anticlericalism from which the Church previously had to defend herself. However, some say that the Church is now crumbling from within. Do you agree? Why?

Only a very small and relatively insignificant minority accepted the implications of the word 'crumbling'; and insisted that the Church was in no way falling apart. They did however point to the major area of discord, and also suggested reasons for its existence. The older clergy, surprisingly enough, were rather reticent to comment on this point. One of them avoided the question by a Latin remark '*rem difficilem postulasti*' and then proceeded to state that one had to take it for granted that the Church's stand had the approval of the Vatican Secretariate of State. Most of the others in his age group acceded to the inexistence of 'organized anticlericalism', but not to the absence of other forms of anticlericalism. 'The Church in Malta has no leader', one complained; and then added, 'We are a fold without a shepherd!' [E.40].

The majority of the clergy in the middle-aged group, although not acceding to the full implications of the word 'crumbling', seemed upset by the internal disunity that existed within the Church when the interviews were carried out. [22] Comments from the interviews are very illustrative of the prevailing mood among the clergy:

It is not crumbling from within. But within the Church there are individuals who are attempting to present the image of the Church to our contemporaries in a way as it can still attract them and hence carry on the massage of the Lord ... [C.15]

Crumbling is perhaps too strong a word. The Church in Malta can dispose still of tremendous forces for good. But unfortunately it is disorganized. Many priests are apathetic and frustrated. A strong sense of purpose and leadership is urgently needed ... [C.21]

One has to admit to the unfortunate crisis within the Maltese Church, and to a certain extent of 'crumbling' of Church structure. The reason is lack of leadership, and lack of ideas even in the whole church community. We lack ideas, we lack community spirit, we lack inspiration ... [A.11]

Indeed the Church has been experiencing some difficulties arising from within. The most serious is the loss of confidence in the Bishops as a result of failure to carry out in time the administrative reform and to produce a pastoral plan, and of impoverishing the diocese to a considerable extent by indulging in some risky transactions ... [D.17] The Church cannot crumble from within; but it can crumble from without because of the human element ... and there are some signs of decay ... [B.24] There is certainly chaos in the Hierarchy's guidance ... [D.11] Yes, because it has been so often buttressed by external help of various kinds (some quite contra-evangelical) that the Church in Malta has grown into the habit of placing its trust more in these inadequate helps than in the Spirit. Now that these are falling by the wayside, the Church in Malta seems unable to recapture and give witness to the genuine Spirit of the Gospel and to God and Christ, especially because its members lack the genuine spirit of Christian love, sacrifice and self-restraint ... [C.11] Yes, this is due to a lack of orientation, vision, involvement, planning, and organization. Maltese people, in general, still look for leadership from the Church. Yet this is missing ... [B.14] No. She is undergoing a necessary change from within. The trouble is that she is leaderless ... [C.17]

The attitudes of the younger clergy, as in other areas, were siginificantly different from those of their older counterparts. They accepted more easily the facts of an internal distintegration of the Church as an organization, and in many cases even expected it; but their evaluation of the process was more readily positive. In their view, the type of church they received from their predecessors restrained the building of a true community; and the new image of the Church as desired by Vatican II could not come about unless within a completely different ecclesiological approach. One particular priest typified this way of thinking very clearly: If you mean the organized Church (or institutional Church), they could be right to say so. The reason is that the Church is run by men who cling to old systems. But the real Christian community is a-building in Malta, slowly but soundly in the parishes run by young priests ... [B.6]

6.42 Ideal Church-State Relationships

Respondents' views on the *ideal* form of Church-State relationships correlated very strongly with their ecclesiological perspectives. This particular area of priests' thinking, it has already been indicated elsewhere, has been particularly crucial in the unfolding of events in Malta ever since Catholics enjoyed 'majority church' status. During April 1974, for example, politicians still considered it necessary to frequently explain the quality of Church-State relationships during public political meetings & conferences. [33] These relationships however had undergone strain during the lifetime of respondents; an analysis of the way the clergy themselves envisaged the existing situation and their earlier experience therefore indicates emerging trends in this delicate sphere of Maltese public life.

The five theories representing five modes of Church-State relationships given by Depasquale provided a good scale and the opinions of respondents were ranked accordingly. [34] The views of the older clergy interviewed were almost exclusively construed around the traditional juridical approach to the problem of Church-State relationships: both Church and State were considered to be perfect societies, each with different purposes and different means to attain them. Respondents in this category pointed out that the Church has true authority not only over strictly religious matters, but also over matters of a temporal nature connected with man's supernatural destiny. Their approach to the problem tended to coincide with the fourth theory — that of the 'indirect subjection of state to church' in those areas connected with the Church's own superior purpose. In traditional terminology, the Church's authority was not said to be exercised *propter se* but *per accidens*. The accent all through was on practical cooperation and coordination between the two societies; and it was frequently suggested that the common good could be attained only within such a perspective. [35]

Strikingly enough, an altogether different conception of ideal Church-State relationships was envisaged by respondents in the younger age groups. To a certain extent, the accent was still on coordination and harmony between the two 'organizations', but the perspective had changed. Only one respondent came close to endorsing the view that ideally the Church should wield indirect but true juridical authority over the State when he said:

In Malta, where all citizens are also Catholics, there should be perfect harmony and a sincere wish to follow the teachings of the Church ... [D.24]

With all the others the accent was on separation of Church from State, with freedom for the Church in the exercise of its mission. The Church's aim, for these respondents, should never be to wield power and authority over the actions of the State, but should be rather to show the way for those who wished to follow. Respondents' own remarks illustrate the point:

Cooperation *cum* separation ... [A.17]

The Church should insist on her freedom to:
(a) proclaim the Gospel of Christ even in concrete situations;
(b) exercise this freedom with clarity and especially by giving positive
    live witness to the *whole* Gospel and *all* the time through her
    members. This is important for its credibility. And I think this is
    where it is failing miserably.
At the same time the State should be free to exercise its authority
in its spheres. In 'mixed' issues (marriages, education, etc.) the Church
should not insist on privileges, but only on its right for freedom as
in above; the State should take heed of both the changes in Maltese
society (with a tendency towards pluralism) and also of the links
between Christian and Maltese culture ... [D.11]
Mutual respect, cooperation for the common good, separation ..
[C.17]
I want a free Church in a free State. Cooperation in all that is to
the good of the 'whole man' but a free Church means a Church
capable of excercising its prophetic function without any limitations
or pressures ... [A.11]
friendly separation ... [D.24]
Both serve the same human beings. Therefore they have to collaborate
to help every being fulfil himself as a person morally and materially.
In a pluralistic society the Church should not have, and should not
seek to have, privileged status unless this is necessary for the general
welfare of the particular community which both Church and State
are serving ... [B.14]
Each has its own sphere of activity. No paternalism either way. The
Church has to retain its position as the guardian of the Faith and
Morals of its members ... [C.14]
Mutual help and understanding but no political alliances ... [A.11]
Consensus on the theoretical aspects of the ideal conditions for
trouble-free Church-State relationships did not necessarily mean consensus
on the ways by which the ideal was being realized in the daily experience
of incumbents. In order to test for divergencies of this kind, respondents
were asked to comment on the old disputes with the Malta Labour Party,
on developments under the Nationalist government, and also on the actual
effectiveness of the peace agreement signed in 1969 between the Labour
Party and the Church; and its practical application since Labour was
returned to government.
    The replies of the diocesan clergy to the question, 'The biggest
dissension in Malta during the 1960s was the politico-religious crisis. What
were the real issues?', were rather diverse; but all pointed out that the

issue centred on Mintoff's attempt to secularise Maltese society, and to reduce the Church's influence over social institutions — an influence which had until then been all-pervasive. Most priests felt that Mintoff was then propounding laicist tenets in socialist garb, which could not be accepted by the local hierarchy which were bound to abide by the Papal dictum that 'all forms of socialism must be rejected'. [36] Socialism was at that time considered to be the first step to communism, and fears that Malta could become a second Cuba, particularly as a result of the Malta Labour Party's association with the allegedly Communist-dominated A.A.P.S.O., further complicated the issues. [37] Mintoff's leftist tendencies were traced back to his university days, and his early letters to *The Daily Malta Chronicle* in 1938 and 1939, which gave Marx and Christ equal status, were often quoted and attacked. [38] Quotations from the survey material illustrate the points priests sought to make:

> Judging by Mintoff's six points, the main issue was whether and to what extent the then eminently catholic island of Malta (*un' isola nobilissima e cattolicissima* — Paul VI) was to be secularized ... [E.39]
> should a political party present proposals which the Church Hierarchy considers not to be compatible with integral Catholicism ... [C.9]
> Labour Party leaders wanted to create a socialist state based on traditional socialist beliefs ... the Church finding itself and its traditional role threatened, retaliated ... [D.11]

When asked whether they still endorsed the position then taken by the Church, priests generally agreed that the Church had been rightly critical of MLP attitudes, but felt that the experience had been too traumatic to be cherished. With the exception of a small minority who gave their absolute approval to the policy and procedure adopted by the Church, those diocesan clergy who were interviewed revealed their serious reservations, especially about the methods used by Church people to combat the positions of the MLP during the dispute. Two priests from the middle-aged group admitted they had never endorsed the position taken by the Church, even during the hectic days of the early '60s [A.17 and C.14]; and a substantial number pointed out that Vatican II theology had changed the outlook of the Church towards people who did not fully agree with her teachings, and that the Church had become more tolerant towards them. A few quotations from the replies of the priests demonstrate this point:

> To a very great extent yes, but we now have a slight increase in the number of unbelievers. Of course, I do not approve of some weapons imprudently used in the fight for a just cause ... [E.39]
> I still hold the views that I held then, viz. that the Church authorities

were rightly critical of MLP attitudes, but were often misguided in rebutting them ... [C.9]

Although *at the time* the Church's reaction was only natural, and although one cannot judge this reaction on the basis of criteria that have become 'firmly' established only since Vatican II, that view can no longer *now* be endorsed *en bloc* in my opinion since it is not in touch with modern social conditions and with the Church's own attitudes to the temporal order and the State ... [F.1]

No. The Council convinced me that our approach was not Christian ... [C.17]

The position of the Church has been overwhelmed by the times. The Conciliar era has made the Church more tolerant. On the other hand, socialism has taken so many faces that one has to distinguish between ideological and practical socialism. [B.6]

Despite the non-infrequent crticism of the allegedly 'hasty' way the MLP-Church agreement was reached in 1969, [39] priests generally agreed that the Church's task now was to live up to the spirit of the Vatican decree *Gaudium et Spes*, and specifically to article 76 on which the whole agreement was reached.

The priests interviewed were also asked to comment on how Church-State relationships under the Nationalist regime contrasted with conditions under a Labour government. On the whole, priests accepted the fact that the Nationalists did their best to accede to (*jaġevolaw*) the wishes of the Church hierarchy, and to do so in a cordial way. But the majority of those interviewed pointed to several instances where this was not done in practice. 'Some decisions taken under a Nationalist administration should have never been taken', one said [E.40]. The tendency prevalent among Nationalist MPs to consider themselves the *protegés* of the clergy also came under frequent attack. The priests interviewed occasionally noted that relationships at the top tended to be 'by and large correct', but at the local level, the close associations of individual members of the clergy with Nationalist MPs was a matter of concern as it created animosity among supporters of the opposing *partit*. [40] It was also pointed out that much more practical collaboration between Church and State could have been procured during the Nationalist administration: 'unfortunately, very often the two bodies contented themselves with artificial ceremonial co-operation!' [B.40]. The lack of public comment on issues like the setting up of the Casino [41] and of the greater laxity in dress made people think that the Church had made a 'coalition' with 'her' party, and would not publicly condemn it. The majority of the priests interviewed resented this and insisted that although issues like the Prime Minister/Archbishop precedence [42] and the visit to Malta of the Czech Minister of Education [43] were relatively unimportant and should never have been commented upon at all by Church officials, there had been cases where the Church's stand should have been beneficial to the setting up of a more ordered society.[44]

Similar feelings of dissatisfaction became evident when priests were asked whether they were satisfied with the quality of Church-State relationships under the Labour administration. Only a small minority of those interviewed answered with an absolute 'no', the majority answered with a qualified 'no', whilst another group gave a very qualified 'yes'. The biggest problem priests were facing in the prevailing condition of Church-State relationships was the lack of knowledge of what exactly was happening, and the simultaneous need to safeguard an atmosphere of *detente* — a situation which contrasted sharply with what had been the case ten years before. Among priests' replies were the following comments:

Perhaps under present circumstances, no better *modus vivendi* between Church and State is possible ... [C.39]

The Church is being accused of not following the same policy it used to have before. I think the Church is now trying to prevent awkward situations but when these arise, it has to tackle them even publicly ... [C.18]

No, definitely not. The Church is too much preoccupied with possible reactions ... [A.21]

Definitely not: I believe we are *really* in a state of no-war, no-peace, but not of *real* positive good-will and collaboration: situation based on mutual fear and distrust basically. Hope I am mistaken, but afraid not ... [C.11]

No, although I think that the Church cannot do otherwise ... [B.6]

There is little information to go by on what is going on. But it is felt that Church authorities are bending backwards not to come into any trouble with the administration ... [C.14]

No: a) Church leaders have not yet learnt to fulfil a 'prophetic' role;
b) Government policy — especially social — is ambiguous ... [C.9]

One is thankful, considering the good of the faithful, that clashes between the Church and the government have been avoided ... [D.15]

One particular priest gave a rather lengthy explanation of the way he viewed the situation:

The government is extremely cautious not to rock the boat, though it is clearly happy with the accelerated 'secularization' process; and every now and then takes its chance to increase the impetus, for example with the Colleges of Education, the Trade Schools etc. ...
The Church is extremely cautions not to repeat the old experience. Nothing bad, if this cautiousness were the fruit of deep and

evangelical conviction, which I doubt. I am afraid it is coming rather from fear of losing its 'prestige', which it loses nonetheless through the process I mentioned before — and the government is very well aware of all this, and it cannot serve him [the government] better!

The Church authorities, on the other hand, are hardly taking any *visible* stand to give real witness to the real human and Christian values. And this is the tragedy, since this is the only way to ensure that Christ and the Gospel will find their place in today's society: see the financial, property scandals, power struggle between Bishops, lack of leadership in the Christian community, failure to talk on *real* questions, e.g. freedom of speech for authors, industrial relations and the General Workers Union, lack of initiative and leadership on pastoral renewal, loss of touch with the grass-roots, preoccupation to 'praise' the government when 'privileges' are accorded — the nomination of Ambassador to the Holy See, the Archbishop's talk on Government action against prostitution — lack of real effort towards evangelical poverty, etc ... [D.11]

Similar, and sometimes identical, examples of the areas where closer collaboration between the Labour Government and the Church would have proved the good intentions of the Labour leaders were commonly mentioned by interviewees: the reform of the training colleges need not have entailed the express exclusion of the De La Salle Brothers and the Sisters of the Sacred Heart who had given such excellent service for so long; more importance could have been attached to the teaching of religion in the new trade schools; and the running of St Philip Neri — a reformatory school for criminals who are minors — need not have been changed. All interviewees were asked to give their reaction to the stand by the Church to three particular issues which had arisen since Labour came to power. The clergy's opinion was sharply divided on the way in which the Church had insisted that religion should be included in the syllabus of the new trade schools. Only a minority showed absolute disapproval; a substantial number indicated approval and agreed that the Church had to accept such concessions as the government was ready to make, whilst the rest pointed out that Church's stand had been rather confused, and the effort weak, insufficient and, to a large extent, inefficiently conducted. Similar reactions were elicited about the stand taken by the Church on the amendments to the criminal code on homsexuality and adultery. [45] Priests generally did not consider themselves against the actual amendments but considered that the bishops' pastoral letter clearly distinguishing crime from sin, and admitting that homosexuality could frequently be the result of psychosomatic factors, was not clear enough. Many criticized the pastoral letter as 'platitudinous'; and declared that a better form of organized follow-up, intended to educate the people on the issue, could have been arranged. One priest pointed out that the stand taken by the bishops was correct; and it was up to the clergy to explain what the bishops meant in their pastoral letter, which, because of its typical elaborate style, might not have been fully comprehensible to most.

Opinion on the personal intervention of Archbishop Gonzi in the Anglo-Maltese dispute in the early months of the Labour administration was more dispersed. Negotiations on the rent to be paid by England and her NATO allies for their military base in Malta had come to an impasse and the British had already ordered a withdrawal of their forces and equipment from the island as a result of the ultimatum Mintoff had given them. If things had continued, Malta would have found itself in great difficulties since the transition from an economy based almost exclusively on the employment generated by the Services to a diversified economy was still in its initial phases. [46] Gonzi intervened on his personal initiative, and with both Mintoff's and the Pope's approval was received by the British Prime Minister and the Defence Secretary soon after he arrived in London from Rome. Though he had no executive mandate from Mintoff to conduct discussions for the Maltese Government, his intervention, which he repeatedly insisted did not arise out of his capacity as Archbishop, helped to draw the parties back into negotiation, [47] and eventually to a settlement. In their replies, all the clergy showed appreciation of the positive results of Gonzi's intervention, but quite a number emphatically said he should have kept out of it. Some priests were critical of the Archbishop's intervention because they saw lack of clear vision on the 'Church's proper role' as distinguished from 'its historically assumed role'. The majority of the priests interviewed further pointed out that Gonzi's move had no political implications, and should be appreciated in the way in which Mintoff and his supporters were said to have appreciated it. Gonzi's standing in international circles, and especially the esteem he had built for himself in British government circles, coupled with the backing he got from Vatican diplomacy, helped Dr Luns, NATO Secretary General, to bring matters to a settlement. [48] The priests who showed their appreciation of his action also pointed out that his move was a clear sign from the Church that its intentions were good, that old feuds were to be forgotten, and that a fresh start, built on trust rather than on fear, was possible.

6.43 *Their Vision of the Priesthood*

Within the complex web of changing conditions, and in the light of internal points of strain within the Maltese Church, priests in Malta must continually re-examine their commitments. Had they made the right decision in becoming priests? What were the prospects of the priesthood in the new Malta? And which were the models of priestly life which present-day priests envisaged for the future?

Priests generally agreed that the priesthood was undergoing a crisis. This was not to be attributed to Vatican II, but more to the search for identity. Changing patterns of life and the shifts in Maltese society had eliminated the traditional roles which priests had assumed, and had left them without clear alternatives. Most considered the current stage to be transitory, and a period to be cherished. When asked whether they would still become priests if they had to choose anew, an absolute majority replied in the affirmative, and did so on the basis that the priesthood made sense to them as an institution even though individual priests might at times find themselves ill at ease, very often due to problems inherent in the situation in which they were working. The insistence of many that 'they would still become priests, but with a different outlook in view' was indicative of the new model priests were looking for for themselves; and very often related the need for a new perspective following the new order of priest-people relationships promoted by Vatican II with its added emphasis on the laity's role in the life of the Church.

Priests considered that people at large had become conscious that the priesthood was increasingly less attractive as an avenue to higher status, and attributed its remaining popularity to other factors. The family, faith in the office as an optimum way of continuing the spread of the Gospel, as well as the spirit of service and generosity, were repeatedly considered to be factors that still attracted young men to the priesthood in spite of the dificulties inherent in the office. Priests said:

The priesthood still gives status, although much less than formerly. Young men are drawn to the priesthood by the desire to serve God, to help their fellow men and to save their own souls. Vocations are fostered by good family upbringing and religious formation in the Catholic organizations ... [D.17]

Previously the priesthood in Malta could have meant a change for the better in the social sphere for the family of the individual concerned. Now times have changed considerably when other openings for such an amelioration are to be found. Neverthless the Faith factor is still important in the Maltese family and has an influence on our vocations ... [C.14]

1) Faith; 2) Generosity; 3) the influence of lay associations and good families. I do not exclude mixed motives in particular cases, such as the (mistaken) notion of an easy life ... [C.21]

I find that those going in for the priesthood in Malta believe that in the local context, it is one of the major avenues through which one can serve others. Yet the status symbol is, unfortunately, still an attraction for some ... [C.14]

Activities of future priests were, the interviewed priests insisted, bound to be different from and less easy than those of their predecessors. Certainly they should never meddle in politics. When it was suggested to interviewees that in other countries priests took an active part in politics, and when they were asked whether Maltese priests should do the same, the majority came out forcefully against the idea. 'Maltese politics is too much bound with party interests', one priest remarked. Every priest interviewed affirmed his right to have political opinions, but most could not envisage a situation in which people would accept priests as actors in the political arena. Several priests independently came up with the idea that there might conceivably be a particular instance where a priest, or group of priests, might join a party, or even form a new party to provide an alternative if the need for it arose, but they all insisted that such priests wherever they were would have to abstain, at least for a time, from exercising the priesthood. [49] Such a development however was considered to be possible only in the event of extreme circumstances: the priesthood as visualized by many diocesan priests for the future within the Maltese context was to be emphatically a-political, and with much less access to direct socio-political power than previously. The priest's economic position vis-à-vis other professions or occupations which demand a similarly lengthy training period was also expected to become less favourable. Vocations would tend to decline, and, as the still lingering connections of the priesthood further melt away in the new openings created in larger society through social advancement, the repository of dispositions for service previously attached to the priesthood may easily find themselves being channelled to the new lay leadership services and occupations. Priests do not however think this should in any way be considered to be a direct threat to the priesthood, but rather, as one priest put it,

> all these factors [the process of secularization, the disharmony within the Church, and the uncertainty surrounding the priest's role in the emerging welfare state], far from being negative aspects, are serving to purify the image of the priest, making it more beautiful, attractive, and challenging [D.11].

In many ways, the emerging vision for the priesthood as envisaged by the most committed members of the clergy — especially those in the younger age groups — was clear and uncompromising: it is not quantity but quality which matters; and quality depends on the priest's understanding his role not on a par with any of the other lay professions — concerned as they often are with gain as much as they are concerned with technical skill — but as a vocation to provide service on the pattern of that provided by Christ. As one priest pointed out,

> So far we had a lot of 'mass' priests. Wo we need them in future? If not, it would be perhaps a blessing in disguise to have a smaller number of priests totally dedicated to real priestly activity and provided for by the Maltese Church. Otherwise we will continue to have many frustrated individuals who are only good at causing frustration to others ... [D.18]

6.5 Developments in Disharmony

The intimations of possible divergencies among the Maltese diocesan clergy which were suggested at the end of Chapter V have been fully realized by the foregoing summary of the opinions of the priests' way of looking at the world, and at themselves in that world. Each of the preceding sections has attempted to dissect into its various component parts the life-styles, aspirations, and ideological orientations of the clergy; and what has resulted is a web of disparaging comment on a substantial number of issues which had assumed — and still continued to assume at the time of writing — sustained relevance in the development of social life, and of societal organization, on the island over the last few decades. Priests were in fact found to be in disagreement on issues very intimately connected with the daily exercise of their ministry, and although patterns of similarities on certain issues (the need for self-assertion, the role of the Church in the provision of an end to society, the need for better communication channels within the Church) were becoming more diffused across the whole specrum of clerical opinion, the existence of disharmony on issues which formed the basis of the priest's involvement in life, and of his self-fulfilment therefore, could not be doubted. This disharmony must be further explained, as must be the forces that, paradoxically enough, have maintained the 'clerical ethos' despite the widespread elements of dissent and disagreement that have been noticed. The preceding sections admit a three-pronged typification of the more relevant orientations to life, to religion, and to the place of the Church in society, adopted by the Maltese clergy. Undoubtedly, none of these world-views is held in this form by any one particular member of the clergy; and their introduction at this stage of our discussion is meant to be only instrumental, each being indicative of a possible framework in which a priest might operate, rather than a prescriptive analysis of mutually exclusive modes of thought and behaviour. In real life the views of an individual priest might fall somewhere in between any two of these types, or he might even apply more than one perspective, simultaneously or at different times. The three orientations will be called (a) the 'integralist', (b) the 'liberal', and (c) the 'dialogic', respectively.

(a) *Integralist* A priest operating within this perspective would consider religion, specifically equated with Roman Catholicism, to be the unique means whereby God's message to the world might be transmitted and received by man. The world of the non-rational posits no epistemological problems to him, and has to be accepted as part of the 'gift of faith', in such a way that actions based on it have the same force and effect as actions derived from a logically coherent process of thought. The unknown is a given datum, but although knowledge of such a datum is itself based on a non-rational deductive process, it has the capacity to become what, in the terms of Aristotelian logic, would be called 'the major premise'. The eistence of God, man's dependency on this God, and the existence of the Church as the sole medium of communication between man as dependent and God as creator, are instances of such basic data. Man's responsibility in religion is seen to extend only as far as he is able to abide by the rules of conduct, and by the precepts of behaviour originating from, or endorsed by, the institutional Church — itself the bearer of the *only* possible truth. The word of the Church is to be taken as ultimate, beyond doubt or discussion. Guardianship of the eternal dicta is the responsibility and the prerogative of ecclesiastical authority, and, specifically because of the divine mandate enjoyed by this authority in the exercise of its teaching prerogatives, everyone is expected to accept and abide by the official interpretations of the truth as the Church propounds them. The individual priest would consider himself not simply as the officiator in religious services, but, because of religion's superintendency of social life generally, as the unique legitimator of society's aspirations and customs. He would therefore not consider the assumption of roles outside the purely sacramental sphere as being incongruent with his calling, but would rather tend to consider his social status as being derivative of the authority he represents, and which is to be ascribed to him by virtue of his office.

(b) *Liberal* A liberal priest would approach the problem of religion and its place in society in a way markedly different from that of the 'integralist'. To him, the realm of the non-rational does posit an epistemological problem, and one which every individual should be left to solve for himself. Each person should have the greatest possible freedom to choose between a rejection of the alleged relevance of non-rationality, and its acceptance — the latter possibility eventually leading to, and culminating in, the free, privately reached and maintained, profession of faith. To a liberal priest, too, social mores should represent individual decisions, not the mere conservation of inherited behaviour based on unquestioned dicta. The Church, which to him should extend beyond the institution pyramidally ordering the distribution of power, should disengage itself completely from involvement with matters not strictly relevant to its primary tasks as understood by the individuals who associate with one another because they accept the same premises for the ordering of their action. Their action and behaviour should be clearly related to the pristine kernel of truths as found, primarily, in the 'Book'. Areas such as public decency, and fashion trends, should be beyond its corporate interests; it should especially dissociate itself from politics and in no way indulge in a debate on the philosophy upon which the political community chooses to base its programme.

(c) *Dialogic* A third stance, lying somewhere between the other two, is possible, and actually emerged from the interview material. A priest adopting a 'dialogic' perspective would insist that people should be given the fullest possible freedom of choice whether to accept or reject the idea that there is a God who is active in their lives, and, in the case of acceptance, whether to organize their lives in accordance with such a concept. Such a priest would recognize the reality of the epistemological problems associated with the non-rational, and would insist that these problems are the concern of the individual. Once they had opted for a particular solution to these problems, however, individuals should have complete freedom to assert their beliefs in public, to attempt to influence, in accordance with their ideas, the pattern of social relationships and social institutions. Within the Maltese context, such a priest would be ready to admit that Catholicism could no longer validly claim full super-intendency over Maltese social life and custom, and that secularization, even if still in its incipient phases, was becoming increasingly more widespread; but he would argue that the problem of life's meaning could be solved only within a religious framework, and that recent social change had simply provided a better opportunity and more adequate means by which to engage in dialogue with others.

The existence of these three orientations, at times in muted form, among the Maltese diocesan clergy has been amply documented in preceding sections of this chapter. It is extremely difficult to estimate how they are spread over this spectrum, but it was evident that age, education, and type of work being done, correlated highly with the positions assumed: the older clergy, those who were educated 'once and for all', and especially those who had enjoyed a stable appointment for a long period, tended to opt for the 'integralist' stance; a small minority or priests, mainly middle-aged, but with a history of attachments that brought them in constant touch with foreigners and with values alien to Christianity, could be called the 'liberal' group; the rest tended to fall into the third, 'dialogic' group. Rather than attempt to specify the number of priests which might be classified under each type, what is most important here is to note a basic shift away from the 'integralist' to the 'dialogic' and 'liberal' positions, with the former becoming the more popular. Remnants of the integralist perspective persist, and surfaced explciity even in contributions to the press during the debate on the provision of religion in school curricula early in 1974; [50] but it is primarily the simultaneous existence of the three orientations among the Maltese clergy that not only reflects the disharmony that exists, but which creates situations that protract it.

The shift from a situation when the Church was the unique legitimating agency in society to one in which it has to compete with other agencies which are providing alternative models of life-styles, based on different, perhaps less demanding, values, is undermining the 'integralist' stance, and considerably affecting the security of the clergy. Not only is a multitude of varying life-styles being offered to the people, but the very way in which these are projected is increasingly more attractive. No individual is left unaffected. The facilitating role of the media in the process of social change has already been discussed elsewhere, and needs no further elaboration here. From the clergyman's point of view, the media are a force with which he has to compete, even though his educational background (based on 'trust' as a datum rather than 'trust' as an achievable end) was never intended to turn him into a 'hidden persuader', endowed with a special flair for communication. Other agencies, enjoying more developed techniques, compete for individuals' time and seek, often quite consciously and deliberately, to change the norms and values traditionally accepted and religiously legitimated. Against this, the community has had only the parish priest and his assistants to reinforce received orientations and value-systems. The observation that the media are constantly robbing the Church from the time traditionally allocated to the sacred cult does not imply necessarily that the Church will suffer complete destruction; and the clergy, even those most liberally minded, emphatically rejected the idea that the Church could ever fall into ruin. And yet, several factors were undoubtedly creating for the Maltese priest a crisis of identity: social change undermined the uniform social substructure from which the priest's traditional authority was derived; Vatican II ideas made him more aware of the positive values existing in secular society, and generally in other value-systems too. The sense of security among the clergy was not however undermined solely by these ideological factors, most of which reached Malta from abroad through education, the media or tourism. Internal factors within the Maltese Church, too, had accentuated the loss of traditional security, for the individual priest. When the interviews for the purposes of this chapter were held, the leadership of the Church in Malta was known to be divided, and the bishops were known to be in disagreement among themselves on issues of vital importance. Disharmony had grown gradually, but it had then come to a stage when it was discouraging for priests even to think of communicating with one of the bishops to the exclusion of the other because of the gossip which circulated about each of them, and the unattractive situation in which the Curia itself was divided into two *partiti*, each built around a bishop. Evidence of this has already been forthcoming in preceding sections, and the explosive situation was defused only when Bishop Gerada was promoted to an Archbishopric and invited to rejoin the Vatican diplomatic corps. This did not, however, mean the end of disharmony, and the consultations which started to be carried out by the Archbishop and by the Apostolic Nuncio to Malta about who might eventually be nominated in Gerada's stead, gave rise to a further crystallization of interests around a group of favoured candidates for the appointment. It was precisely during this interim period that a substantial number of the clergy signed a petition addressed to the Pope, asking him to nominate an Apostolic Administrator to run the diocese. Meanwhile, many names were mentioned, the Archbishop and the Nuncio making independent consultations, proposing their own candidates, even approaching their own men. The seed of disharmony had however grown into a tree, and it was practically impossible to obtain a consensus of opinion as each priest mentioned as a possibly suitable candidate found himself bitterly criticized, as his detractors enlarged his defects and minimized his credentials. In the end, the Vatican took one of its favoured options, and nominated someone almost completely unknown on the Maltese scene.

The nomination of Mgr J. Mercieca came as a complete surprise to most members of the clergy in Malta. [51] It had never occurred to the Maltese priests that the diocese of Malta, with so many priests, could not produce a good candidate for the bishopric. Mgr Mercieca was virtually unknown in the larger diocese, and he had never been involved in the main issues that had assumed such importance in that diocese. Mercieca's nomination provoked little enthusiasm among the clergy; and some believed that the Vatican had failed to deal with the complexities of the situation.

The clergy hoped that the man could do well, but they adopted an attitude of expectancy, without allowing themselves to move either for or against him. A few days after the nomination, three prominent members of the diocesan clergy publicly made a declaration on the issue, and though this declaration was not publicly endorsed by many others it certainly reflected the opinions and frame of mind of a substantial number of the Maltese diocesan clergy. The declaration stated:

We, the undersigned, although we do not know Mgr Joseph Mercieca, would be ready to believe that he has all the necessary qualities to make a good auxiliary bishop. What we are going to state therefore should in no way reflect on his person.

We would like to remind everybody that Archbishop Gonzi had appealed for a consultation on the choice of a new bishop; and that several priests and laymen had given their opinion on the matter to the Archbishop personally.

We would also like to remind that the Christus Rex Society also organized a consultation, and all the diocesan priests were asked to forward their opinion on the choice of a new bishop to the Apostolic Nuncio and to the Archbishop of Malta.

We are therefore surprised by the fact that the choice for an auxiliary bishop for the Malta diocese has fallen on a priest who has never worked in this diocese, and who is not sufficiently known here.

We are afraid that as a result of this future consultations held by the Ecclesiastical Authorities among the clergy and the laity will be increasingly taken with less seriousness.

> Signed: Fr L. Cachia, Archpriest of Zebbug
> Fr M. Camilleri, President of Christus Rex
> Fr P. Serracino Inglott, Professor of Philosophy [52]

The effect of these circumstances on the individual priest is to create a somewhat traumatic situation. A very articulate comment from the interview data may further elucidate the feelings of an individual who could not easily come to grips with this sort of inharmonious situation:

> In 1956 I behaved as a natural leader, disinterested protector of all around me from all sorts of real and imaginary threats, then between 1962-65 I had a glimpse of a future when the Church will be re-going through a vacuum, in disarray, not knowing what is worth doing. I was trained as an intellectual, I feel I have to be pastor. Meanwhile I am adrift, in search of a meaningful role ... [C.21]

Such a feeling of crisis of identity, and of lack of specific commitment — so different from previous situations when every priest knew what the community expected of him — tended to dilute the previously strong links of *esprit de corps*. Even though frequently not in full accord among themselves, priests had always been equally treated by the people, an aura of sacredness encapsulating in equal degree the members of the same caste as it were. But with the gradual erosion of this respect, and in the absence of sustained leadership, priests came increasingly to endorse divergent, and at times conflicting, world-views. They no longer hesitated to criticize fellow-priests, even the bishops, in public. [53] Allegiance was no longer directed towards an abstract reality known as

'Mother Church', but to a body of individually-held principles, the legitimacy of which — as in the emerging national ethos — was not derived from man-made institutions, but from individual consciences. Respect for ecclesiastical leadership, once apparently so deep-seated, had largely gone: the authorities could make mistakes. Priests gradually began to find it easier to give advice — especially from the confessional — which at times was not clearly in line with established norms. In many ways, this emerging process could be easily called the 'protestantization' of the Maltese clergy, a clear, if silent, movement of dissent, the like of which Malta had never experienced before.

The priesthood as such, and the Church as such, was apparently losing something of the support and affection that, traditionally, it had enjoyed. The priests themselves were, apparently, increasingly aware that they could no longer take for granted their own sense of belonging. A process of alienation, in however mild a form, might be not too strong a description for what was occurring. Perhaps one indication of this changed sense of one's place can be observed in a quite different development. For a long time priests, enjoying considerable social esteem, lived with their near kinsfolk rather than in presbyteries, and in their homes found the natural affective support for a celibate cleric. As manifestations of traditional esteem and affection diminished, so some substitute for the old pattern appears to have been felt necessary, at least by some. Small groups of priests began to work in teams. The *focolarini* movement (which asserts that Christian love has to be outwardly expressed so that it can be properly perceived) became suddenly pupular. In their own way both trends suggest a reassertion of the demand for an expression of the affectivity of the priest's role in new forms.

The foregoing phenomena that bring the Maltese diocesan priesthood to an impasse in its own development vis-à-vis the society it serves have, in some measure, already been experienced abroad. [54] Rapid social change, most especially the cultural revolution that restructured the distribution of leadership roles and gave rise to an increasing number of professions, repeatedly brought great pressures to bear on the clergy as they, gradually but persistently, realized that their theological universe could not continue to cater for the problems created by modern societal developments. The result of course was that the clergy, too, came to consider themselves as members of a profession, interested in a very specific area of human activity, and claiming exclusive control of only a section of what previously had been a domain fully and exclusively legitimated by their ideological stances. In a way, such a process of 'professionalization' of the clergy helped to re-create the claim for exclusivity, even if within a set of much limited role performances. The priesthood as an institution seeks to emerge from the experience of rapid social change in a new livery, affirming the continued indispensibility of its functions, even if in considerably changed form. The former universality of the clergyman's role has been undermined and its scope has become restricted; but by virtue of his theological training, and — perhaps even of the new emphasis on a more restricted sphere of specialisation — the cleric may be considered as a 'professional' in ways which are perhaps closer to the usual model than was formerly the case. [55]

Circumstances in Malta were in many respects different from those prevalent in other countries, and the clergy did not experience the greatest threat to their survival from the development of other professions. The traditional professions had always functioned in complete harmony with the priest: clergyman, doctor and lawyer frequently knew each other from their boyhood years, they had advanced socially together, they had frequently rubbed shoulders at the *alma mater* (itself more like a family school rather than an anonymous institution because of its essentially limited scale), and they had provided each other with sustained cooperation and friendship all through their formative years. On crossing the threshold of their respective professions, they continued to cooperate, providing patronage to the people around them, and finding in each other an oasis where the experiences of the community they were serving and leading could be theoretically evaluated and discussed. Corrective, educational, or any other form of communal activity frequently, if not exclusively, stemmed from their conjoined efforts, and, at a time when the value system of the community around them was essentially unitary, their contribution to the smooth running of affairs was always accepted and appreciated by the people at large. [56] Such close collaboration sustained the Church's position of monopoly, put her in a better position to resist the effects of secularization, and in a variety of ways helped her to come to terms with them. Even when, as a result of foreign influence primarily, the call for a diminution of the clergyman's domain was made in local circles, the general population reacted and tempered what might otherwise have led to the end of the Church's hold on social life in general. The absence of a regimented structure of priest deployment and organization readily allowed those clergy who so wished to embark on initiatives, and to adopt ideologies not strictly in line with canonical teaching practice in the various fields of responsibility within the Church. [57] The clergy, consequently, did not find themselves isolated from the major areas of social life; the priesthood is still a significant form of leadership among the Maltese, and an agency of substantial influence not only through its activity, but also through its influence on opinions in most areas of social life, not excluding — despite the increasing forces against its being so —

the political domain. Undoubtedly, several factors put Malta at an advantage over other countries in this respect: Vatican II theology anticipated social change in Malta as much as it acknowledged it elsewhere. The post-Vatican atmosphere of inquisitive freedom has considerably affected the way of thinking of Maltese priests, and has allowed the individual priest to attempt an unconstrained re-interpretation of his life experience, and has probably made some individual priests much more forward looking in respect of social change than is the case elsewhere. The experience is still too new to allow judgement, or any form of quantification, but the ideas expressed by some of the clergy interviewed — ideas undreamt of a decade ago — is a clear indication of some of its possible dimensions. In many respects, of course, all this adds to the disparity and disharmony within the clergy ranks; it explains the bewilderment of a considerable number of laymen who at times feel they have been betrayed by the new positions adopted by the clergy (in matters of birth-control, and of Church-State relationships, for example). The new forces that are now making themselves felt are recognized by the Church — at least by progressive elements within the Church — and many priests try to harness them in the restructuring of the Church according to a new model based on more openness, and on the added recognition given to lay opinion. The younger clergy especially are oriented much more to the future and to change than to tradition and the past and, in a variety of ways, seek to defuse the old bureaucratic power structures in favour of communal relationships. The whole process — and this has to be noted — is not coming about through a process of polarization. Conflict, younger priests claim, is contrary to the Christian ethic. They wish to bring about change by initiatives that retain the priest's social base, perhaps even enlarging it, not through coercion or the forceful assertion of priestly prerogatives, but through a peaceful assertion of the Christian values of love, tolenrance, and hope, which they claimed could bring about a new social order.

The emerging situation of course posits several difficulties. Will the Maltese clergy seek — and if seeking will they succeed — to hold on to their position of relatively high status? Strikingly enough, none of the priests interviewed wanted to talk of the priesthood in terms of status, neither did they consider the priesthood to be any longer a comfortable 'status route'. They agreed that in the past men might have chosen to become priests for social advancement, but they no longer considered it possible that any young man — in an era when the costs of becoming a priest were so much higher and the material benefits associated with it lower — could be attracted by the social prestige of the priesthood. These expectations were in fact borne out by the description of an ideal priest given by almost all the priests who had been ordained for only one year in 1973. [58] The ideal of a good priest which emerged from this group, in spite of the difficulties they were encountering in their attempt to translate their ideals into hard reality during their first few post-ordination months, was that of a person in low key, humble, lovable, determined to do good wherever he was or went. Status and prestige were never mentioned by these priests as positive features of the priest's life; but rather as negative ones. When they were mentioned in fact they were mentioned as the things which the people expect *least* of a priest, and therefore as things which every individual priest should strive hard to avoid. Some examples of the descriptions given by the priests themselves might explain the shift towards a new model of the priesthood:

Lovable and humble — somebody who keeps his dignity, but with no sense of pride. A person continuously seeking to be of help. A busy person — always prepared to say yes when asked to give talks or deliver homilies. Somebody who prays a lot, and does so with the people ...

A sincere person, good-hearted, dedicated to his work, and prepared for his task ...

Somebody who continuously seeks to bring people together without consideration of his own personal interests ...

A spiritual, humble, happy person. Somebody who is nice and homely with everybody ...

A man of prayer, who loves his companions and the people, and who would therefore be ready to help them as much as he can ...

Somebody who is frequently in Church, who works a lot especially among those who need his services most: young people, children, the sick. He must do all this without concerning himself with his personal interests and with money matters ...

A person who is able to orientate the individual and the community to God — the absolute value. He must have the ability to this by way of service to the community in general, and to every individual in particular ...

Almost identical replies were given by the seminarians who were independently asked to give their views on the same issues: [59] an ideal priest, it was repeatedly pointed out, must be one who considers himself 'lost' to himself, and 'totally given to the service of humanity'. He must not allow the lure of politics, or of financial advancement to lead him away from an ideal of service to humanity, for whom he might work only if he is humane, lovable, and ready to sacrifice himself for the benefit of the other — always remembering that he is dealing with persons, not just with an anonymous number in a crowd of identical units.

Of course, for the priesthood, the search for a social status is always an unworthy motive. Priests do have a normative commitment, strongly reinforced by the process of both formal and informal socialization to the profession, to disavow wordly considerations, whether of status, power, or wealth. This element is to be found in all professions, and, in a way, it is entailed in the fiduciary relationship that a professional man must cultivate with his clientele. He is offering service, committing not only his skill but also his disinterested goodwill to the service of those who engage him. In the case of the clergy, skill is perhaps less at issue, but goodwill is to be more than disinterested, and in consequence reward, in whatever terms, is to be of very much less account, if of account at all. Priests are taught that the relationship with those they serve is to be not only unexploitive but positively self-denying. It is therefore to be expected that in interviews, priests will be most likely to reaffirm the ideological and normative demands of their role. It is also clear that in practice, over the centuries, the performance of priests has often fallen far short of the ideals to which they have subscribed. But the impression remains that contemporary younger priests in Malta — and perhaps elsewhere — have rededicated themselves (and they are of course not the first generation of priests to do this) to the more vigorous affirmation and realization of these goals. Nonetheless, the choice of the priesthood in such a troubled period of the Church's life — when, both in Malta and abroad, disharmony rather than stability has become normative, and the spirit of group-belonging that the younger priests and seminarians are trying to foster — suggest that they are not motivated by social forces related to prestige, to status, or to social advancement, but rather by a sincere belief that there is something worthwhile that a priest — if dedicated — might achieve.

It does appear that there has been a significant reappraisal of the very nature of the priesthood. The shift towards the dialogic perspective suggests an awareness that the Church and the priesthood cannot remain as they were. In a stable and non-technologicalised society, the social kudos, the comfortable life, and the social influence of the priesthood undoubtedly made it an attractive social postition, and may have been considered 'worthwile' side-effects accruing to an occupation primarily concerned with the perpetuation of religious ideology as authenticated by a mass of inherited cult and liturgical ceremonial. These status advantages are now available in other spheres of social life, and the priesthood no longer enjoys the relative status, respect, or comfort that once it did. In part, the loss of status is no doubt a consequence of the loss of function, evident even in Malta in the growth of other (at times new) professions, although perhaps less evident there than in some other societies. The old incidental functions of the priest, the caring, nursing, chiding, punishing, counselling, have in large measure become the work of other functionaries who have subjected these activties to narrower and more specialized and routinized techniques. In the context of what must be called relatively amateur competences, the priest brought dedication and affectivity to his work, and it was on the basis of these qualities that his status — the esteem of others and his own self-esteem — rested. The loss of these functions has made a new image of the clergy indispensable. The diffuse role has lost the contexts in which its benefits were realized. The pressure in other countries — notably in Britain [60] — has been to rationalize the priest's role. To some extent such a pressure existed also in Malta, as was made evident in foregoing pages. But inevitably, such a prospect encounters opposition in the ranks of the clergy. Rationalization militates against the primary affectivity of the priest's task as traditionally conceived. It is difficult to reconcile with the ideological commitment by which priestly motivations have previously been summoned. It is against this background of the contemporary crisis of the priest — a crisis that is more acute in other societies than in Malta, perhaps — that there appears to be, among a substantial number of the Maltese clergy, an attempt to revitalize the conception of their work in society. That mood, if it is correctly detected by the interviews undertaken for this book, is in part a demand for a return to a more charismatic and prophetic element in the priesthood. In some respects it appears to stand over against the trend of the times, and it is of course very difficult to establish to what extent this mood is consistent with the Church's own organizational structure; but the attempt to conceptualize the priesthood in this way is a clear alternative to the professionalization of the priesthood noted elsewhere. The quest for a vision undoubtedly creates concern to the leadership of the Church, and could eventually result in further developments in disharmony. It could, on the other hand, re-create a new pattern of ecclesial commitment, one in which veracity resides in the remnant few, who, proud of their ideological commitments, try to re-enact them in conformity with the demands, the pressures, and the signs of the times. But the prospects of the realization of such a mood — paradoxically enough developing as it is in a period of quasi-structured disharmony — lie outside the scope of the present discussion.

Conclusion

1. Politics and the Maltese Church: a Transient Ideological Vacuum?

Over the last few decades, the process of social change and modernization in Malta has resulted in the development of a new society, altering not only social structure, but also the very fibre of social life and the mode of social interaction among the Maltese. The symbolic universe of the islanders, their mode of communication — among themselves as well as with foreigners — were very different in 1974 from what they had been two decades previously; and had changed in accordance with the conceptions that the Maltese gradually developed about their place in the twentieth-century world. Calls for change in Malta's social structure, and especially for a more equitable, and more directly productive, society, had for a long time been made by various Maltese intellectuals and leaders, but without much success. [1] The major stimulus for change, as has already been argued, had always been dissatisfaction with a condition of economic dependence, but until the Second World War the need for change had never been properly rationalized, and attempts to improve conditions had often been nullified by factors beyond the control of the islanders. Only after the Second World War was there a possibility of rationalization of the economy, and, perhaps more important, only then did a process of vigorous politicization occur in Malta — extensively facilitated by the growing disapproval throughout the world of colonial government. But as early as 1939, in the course of Mintoff's earliest political debate in the Maltese press, the basic problem of inequality among Malta's population had been clearly articulated, and these ideals came increasingly to dominate the Maltese political scene in the following decades. [2] In the postwar years, political power was gradually transferred to the indigenous population and, more important, to the peasants and the workers. The politicization of the masses, and the concomitant rise of democratic political hegemonies, gradually gave to the workers a distinctive claim to power. Through unionization they have today become one of the most powerful organized forces in almost every sphere of activity on the island. Clearly, unionization was possible only as a result of structural differentiation in the economy resulting from the deliberate shift from the autonomous, family-centred, farm, fishing, and commercial activity, to the more stable, if at times not so lucrative, jobs in industry. Unionization and politicization developed together, especially as the workers involved in Malta's largest industry — the dockyard — sought strategically to politicize their claims within the up-and-coming Malta Labour Party which had, especially since Mintoff's break with Boffa in 1949, gradually created a vigorous political machine, supported by its own media. The Labour Party constantly called for improvement of living standards and life-chances for the more deprived segments of the community. It was this party that, as early as 1949, introduced the first measures for a more equitable distribution of wealth through income tax, old-age pensions, and other similar measures intended gradually to introduce the welfare state. The process of politicization of the masses was not of course the sole prerogative of the Labour Party. The introduction of universal suffrage in 1947 necessarily forced the leaders of the Nationalist Party to take more seriously the question of re-thinking their political programme in terms of a wider and a more differentiated electorate, but it was primarily the Labour Party which made people aware that the old language question was really not a matter of importance; it was that party which made a serious attempt to develop a political strategy away from the thrust political debate on the island had followed in previous decades; and which made articulate demands for immediate social reforms.[3] This development had consequences for the Church. Although the Church had not acted formally as a political agency, its direct influence over the lives of many, its standing as the primary organized identification for the Maltese (over against the occupying power), its ubiquity in the island, and its hierarchical structure, had given it a political significance in former times which, in the face of the mass party system, it now lost. In some ways, the struggle with the Labour Party, documented in the foregoing pages, was itself an indication of the latent political significance of the Church. That struggle was in its own way also an indication of the changes occuring in the Maltese political arena, and, quite without regard to the temporary victory claimed by the Church, perhaps the long-term message of the Church and the people was that for the religious institution to become so overtly embroiled in political affairs, in an age in which democratic politics had been established, was to run the risk of serious divisions among the population at large and the prospect of diminished efficiency of the Church itself, as normal spiritual life was invaded by extraneous political concerns. Although in 1969 a reconciliation of interests was effected between the MLP and the Church after the dispute of the early sixties, the generally secularizing tendency of the Labour Party may remain a ground for futre distrust. Even so, the likelihood of the Church mobilizing its following for confrontation with Labour at the polls has certainly diminished, and in this sense Maltese politics have been secularized.

In the background of these changed institutional relationships, there were, of course, changes in social structure. The old patronage system had been considerably altered, and although in respect of social status the professionals retained the prestige and esteem they had previously enjoyed — they remained highly educated men in a society with a very short history of mass literacy — the political implications of their status came to be more restricted. Increasingly it became apparent that the influence of professional men now also operated through a party system: when the political party of an individual 'professionist' was out of power, his political stature was usually negligible, leaving him with the status he enjoyed by virtue of his individual capacities as a specialist within his particular field. His political opponent, especially in the case of the Labour Party, might be an illiterate committee member on the village level, and this man would now wield the political influence once the virtual monopoly of the professional group. Thus a new distinction has arisen between social standing and political influence. The same process had, insofar as it was relevant to their case, also affected priests. Once, they had exerted a considerable amount of local social influence which at times had also extended to politics. The general loss of social influence by professional men had also occurred with the priesthood as the domain of politics and religion had become more clearly distinguished. Although priests had done a great deal to win support for the 'umbrella parties' in the 1964 election, they had been drawn into the political debate because explicitly religious issues were at stake. On strictly political matters, as these became more emphatically distinct, the priest was, in the future, less likely to influence his parishioners.

The two major political parties were also seriously affected by social change, and particularly by the new approach to the world entertained by the 'reformed' Church. For a generation at least, the Malta Labour Party had tended to be the party of dissent, seeking to replace traditional authority by a legal-rational type of authority, and proposing to the electorate a universalistic creed which for a long time appeared to be in direct conflict with the creed undergoing most social institutions on the island. Its roots of support, especially among the illiterates or semi-literate majority of its supporters who could not rise to the rationalistic reasoning of their leaders, had tended to be grounded, paradoxically enough, in elements of dissent already existing in the various parishes, cyrstallized as it were around a Church-legitimized institution — the secondary patron saint and the secondary *partit*. [4] On the other hand, the Nationalist Party had, for some time, tended to lose the vigorous mass appeal which its founders had inherited from the elite group of people around Fortunato Mizzi (who had thought of making the Maltese seriously aware of their political condition during the nineteenth century); and had tended to appear instead as the party of the *literati* and of the establishment. During the 1920s and the 1930s, the constitutional issue had become blurred as a result of the extensive importance given to the language question; and since Italian was the language of culture and learning, Nationalist Party politics were inclined to become mainly beneficial to the cultured minority. The Nationalists' avowed defence of religion — traceable to the commitments of F. Mizzi himself — had perhaps made them appear over-associated with the established order and with traditional values. Though their close association with the Church certainly helped them to become increasingly popular among the traditionally conservative peasantry, their other calls for social reform were hardly audible during the heated discussions on language and religion. The motto of the party, *Religio et Patria* (inherited from the Democratic Nationalist Party), was of course an attempt to unite the two political themes of the time; but when *religio* came to be most at stake, *patria* lost much of its earlier significance. Language and religion were both surrogates of national identity, and were both used by the early Nationalists in their claims for more extensive home rule. When national identity was asserted in constitutional terms in the 1960s, only religion remained as the major issue. Recent changes in the Church, however, have given to the Party motto a somewhat antique ring: the Church and religion increasingly feel they have to disentangle themselves from the political arena. Without religion as the issue, following successful peace negotiations between the Labour Party and the Church in the late 1960s, political debate in the early 1970s seemed to be devoid of clear ideological cleavages. Even though slogans like 'democratic socialism' and 'christian democracy' were then already being attached to the MLP and NP respectively, the essential similarity of the policies they put before the electorate before the 1971 election, was evident. During its nine-year tenure of office in the 1960s, the Nationalist Party had to forsake, for the sake of electoral support, the latent 'class' pretentions which had developed earlier; it had to let die, also, the old language question which so manifestly differentiated its cultured leadership from the social base. It grappled with major economic problems, but could not employ a pure capitalist model, and was obliged to follow broadly socialist principles, since they were the only viable possibilities for a small state which had been established as a modern democratic welfare society. Malta had, surprisingly enough, two parties which agreed on economic objectives; and which realized that these objectives could be attained by a measure of government ownership and economic planning. Paradoxically enough, it was the party of the *literati* in government, and not of the socialists, which nationalized Malta's largest industry — the drydocks; which extended free secondary education and introduced a free University; and which, when the Services' run-down was threatening the employment of the workers in that previously all-important sector, did not hesitate to intervene, and eventually to shift a number of them to direct government employment.

Such a situation was already forseeable in the sixties. Other than the religious question, political debate in the pre-Independence period especially, related primarily to matters of emphasis: whether Malta should become a Constitutional Monarchy or a Republic; and after that period, to such matters as the exact increase to be given to old-age pensioners. The decline of ideology in Maltese politics, as a result of the forceful disengagement of religion from the political scene, may not be compared in its overall effects with similar tendencies in larger countries. In a way, of course, the absence of extremists (except for the recent emergence of a small extra-parliamentary Marxist group) indicates that the fundamental problems created by industrialization in bigger countries — the need for the political and economic citizenship of the workers, and the need for restraint of uncontrolled capitalist enterprise — apparently had been understood and at least conceptually solved by the the Maltese leadership elite throughout the 1960s in the early 1970s. But this very fact points to some other important features of the Maltese socio-political scene. First, the politicization of the Maltese, unaccompanied as it was by a tradition of widespread knowledge, did not involve widespread specific ideological commitment at the grass-roots level. Marxism was anathema, and even though conflict occurred among supporters of the different parties themselves, and against the Church during the politico-religious disputes, it was not generally understood in ideological terms. With the exception of those most intimately involved in the party machinery, the major conflict of the last decade was generally regarded as a struggle for power between Mintoff on the one side and Borg Olivier, 'aided' by the Church, on the other. This was, at best, the old patronage system endemic in a closely-knit small society, with its *pika* and *partit* system recrudescing in a different, 'nationalized' form, and geared to defend itself from an often 'sloganized' aggressor. The implications of this fact lead to a further consideration: Malta emerged in the 1970s with a social structure, and with social institutions for which there had never really been any popular demand. Social change in Malta does not simply happen: it is 'engineered'. This fact emerged quite clearly in the course of research on workers' participation in industry in Malta carried out by the Institute of Social Studies at The Hague:

In Malta, workers' participation in management and ownership was both for the country and the Trade Unions a rather unexpected phenomenon. It was initiated as an *ad hoc* response to particular situations rather than a result of premeditated policy ... In many countries this is rather the opposite: legal regulations define the forms of participative institutions, set rules for their composition, their activity areas, the extent of their authority etc ... workers' participation was not introduced in Malta under pressure of workers or unions: there was no prior ideology of participation ... [5]

In some ways, as the researchers from The Hague suggested, such a situation could be advantageous since 'without a prior ideology one is more free to make up one's mind', [6] but, to a people seeking a condition of self-reliance, this might also entail a traumatic experience for which they might not have been prepared well enough. Over the 1970s, and especially in the course of the 1976 electoral campaign, novel ideological cleavages were already in evidence. Now that 'religio' questions had been more or less settled, or kept in abeyance by parties who were realizing that such issues could be bitterly divisive, 'patria' themes re-emerged. The political parties, now considering themselves unconcerned with issues of religious structures — an attitude very much condoned by a Church undergoing a period of uncertainty and critical self-appraisal — were promoting allegedly different world views. Such world views had, as in earlier days, the creation of better welfare conditions as their primary concern, but the mechanics for this creation were presented as different, with the individual and the community promoted as the respective starting points for Nationalist and Socialist economic and political planning. Even so, ideological cleavages were fast emerging, each party obviously engaged in a conscious effort to use its party machinery to project and to consolidate a divergent world-view from that of its opponent. The nascent character of these developments — a lull in ideological debate in the early 70s followed by a metamorphosis in content in the second half of the 1970s — does not yet allow proper appraisal. But, in the context of our discussion, it is not their extent that matters most, but the fact that this has come about at all, and that it has done so at a time when (a) the traditional proponent of ideology on the island — the Church — is itself attempting to remould itself within the framework of a community which no longer needs protection from a foreign overlord, but which needs credentials of its own in its new dealings with the world at large; (b) when the Malta Labour Party — for so long the promoter of social change through mass politicization and unionization — had been governing the islands for more than one term of office; and (c) when statutory fusion between the MLP and the General Workers Union had been affected.

2. Changing Life-Styles and Religion

If developments in politics have had an influence on the islander's traditional mode of thinking, bringing a shift away from the strict ascriptive system of previous generations, so, too, economic developments have had their own effect — particularly in eradicating the previously well-delineated divisions of town and country. What emerges most sharply from a study of social change in a relatively small, but until recently diversified, society is in fact the blurring of the old urban/rural distinctions. The urbanization of the countryside was, in 1974, a matter of fact; and even though the process had not reached a uniform stage of development in each of the settlements and villages, the basic shift to a different, more elaborate, way of life was unmistakable. Urbanization was most impressive in respect of the cultural artefacts that had reached the country-side, and in the images of 'how to live' which were produced in the most urban, most sophisticated, and most commercial centres and which — primarily through television and the other media — are instantenously transmitted to the most dispersed areas. [7] The electricity pylons that reach into the countryside, and to such previously untouched areas as Bahrija and Imtahleb, are symptomatic of the incidence of change. They have followed the influence of the books brought home by children who, since the introduction of compulsory education, have moved everyday from family farms into the more urbanized environments of the village for schooling. Today, they constitute the young adult population of their respective communities; and they are followed by another generation of boys and girls whose prospects in education by far exceed that of their slightly older brothers and sisters. City life and customs now, perhaps more than ever before, have become identified as the better way of life. Country people are increasingly aware of the possibility of benefitting from tech-nological advancement, and of the possibility of social mobililty and achieved status. Even if ecological settings themselves have not changed, what it means to be a countryman has been radically transformed — both by daily commuting to factories, as well as by the diffusion or urban values to rural areas. [8] The new availability of town life-styles, and the vigorous publicity which — because of the bias and provenance of radio and television material — they receive, has profoundly affected country life. The aspiration of (especially young) people is increasingly informed by ideas and values from the town and it was this which was in the mind of the priest who suggested that rural youth no longer had any tolerance for the differences between country life-styles and those of the city. He was commenting on the prestige of city life with country dwellers. There had been a time, in Malta as elsewhere, when countrymen had their own sources of pride, in their craft, in their productivity, in their festivities, in their nearness to what they could define very readily as the realities of life. The city often appeared to them as little more than the seat of authority to which their only relationship was that of paying taxes. City life-style was un-appealing and certainly out of their reach, and its festivties (like Carnival) and recreations (like the theatre and the opera), were quite often to be scorned as the 'sources of evil, and of sin'. With the massive impact of education and of television, with the high prestige of technology, electronics, and the glamorous life of fashion and luxury which could now be seen more intimately than ever before, and which, in a democratic age, are more readily available, the confidence of rural man in himself, and in his institutions — and particularly the confidence of the rural young — was undermined. The members of Malta's new generations of country people have been readily socialized into the new way of life projected through the media and read about more frequently in papers and magazines. 'Cultural differences — unless freely chosen — are intolerable', is virtually the message of the present situation. There is a powerful rejection of the idea of being 'culturally retarded' or of living in a culturally retarded area. It is primarily for this reason that the rural young are often extremely suggestible and vulnerable to the blandishments of the media, commercial promotions, and advertising, since, living where they do, they cannot afford to be left out of what appears to be the latest trends and fashions. Equally, of course, because of the need to compensate for a less rich cultural environment, and because there is little basis for discrimination with respect to the value of the new titillating material of the media, the reactions of country youth are often and paradoxically more extreme than those of youth in the suburbs or the cities. These developments lead of course to the dominance of city life-styles over those of the countryside, so that for the brighter there is a high inducement to seek promotion in the city, while others are stimulated to demand vociferously that the countryside should have the same facilities as the town.

This particular process of social change has clear consequences for the Church and, if as yet only incipiently, for religion. The Church in Malta has been deeply entrenched in community life, and in many respects it had long become adapted to the rural values and country practices of the people. Some of these values were indeed legitimated in religious or quasi-religious stereotypes; country life had been underwritten with religious prescriptions, and the content of that life was in some way sanctified and validated as the way in which men should live. The evil city was not perhaps a conspicuous point of contrast in the Maltese context except insofar as it represented the inevitable and at times sinful service facilities developed to cater for a foreign soldiery (and which could in consequence, therefore, be at least partially identified with the foreigner, his 'untrue religion', or, as was often the case, with his lack of true religious and moral values). The diffusion of new ideas for living, of new attitudes to social arrangements, social obligations, and social relationships, and even to physical comforts and luxury, have all disturbed an earlier pattern in which the practice of countrymen appeared to have, by and large, and at its best, the sanction of divine authority and the protection of the Church, through the agency of the local clergy. Local allegiance was all part of this pattern of course, as evidenced in the *festa*. But all of these value assumptions have been challenged in the diffusion of urban ideas and standards. Local allegiance has been diminished, and the local life-style, consolidated over generations, has itself undergone attack — and with it, implicitly rather than explicitly, the religion which warranted it. To say this is not to suggest that the Church cannot adapt to new social arrangements: in time perhaps it might. But at least the disturbance of the relationships between folk religion and folk life-styles, and the spread of new attractive ideas, could not occur without some weakening of the hold of the Church over the minds of the people. The very idiom employed by the Church had become inextricably intertwined with the experiences of country life, and although the content of the religious message ought to be distinguished from its convenient idiom, initially at least, the effect of the dissolution of this relationship must be acknowledged. The city was long regarded in Christianity as a location of dubious morality and sceptical attitudes: if images of city life were to be diffused to the countryside and presented as an attractive model for countryfolk, some effect on Christian teaching must be expected.

3. The Change from Tradition

Both politicization and, even if to a lesser extent, urbanization depend, especially in the context of a society with distinctive traditions and values, on the diffusion of rational procedures, as these replace the traditional. Poverty and scarcity are, of course, always relative, but in traditional societies they are not condemned in themselves unless they become exceptionally oppressive. But in the non-traditional, rationally-oriented society, effective use of resources for maximization of product becomes a principal canon of man's way of life, and discontent with poverty, even with relative poverty, becomes a fundamental attitude of men. The concern is to increase the benefit of basic resources and the sense of poverty and the evil of poverty gains not so much because of any decline in wealth (indeed there is in absolute terms usually a growth of wealth) but because of the increase of want, and the assumption that demand for more is a right attitude of mind for all. In folk societies, any departure from traditional practices, procedures and relationships usually raises suspision and resistance, the more so when tradition is legitimated by religious belief. An important element in the change that occurred in Malta's social structure was a strong attempt to break away from traditional procedures and to adopt rational thought-processes conducive to a more regularized and controlled environment. This particular orientation away from *Wertrationalität* to *Zweckrationalität* — from a kind of evaluatively rational action to purposeful or instrumental action — could be illustrated, by way of example, from some of the letters to the press written by Mintoff at the beginning of his political career. [9] He then gave voice to explicit demands for a shift in Maltese thinking, seeking to eliminate traditional authority and urging instrumental and ordered procedures by which to attain well-specified social goals. Obviously these orientations were not entirely new: other Maltese leaders had adopted a self-consciously rational standpoint before. [10] But in this case the demands came from a man who was to be the Prime Minister of the country and who was to enjoy far wider powers — those of an independent state — than had any of the Maltese leaders before him. His demands for rational action came, too, at a time when earlier hindrances — not only in the political structure, but also in the social structure — were being swept away. What was original in the Mintoff approach at the time was his understanding of socialism as an economic and philosophical programme transcending particular religious beliefs. And yet it was this same universalistic claim that Mintoff made for socialism in the context of mass Catholic belief that was to prove the main issue of contention for the actualization of his plans later on. By its nature, Catholicism had always tended to be an exclusive belief system, intolerant of variations, and, as Kingsley Davis put it, 'irreconcilable even with democracy' since 'it attempts to control so many aspects of life, to encourage so much fixity of status and submission to authority, and to remain so independent of secular authority that it invariably clashes with the liberalism, individualism, freedom, mobility and sovereignty of the democratic nation'. [11] It was, therefore, not surprising that during that same public controversy in the late thirties, the semi-official organ of the Church, *Leħen is-Sewwa* commented editorially in very harsh terms on Mintoff's proposals:

> Such a poor mentality is the key to all [he said] ...such a superficial mentality would not have been expected — to say the least — from a student, especially from one who pretends to be so superior to our fathers, and who insists on the need of persons — naturally enough,

like himself — who could make of Malta a torch that gives light to men.

It is not surprising that this lighted torch sees Jesus Christ, Disraeli, Einstein and Karl Marx on the same level ...

He told us something really novel ... that socialists pertain to all nationalities and to all religions — 'to every creed'.

Really novel ideas which we would have expected from somebody with no knowledge of sociology ... and not from someone who should have read (if not studied) the encyclicals of the Pope. If he read at least *Quadrogesimo Anno*, he would have clearly learned that a Catholic cannot be a Socialist. Therefore either this Mintoff is a Catholic and not a true socialist, or a socialist and not a true Catholic. In order to be both, he has to be a 'pecked-out' Catholic as much as he has to be a 'pecked-out' socialist. And these people who simultaneously profess to be one thing and another, without being either, cannot easily become torches that enlighten humanity, and they cannot fix the bearings of their mind, most especially when they are filled up with themselves to the very brim ... [12]

This negative response to Mintoff's appeal for social reform as an absolute value, to be sought irrespective of particular traditions — religious or otherwise, was the exact echo of Catholic thinking throughout most of the earlier political debate in Malta; [13] and it was that attitude which eventually precipitated the open conflict of the Church with the Labour Party. [14] In some respects, the confrontation which eventually took place was a dramatic way of making apparent to at least the more politically and socially conscious that the social framework was now to be actively, openly, and explicitly considered. A demand for reform, the specification of social goals, the articulation of policies, was a way of making political debate much more self-conscious. Whereas for so long the whole political aspiration of the people had been channelled into the deeply emotional demand for national autonomy — a cause that could readily fuse ethnic, religious and political aspirations in one relatively unreflective demand — now political goals, and the means by which they were to be attained, were brought deliberately into the forefront of the public mind. Such a procedure must of necessity result in a challenge to the traditional-religious approach to society. Even had the policies propounded by Mintoff been relatively conservative, and even had he been a defender of the Church, such an explicit statement of aims would have made politics a more conscious social process. As it was, his differences with the Church, and his socialist onslaught on tradition, intensified the rationalizing effect of his activity. Instead of receiving intimations of the approprateness of particular goals and particular practices in a veiled way, from religious functionaries, older generations, and higher classes, the people were now being made to deliberate on just what Maltese society might be like. It was, in the very rationality of the assumptions which such a campaign made, a thrust against the older, traditional, 'received' ways of proceeding.

Of course, such a heightening of the rationality of the political process accompanied other developments in which the ordinary Maltese was increasingly involved in activities that demanded at least a response to rational methods, particularly as encapsulated in machinery and technical apparatus. The war, for example, had been an enforced education in this respect, as men had to become acquainted with the principles behind a wide assortment of equipment, behind the machinery of military forces and of bureaucratic government. In many respects, the Maltese had been somewhat socialized for more rationalistic ways of thinking and acting long before the explicit process of political socialization occurred. [15] This process was in turn extended by rapid postwar development; and such facets of development as industrialization, the expansion of technical education, the development of a variety of new consumer involvements (especially television, the epanded use of telecommunications and of motorized vehicles, and the increasingly widespread acquaintance with foreign travel) are all elements of this new consciousness.

All these factors and the attempted resolution of the politico-religious dispute — itself an indication of the loss of centrality of the Church at least in political affairs — was not without consequence to the three major institutions of social and political life in Malta: the Church, the Nationalist Party and the Malta Labour Party. Social change in Malta had brought a transformation of Church life on the island, and Vatican II ideas about *aggiornamento* had intensified the need for a re-examination of traditional procedures and customs. In 1838, so much had been the control of the Church that the Royal Commissioners had reported that despite the privileges and the money accorded to 'the Protestant Missionaries to convert the Maltese from the Catholic faith, their endeavours had been wholly or nearly fruitless ... the attacks which they made on the Catholic faith, in writings imported or printed at the Missionary presses, have scarcely met with a reader amongst the native population. We were informed ... that the conversions from the Catholic religion ... have been extremely few (not more than five or six) ...' [16] The situation had virtually remained the same throughout the nineteenth and early twentieth century. Strickland, indeed, commanded a following, and, as political issues had become blurred with religious ones during the Padre Carta case, he managed to attract the anti-clerical elements from the then dwindling Dimechian movement. Mintoff, for a time, seemed determined to re-create the old brand of 'anticlerical irreligion', [17] but in spite of his substantial following it was known that, even at the height of his dispute with the Church, a substantial number of his supporters followed him because of his charismatic appeal, and of his previous emphatic involvement in the workers' cause. Even so, the Blood Commission could still state in 1961 that 'the Church is still a potent, if imponderable factor in Maltese life'. [18] Since then, the Catholic Church has greatly changed, and although in 1978 the Church's presence in social life in Malta was still massive, there was a widespread feelings that its previous claims for exclusivity, and the almost 'sacred avowal' to view any form of change negatively, were no longer as marked as they had been previously. The diminution of the Church's legitimating power occurred as the rural context — in which religious virtues and morality had been primarily conceived — became a context in which men feared cultural deprivation. As man's social relations widened, the Church could rely less and less on the basis of face-to-face relationships as the normal contexts of life, for which its moral teachings were especially well-adapted. The symbolism of traditional folk-life, and especially those elements of it which came to be advertised as a tourist attraction, steadily lost its earlier significance and ceased to be intrinsically justifiable or beneficial. The clergy themselves began to take a new view of them within the new ecclesiology disseminated by Vatican II. Extensive as the changes were, however, not everything disappeared at once: thus the at times forceful opposition by conservative elites in the different parishes, and the demand to exploit the past as a commodity with which to lure tourists, combined to preserve the traditional *festa*. But even this festivity, and such other previously purely religious activities as the Good Friday processions, underwent the accretion of instrumental and pragmatic values that had been quite alien to them in earlier times. People became more self-conscious about such festivals, and from natural parts of social life in its various manifestations, they became regarded less as coherent elements in everyday activity, less as essential features of the community's symbolic universe, and more as isolated, saleable artefacts of culture, to be produced and performed 'to order' for outsiders for whom they bore no intrinsic meanings but only the qualities of spectacle. This process, too, can be seen as a very evident growth of instrumental, *zweckrational* elements in activities that were once intrinsically self-justifying and self-legitimating. What once was sacred, jealously-guarded, and good-in-itself, had become another item to be put into the balance of payments as a credit-earning product.

4. The Metamorphosis of Maltese Catholicism

The combination of these factors in social life in Malta has important consequences for religion. In whatever way it occurred, the pressure of social change has altered, modified, and in many ways 'disenchanted' social life and institutions in Malta. It has brought about a decline in ascription; accentuated the need for rational procedures; and stimulated the swift establishment of a meritocracy. And yet, several factors in social life — the fact that patronage continues as an underpinning for most political life, and the very size of Malta itself, for example — seem to be working against such tendencies. The sudden establishment of an indigenous government coincided with the dissemination of new life-styles, but government was not able to meet the new needs arising from the new social currents, and was certainly unable to prevent the breakdown of the organizations that were rooted in local community life. It was the Church, already a custodian of morals and manners, a socializing agency, an agency of social control, often an arbiter, theoretically at least a keeper of peace among men, and an agency ready to assuage grief, to encourage righteousness and protect the defenceless, which entered the social scene and established new facilities in an attempt to satisfy the new demands. In Malta, the Church could do this because it was already there, a ubiquitous and properly distributed agency, which operated without competition in most local communities. The development in more coordinated and integrated forms of traditional church functions, such as counselling (as in the Cana Movement, and, in a more specialized context, in the Emigration services), was the effect of some process of rationalization within the Church itself, necessary to meet the more complex demands of a people now liberated from the local community, and requiring more sophisticated, more specialized and more technical forms of advice. Such functions, in advanced countries like Britain, would probably fall under the provision of the government (national or local). In Malta, no less ambitious to be a welfare state, they remain the function of the clergy — who, in some respects, are getting used to the idea of the 'welfare church'.

The adaptation of church concerns to the changing society that is developing in Malta is perhaps best illustrated by the various diocesan commissions, but it is also clear that today's clergy entertain changing conceptions of their own role in society. In some respects the possibility of enhancing the strictly service aspects of that role is evident. For that to occur rather more technical education, or acquaintance with technically influenced areas of social life, are increasingly necessary. The Church may, therefore, come to include new types of priests, and this process of specialization is already becoming evident. If in Malta, various functions fulfilled by bureacratic agencies, government agencies, or free enterprise concerns, in other societies remain within the purview of the Church (largely as a consequence of the small size of this state society), then a process of structural differentiation might begin within the Church rather than outside it. The Church might thus make possible the maintenance of a welfare society that the State alone could not — being without economies of scale — afford. The service ethic has, of course, always been in evidence in the Church, but that service has, in the past, been predominantly spiritual in character. Today the very concept of the spirtiual might be extended, and there are those among the clergy who wish to see, for example, a rapprochement between Marxist ideology and Christian practice, who seek an ideological underpinning for new forms of clerical service to the laity. [19] There are, inevitably, problems in this type of development — not least, in the diffusion and transmission of commitment which, hitherto, appears to have depended on a powerful supernatural referent of a kind uncongenial to Marxist analysis. There is, beyond this, the conflicting images of professional work, and the usual connection of high salary and status for long training and specialized competence. The clergy, even if accepting some new roles, may not find the balance between diminished social standing and more exacting technical service easy to strike.

The response of the clergy to changed social circumstances occurs at various levels. We have seen the changing attitudes of the younger priests, and we have had reason to mention the development of particular spheres of activity arising from the initiative of various individuals within the Church. Although not seeking a drastic departure from traditional 'sacerdotal' practice in favour of direct involvement in social work, and without necessarily transforming the clergyman into a new kind of professional in the sense in which the term is usually understood in the sociological literature, a shift towards a more specialized ministry appears to be a dominant aspiration among a substantial number of Malta's clergy, and also of those concerned with pastoral planning in Malta. The first draft of the plan for the pastorate set out to direct the activity of the Church to twenty different social sectors or social groupings, most of which have become clearly articulated in the course of the recent transformations of Maltese society. As initially conceived, the plan intended to adopt the 'see - judge - act' model as the basis of pastoral action, and sought, in particular, to organize priestly activity and such other human or material resources as were available according to the demands and needs expressed in extensive opinion surveys and situation analysis. The 1966 draft of the Pastoral Plan was never systematically applied, nor, in spite of several consecutive commissions on the matter, has an alternative plan been drawn up. The pattern of pastoral action put forward in the drift plan has, however, been followed in sporadic instances, and attention is increasingly being given by Church officials to the problems created by specific forms of social interaction and in particular situations — all of which are a direct result of the process of structural differentiation in in society at large. Since the publication of the draft plan, new pastoral initiatives directed towards special categories of people have been taken up on the diocesan level. Parish councils, too, have tended to abandon the model of the 'task force' on which they had been initially conceived, towards a new conception of their composition, role and function — in particular, towards a more communitarian rather than a hierarchical structure, with goals more related to catechism and evangelization than to mere parochial organization. Lately the emphasis has been on 'adult catechism', which tends to follow the group system. The younger priests especially like to share experiences about the extent to which they have managed to work through occupational groups, family groups, or other 'natural' groupings. Such changes in ecclesiastical structure and pastoral strategy are a definitive departure from the previous hierarchic organizational system, and in many ways reflect the influence on the Church of the social forces in society at large.

This re-structuring of the Church reflects the recognition that its mission cannot now be achieved through an organization that reflects the status divisions of a form of society that has largely passed away. Not only has structure changed, but liturgical practice has also changed, and these changes have some consequences for the place in society which the Church occupies. The shift from authority and command relationships between clergy and laity to a position of dialogue, counsel, suggestion, and especially the shift from the mass approach in packed churches to family masses and meetings in small groups, without a strict body of rules regulating every movement, tends to make the Church much less visible on the macro-societal level than previously. *Ex opere operato* sacramental action celebrated with due pomp is given less weight as the emphasis is placed on 'learning and understanding'. The features of traditional religion persist only as a symbolic remnant of a dying culture. This is not to suggest that churches are no longer full, or that mass celebrations and behaviour patterns are no longer derived primarily from these activities, but from other more personalized encounters with the proponents of the religious ideology. Such a replacement of mass church education by more personalized, nucleated meetings (as evident, say, in the newer parishes such as Santa Lucia, and in those of the older ones with a more progressive orientation such as Zebbug) is undoubtedly one of the more important aspects of the impact of social change on religion in Malta. To a large extent it arises out of the new needs created by the emerging societal ethos of a Malta the population of which begins to suffer from the ills of compartmentalized education, work-conditions and leisure activities: in a word, of the loss of person-to-person interaction associated with the decline of *Gemeinschaft* and the rise of *Gesellschaft*. The Church begins to reinterpret its role, and to place it, quite voluntarily, less in the public sphere as a commanding presence, and more in the more intimate areas of social life. It retreats from claims to presidency over other social institutions, to more specialized concerns at local level, or as an auxiliary agency in certain departments of life where it supplies a lack that in other societies might be met by functionaries of the State.

It is precisely in this sense that secularization has to be understood in the Maltese context. In the introduction, it was suggested that this study would try to trace the process of secularizaion in Malta as resulting from a process of structural differentiation in Maltese social life generally. The working definition for secularization was that of a process whereby 'religious thinking, practice and institutions lose social significance'. With such a definition of secularization, it can be seen that what has occurred in Malta is a social process that has not been wholly uniform in direction or speed. Certainly there has been a diminution in the socal significance of the religious institution as traditionally understood. The Church has become to occupy a less conspicuous and less presidential place in the affairs of the nation. There is some decline in practice, and religious practice may not be as significant socially as it was, even where it does occur. There is reason to believe that a new type of consciousness, new ways of thinking — manifestly in the extent to which rational orientations have replaced traditional patterns of thought — are growing in importance. But, as we have seen, the Church has not lost by any means all of its functions, and because the religious (of both sexes) are a relatively large body of well-disposed 'service' personnel, they have successfully assumed some new functions in the new type of social system, and over the years have — for want of more specially trained personnel — been recruited by the State to continue to undertake other tasks (particularly in schools and hospitals). Yet, by many of the usual indicators taken to assess the process of secularization, the Maltese remain a profonudly religious people. They support a very large priesthood, relative to the population. They have high, if declining, attendance rates at Mass and Confession. Anticlericalism is, except insofar as the Labour Party's recent campaigns can be subsumed under that term, relatively unimportant, and even the Labour Party's leader appeals to Christian conscience and values. [20] There are no alternative religious bodies of much importance to create a pluralistic situation (which is sometimes seen as conducive to secularization). It has been shown that traditional grandiose church structures and activities are losing their previous universally accepted symbolic content; and the dwindling numbers in churches and in the precincts of the *għaqdiet* system and of the houses of formation of the clergy and the religious, although in no way comparable to similar patterns in bigger, more pluralistic, countries, do seem to chart the trend of the future. Traditional church gatherings, festivals, and activities can no longer claim exclusively to portray national identity and solidarity. Maltese social life has become too differentiated by the new work and leisure conditions for such religious festivities to command exclusive support. The interests of the population have many other outlets in addition to those provided by, or presided over, by the Church.

It would of course be altogether surprising had Malta remained immune from the process of religious change affecting other Christian, and more particularly other Catholic countries. The same broad processes of social change that have affected them have, allowing for cultural and economic differences, also affected her. Obviously there are also other differences. Her priests have not been manoeuvred into the types of political activity characteristic of some Catholic priests in Spain or Latin America. They have not been affected by radical and Protestant ideas as have many of the clergy in Holland. And they have not been so infected by the enthusiasm for the Charismatic Renewal movement and speaking in tongues in inter-denominational prayer meetings which have influenced a section of the Catholic clergy in the United States. All of these aspects of religious change are relatively country-specific. We have already alluded to facets of religious change that are unique to Malta, and some of these cannot in themselves be regarded as instances of secularization. Malta, by its size and relative isolation, provides in some ways a useful laboratory in which to observe the incidence of change, in which endogenous and exogenous elements can be in some measure distinguished, and in which particular local conditions can be specified with some accuracy. Allowing for local peculiarities, and for some reverse effects, it nonetheless appears that a process of secularization has occurred, and is continuing, in the island, as is documented in the foregoing pages.

Appendices

APPENDIX A: 'MAJOR ECCLESIASTICAL BODIES AND INSTITUTIONS'

The Archbishop's Seminary
Cana Movement
Cathedral Chapter
Catholic Institute
Catholic Relief Services
College of Parish Priests
College of Vice-Parish Priests
Collegiate Chapters (Cathedral, B'Kara, Senglea, Vittoriosa, Rabat)
Diocesan Communication Commission
Diocesan Liturgical Commission
Diocesan Representative Council
Diocesan Orphanges Commission
Diocesan Youth Commission
Ecclesiastical Tribunal

Emigrants' Commission
Għaqda Biblika Maltija (Malta Biblical Society)
Il-Hajja (Press & Newspaper)
Kunsill tal-Lajċi (Laymen's Council)
Missjoni l-Kbira (Big Mission)
Missjoni ż-Żgħira (Little Mission)
Pastoral Council
Royal University Students Theological Association
Senate of Priests
Social Action Guild
Social Action Movement

Religious Orders (date refers to establishment in Malta)

Male

Minor Conventuals (1310)
Carmelites (1370)
Dominicans (1466)
Capuchins (1508)
Discalced Carmelites (1526)
Jesuits (1582)

Salesians (1904)
De La Salle (1903)
Augustinians (exact date not known, but present in Malta early in XX century)
Society of Saint Paul (1910)

Female

Enclosed:

Benedictines (1418)
Gerosolomites (1583)
Discalced Teresians (1726)
Augustinians (1854)
Poor Clares (1914)
Franciscan Sisters of Mary (1910)

Sisters of St Dorothy (1911)
Dominican Sisters (1916)
Missionary Nuns of Jesus of Naz
 areth (1914)
White Sisters (1957)

Not enclosed:

St Joseph of the Apparition (1845)
Sisters of the Good Shepherd
 (1858)
St Vincent de Paul (1867)
Little Sisters of the Poor (1877)
Franciscan Missionaries of Egypt
 (1886)
Maltese Franciscan Nuns (1890)

Ursuline Nuns (1892)
Ta' Nuzzu (1894)
Little Company of Mary (1894)
Augustinian Sisters (1896)
Sacred Heart Nuns (1903)

'Għaqdiet' and other Lay Associations

Apostolat tat-Talb (Apostleship of Prayer)
Catholic Action (four sections: men's; women's; young men; and young
 unmarried girls)
Għaqda ta' San Vinċenz (St Vincent de Paul Society)
Legion of Mary (different 'praesidia' could be found in the same parish)
Marian Congregation
MUSEUM (two sections: male and female)
Ommijiet Insara (Christian Mothers Association)
Opri Missjunarji (Missionary Society)
Xirka tal-Isem Imqaddes t'Alla
Żgħażagħ Ħaddiema Nsara (Young Christian Workers)

APPENDIX B: 'SUMMARY OF QUESTIONNAIRE FOR THE CENSUS OF MALTA'S DIOCESAN CLERGY'

Name and Surname

Date of Birth

Date of Ordination

Place of Birth

Where did you receive your secondary education? Please give details of school(s) attended.

Where did you follow your pre-ordination studies? Please specify for Philosophy and Theology.

Did you follow any studies in non-ecclesiastical subjects? Please specify any academic qualification obtained.

Did you follow any further studies in ecclesiastical subjects? Please specify any academic qualification obtained.

Were you a member of any lay association movement before entering the Major Seminary?

Where do you exercise your priestly ministry? Give details of your pastoral commitments.

APPENDIX C: 'GUIDELINES FOR INTERVIEWS WITH A 10% SAMPLE OF MALTA'S DIOCESAN CLERGY'

NOTE: The interviews were carried out in Maltese; and it was made very clear to respondents that the set of questions which I had were only intended to serve as guidelines for a friendly discussion, rather than a set of structured questions intended to elicit yes/no answers.

1. What, in your opinion, are the most important changes in Maltese social life since 1947?
2. Do you notice any difference between the changes that have taken place in the towns and in the villages?
3. Most people seem to think that the cause of all these changes is a result of a better education. Would you like to see educational advance accelerated further? Could there be a danger of 'too much education' in Malta?
4. Do you think that the social changes you mention have had any

special kind of impact on the religious life of the Maltese people at large? Please explain your answer.

5. Has the life of the priest himself been influenced by the changes you mention? In what way?

6. Do people respect priests as much as they did before 1955? 1947?

7. You were ordained in 19—. What used to be the most important items on your day-programme in your first year after ordination?

8. Was there any (a) weekly or (b) annual occurrence you used to consider central?

9. Do you still consider this (these) same item(s) (question 7) as being the most important now? Why?

10. Where do you spend most of your time these days? How does this compare with your first post-ordination years?

11. What, in general, would you think the people expect of you in your priestly office?

12. What would they expect least? (both in terms of experience and ideal)

13. Some time ago I had somebody call on me to write a letter to a relative of his who is living in Australia. Another came for a reference. Is this the sort of service for which you are frequently asked?

14. Maltese is now the language of the liturgy and all liturgical celebrations are now being conducted in the vernacular. What particular difficulties do *you* meet with — e.g. is it difficult to express certain ideas in Maltese whilst preaching?

15. Do you think that one can easily create an atmosphere of communitarian worship with the new rite? Why?

16. Almost all the sacraments have now been included in the Mass. Do you think that these 'ritual Masses' (wherein Baptism, Matrimony, etc. are celebrated) are more of a nuisance to parish life than a help? Why?

17. Some people condemn the new liturgy because it is stealing from the people a tradition of grandeur and mystery, especially on special occasions like the village festa when traditional music used to have such a great importance attached to it. Others on the other hand are enthusiastic about the liturgy because of its informality and what they see as its greater didactic content. What do you feel yourself?

18. It is said that Mass attendance and Confessions are decreasing whilst the reception of Holy Communion is increasing. Do you yourself find less people coming to you for confession and do you distribute Communion to more people? What, in your opinion, are the factors that have brought about this kind of shift?

19. In my childhood I remember occasions when one had to queue for more than an hour before one's turn for confession arrived. With

some exceptions this is quite uncommon today. How do you explain the change? Which are the occasions that generally attract most people to go to Confession?

20. Do you notice any difference between the way people of different sexes and ages approach Confession?

21. What do people show most anxiety about in general in the Confessional?

22. Would you agree that penitents tend to confess more sins related to the sixth commandment? Is it true to say that one rarely hears a mention of sins against charity, faith, other people's property, etc.?

23. The biggest dissension in Malta during the 1960s was the politico-religious crisis. What were the real issues?

24. What were the arguments upon which the Church based its stand?

25. Do you still endorse the view then taken by the Church? Why?

26. How do you look upon the whole experience now that some years have gone by since the peace agreement was signed?

27. What form, in your opinion, should Church-State relationships take?

28. Do you think that this type of relationship was observed during the Nationalist administration?

29. Did a process of secularization take place then? What do you think of issues such as:
    a) Prime Minister/Archbishop precedure?
    b) the visit to Malta of the Hungarian Minister of Education — an ex-priest?
    c) control of decancy in dress?
    d) the setting up of the Casino?

30. Are you satisfied with the way things stand under the present administration?

31. What is your reaction to the stand taken by the Archbishop and the Church in general on the issues of:
    a) religious instruction in the new technical schools?
    b) the amendments to the criminal code on homosexuality and adultery?
    c) the intervention of Archbishop Gonzi in the Anglo-Maltese dispute on the rent to be paid by Britain for its military base on the island?

32. Throughout the rest of the world (USA, France, etc.) more priests are taking a more direct part in politics — with their Bishops' permission. Would you favour this in Malta? Please give reasons for your answer.

33. Up to some time ago, Maltese priests used to take active part in

politics. What was the reason for the change of policy from the side of Ecclesiastical authorities?

34. Do you welcome the prospect of tourism as Malta's future major industry? Why?

35. One often hears that after Vatican II 'the priesthood is in a state of crisis'. Do you agree that this is so? Why?

36. In Malta the priesthood is increasingly less attractive as a status route. What are in your opinion the factors that still attract candidates to it?

37. Having lived the life of a priest for ... years, would you repeat your choice to the priesthood if you had the chance to do so?

38. The end of the MLP-Church dispute has at least put an end to an organized form of anticlericalism which the Church previously had to defend herself from. Some say however that 'the Church' is now crumbling from within. Do you agree? Why?

39. Do you notice any changes since your ordination in the form of parish-priest/priest relationships in your parish? How do you account for this change or the lack of it?

40. I was ordained about a year and a half ago, but I have lived in Malta only for very brief intervals. What, in your opinion, are the greatest problems a newly ordained priest has to face? How can he best tackle them?

41. So much has been said on the financial reform. What is the general financial situation of the Maltese clergy? Would you like to see any particular form in the proposed reform? Explain the objectives and the methods you think one should use to reach a good reform.

42. Unlike the Seminaries of many other dioceses, that of Malta is still full of Seminarians. Do you think this is going to stay like this for long? What are the prospects of the priesthood in Malta's future?

APPENDIX D: 'POSTAL QUESTIONNAIRE ADMINISTERED TO PRIESTS WITH ONE YEAR EXPERIENCE IN THE MINISTRY' *(in translation from Maltese)*

1. Where do you spend most of your time?

2. Is there any particular weekly event which you consider to be central, and which you look forward to? If YES, please specify.

3. What was the toughest problem *you* had to face during your first year of pactoral activity?

4. What do you think people expect *most* from the priest?

5. What do you think people expect *least* from the priest?

6. Is there any particular aspect of a priest's life about which you were not too sure before you were ordained? If YES, please specify.

7. How would you evaluate this aspect (question 6) now that over a year has passed since your Ordination?

8. During this last year, have you been involved in anything in particular for which the Seminary did not prepare you, and for which you would have preferred to have been prepared?

APPENDIX E: 'QUESTIONNAIRE ADMINISTERED TO STUDENTS AT THE MALTA MAJOR SEMINARY'
(in translation from Maltese)

1. How long have you been in the Major Seminary?

2. What, or who, influenced you most in your decision to enter the Seminary?

3. Since when did you start to think on the priesthood as a possible vocation for yourself?

4. How old were you when you took your final decision to enter the Seminary?

5. Before entering the Seminary, were you a member of any *għaqda*? If YES, please specify.

6. What do *you* expect *most* of a priest?

7. What do *you* expect *least* of a priest?

8. What, in your opinion, do *people* expect *most* of a priest?

9. What, in your opinion, do *people* expect *least* of a priest?

10. What do you consider to be the major problems in the life of the Maltese priest today?

11. Do you think that these will be the same problems you will have to face when you have been ordained?

12. What do you think the greatest difficulty will be in the first months after your ordination?

Notes

NOTES TO: 'INTRODUCTION'

1. See, e.g., S.N. Eisenstadt, *The Protestant Ethic and Modernization — A Comparative View* (N.Y., Basic Books, 1968), the SCM volumes on *Religion and Social Change*. The theme of the CISR conference for 1975 was precisely this; and there is even an 'Institute for Religion and Social Change' in Hawaii.
2. An individual's religious affiliation is taken for granted in Malta: in the decennial census the question has never been asked. When asked for the reason for this, the Census officers did not give a reason related to privacy (as is the case in Britain), but considered the question pointless because everyone in Malta is assumed to have the same formal commitment.
3. G. A. Hillery Jr., 'Definitions of Community: Areas of Agreement', *Rural Sociology*, 20 (June 1955), p.111.
4. For an analysis of this in more detail, see J.F. Boissevain, *Friends of Friends* (Oxford, Blackwell, 1974).
5. See R.J. Cooper, 'An Analysis of Some Aspects of Social Change and Adaptation to Tourism on Ibiza' (Oxford Univ. D.Phil. thesis 1974); and A.F. Robertson, 'The Dynamic Process of Change in a Mediterranean Island Community' (Edinburgh Univ. M.A. thesis, 1964) for a shorter but comparable study of one of the islands near Ibiza: Formentera.
6. This was the basis of the Nationalists' philosophy for a long time, and was still felt in 1954 when G. Borg Olivier, then Prime Minister, had to include the intention of his party to strengthen the Italian language in his main speech during the debate on the budget as a way to hold an influential pro-Italian faction of his party from upsetting the fragile coalition he was leading. See E. Dobie, *Malta's Road to Independence* (Norman, University of Oklahoma Press, 1967), p.157.
7. Surnames include those originating from purely semitic sources like *Borg, Zammit,* and *Mifsud,* those of Italian origin such as *Gonzi, Pace* and *Tonna,* and British names like *Bannister* and *Griffiths.*
8. J. Pitt-Rivers (ed.), *Mediterranean Countrymen* (Holland, Mouton & Co., 1963), p.9.
9. J. Pitt-Rivers (ed.), *Mediterranean Countrymen.*
10. J.G. Peristiany (ed), *Honour and Shame* (London, Weidenfeld & Nicholson, 1963).
11. W.A. Christian, *Person and God in a Spanish Village* (London, Seminar Press, 1972).
12. J.F. Boissevain, *Hal-Farrug — A Village in Malta* (USA, Holt, Rinehart &

Winston, 1969). See also M. Kenny, *A Spanish Tapestry* (London, Cohen & West, 1961).

13. J. Pitt-Rivers (ed.), *Mediterranean Countrymen*, p.10.

14. R.J. Cooper, 'An Analysis of Some Aspects of Social Change and Adaptation to Tourism on Ibiza', especially Chapter V.

15. This point has been made very clearly by David Martin: 'in a general way a nation denied self-determination by another dominating society will either seek sources of religious differentation, or use the pre-existing religious difference as a rallying point'. In G. Walters (ed.), *Religion in a Technological Society* (UK, Bath University Press, 1968), p.35.

16. Thus a study of Malta could not accommodate the religious dimension in the brief space accorded to it in studes such as that of J. Matras, *Social Change in Israel* (Chicago, Aldine Publishing Co., 1965), that ed. by I.C. Jarvie and J. Agassi, *Hong Kong: A Society in Transition* (London, Routledge & Kegan Paul, 1969), or that by A. Inkeles, *Social Change in Soviet Russia* (Massachusets, Harvard University Press, 1968).

17. These priests could be of two kinds: a) priests who had spent some time engaged in pastoral actvity with Maltese emigrants abroad; and b) priests who returned to Malta after a period of further study in a foreign insttution.

18. E. Goffman, *Asylums* (Chicago, Aldine Publishing Co., 1692), pp.5-6.

19. D.T. Hall and B. Schneider, *Organizational Climates and Careers: The Work Lives of Priests* (NY, Seminar Press, 1973), p.23.

20. J.F. Fichter, *Religion as an Occupation* (Notre Dame Ind., Univ. of Notre Dame Press, 1961); *Priest and People* (NY, Sheed & Ward, 1965); *America's Forgotten Priests* (NY, Harper, 1968).

21. B. Michel, *Les Resources du clergé et de l'Eglise en France* (Paris, Editions du Cerf, 1971).

22. O. Schreuder 'Types of Catholic Priests' in *Actes de la IX Conférence International de la Sociologie Religieuse* (Rome, CISR, 1967), pp.33-55.

23. S.W. Blizzard, 'The Minister's Dilemma', *Christian Century*, LXXIII, 17 (25 April 1956), pp.508-10. For Blizzard's other contributions see Bibliography.

24. A. Anfossi, 'Funzioni della Parrocchia e Partecipazione dei Parrocchiani alla vita religiosa in comuni agricoli della Sardegna', *Quaderni di Sociologia 2*, Aprile-Giugno 1967, pp.190-216.

25. 'A working paper on the Study on Patterns of Ministry' (Mimeograph report, World Council of Churches, 1965).

26. A.J. Russell, 'A Sociological Analysis of the Clergyman's role with special reference to its development in the early nineteenth century' (Oxford Univ. D.Phil. thesis, 1970). See also M.G. Daniel, 'London clergymen: the ways in which their attitudes to themselves have changed in the first ten years of their ministry' (London School of Economics M.Phil. thesis, 1968).

27. For a thorough study of the history of the decrees of Vatican II on *Presbyterorum Ordinis*, see H. Vorgrimler (ed.), *Commentary on the Documents of Vatican II* (London, Burns & Oates/Herder & Herder, 1960), IV, pp.183-209. The important interventions of Cardinals Alfrink and Döpfner took place on October 15, 1964 and October 15, 1965 respectively, and are referred to in footnote 25, p.217 of Vorgrimler.

28. For a lucid description on the crisis in the priesthood, see D.P. O'Neill, *The Priest in Crisis, a Study in Role Change* (London, Chapman, 1968).
29. In this book the working definition of 'secularization' employed by B.R. Wilson in *Religon in a Secular Socety* (London, C.A. Watts, 1966), p.xiv, has been adopted.
30. L. Shiner, 'The Concept of Secularization in Empirical Research', *Journal for the Scientific Study of Religion*, VI (2-1967), 207-220. See especially pp.212-14.

NOTES TO CHAPTER 1: 'MALTA IN TIME AND SPACE'

1. Footnotes and references to the relevant sources for this brief section on Malta's historical developments have been kept to a minimum. A list of the most important historical works on Malta is given in the Bibliography.
2. A.V. Laferla, *British Malta* (Malta, Aquilina, 1946), i. III.
3. Laferla, *British Malta*, V, says that the appeal took place on 9 February, 1799, but does not quote his sources.
4. See F.F. Fenech, R. Ellul Micallef and M. Vassallo 'Changes in the Epidemiological Pattern of Disease in the Maltese Islands' in M. Vassallo (Ed) *Contributions to Mediterranean Studies* (Malta, Malta University Press, 1977) pp. 221-231.

NOTES TO CHAPTER 2: 'THE EXPERIENCE OF SOCIAL CHANGE IN MALTA'

1. K. Loewenstein, *Political Power and the Governmental Process* (Chicago, University of Chicago Press. 1957), p. 123
2. C. Lavagna, *Le Costituzioni Rigide* (Roma, Edizione Ricerche, 1964), pp. 19-22.
3. Various Maltese personalities tried to influence the constitutional set-up, by a variety of means. The efforts of the four lawyers, Drs. R. Sciortino, F. Pullicino, P. Mifsud and F. Torregiani, in the 1860, of F. Mizzi and G. Strickland in 1886, and of E. Mizzi and F. Sciberras in the early years of the 20th century are worth mentioning here.
4. For an analysis of the correlation between constitutional developments in Malta and events in the Mediterranean, see J.D. Bugeja, 'British Influence on Maltese Development 1919-1933' (Oxford Univ. B.Litt., thesis, 1973).
5. Cmd. 3993, *Malta Royal Commission*, 1931 (London, 1932), p. 9.
6. J.J. Cremona, *An Outline of the Constitutional Development of Malta under British Rule* (Malta, Malta Univ. Press, 1963), p.1.
7. For further details, see D. Mintoff, *Malta's Struggle for Survival* (Malta, Lux, 1949); Mintoff, *Malta u l-Gvern Ingliż* (Malta, Muscat, 1950); Mintoff, *Malta u l-Patt ta' l-Atlantiku* (Malta, Muscat, 1950); Mintoff, *Malta u l-United Nations* (Malta, Muscat, 1950); and Mintoff, *Malta l-Ewwel u Qabel Kollox* (Malta, Muscat, 1950). See, too, editorial in *Is-sebħ* (M.L.P. organ) of 13 July 1950.

8. See an excellent analysis of the integration issue by D. Austin, *Malta and the End of the Empire* (London, Frank Cass, 1971), pp. 63-108; and Cmd. 9657, *Malta Round Table Conference* 1955 — *Report* (London, 1955)), esp. paragraphs 20, 70 and 100

9 See letter of Mgr Tardini to Dom Mintoff; the Bishops' Joint Pastoral Letter on Integration (22.1.56); and the Broadcast of the Archbishop to the People of Malta and Gozo on Integration. These documents are reproduced as Appendices C, D, and E in the pamphlet by a special diocesan Commission, *The Quarrel of the MLP with the Church in Malta* (Malta, Empire Press, undated), pp. 30-40. *Hansard,* 5th series, 1956, 548, pp. 923-26. See also *Hansard,* 5th series, 545, 2005, for written reply on guarantees given by the Prime Minister, Sir A. Eden.

10. For a full analysis, see D. Austin, *Malta and the End of the Empire,* pp. 55-62.

11. D. Mintoff (e.), *United Nations Debate Independence for Malta* (Malta, Freedom Press, 1964), p. 63, Appendix A. Malta's case was further debated in April 1964, *ibid.,* pp. 32-62, 65-66.

12. See Cmnd. 2121, *Malta Independence Conference* 1963 (London, HMSO, 1963); and *Malta: The Malta Independence Order* 1964 (Malta, Supplement to the Government Gazette, No. 11,685, 18 September 1964).

   For discussions of the issues involved at the time see too: F.P. Mizzi, 'Church-State Relations in Malta', *The American Ecclesiastical Review,* CLII, 4 (1964), 241-48; Mons Isqof Galea, *Inħarsu Dak li Hu Tagħna* (Malta, Empire, undated). Azzjoni Kattolika — Kummissjoni Stampa, *L-Emendi li jolqtu l-Knisja proposti mill-MLP fl-abbozz tal-Kostituzzjoni ta' Malta* (Malta. Empire, undated); L-E.T. Mons E. Galea, *Frak tad-Deheb* (Malta, Empire, 1926); D. Mintoff (ed.), *Il-Kalvarju tal-Haddiem,* (Malta, Freedom. 1964)

13. For a detailed discussion of the changes affected in December 1974 see J.M. Finnis '22 Malta' *Annual Survey of Commonwealth Law,* 1975 pp. 45-50. Finnis opens his comment thus: "The transformation of Malta into a republic on 13 December 1974 is an awful warning to constitutional draftsmen and appears to put in doubt the efficacy of the methods of entrenchment used in many recent Commonwealth constitutions."

14. S. Busuttil. *Malta's Economy in the Nineteenth Century* (Malta, M.U.P., 1969), p.1.

15. M. Abela, *Malta — un' Economia in Via di Sviluppo* (Malta, C.O.S., 1962), p.1.

16. Cmnd. 6090, *Report of the Royal Commission on the Finances, Economic Position and Judicial Procedure of Malta* (London, HMSO, 1912), para. 74.

17. W. Woods, *Report on the Finances of the Government of Malta* (London. Colonial No. 196, 1946), para. 8.

18. *Ibid.,* para. 13

19. The first five-year plan was conceived and launched when Malta was under direct Colonial rule. (Order in Council of 15 April, 1959 had revoked the 1947 Constitution and ended the State of Emergency which had been declared soon after Mintoff's resignation (tendered 21 April; accepted 24 April). For details of a political nature, see D. Mintoff, *Malta Betrayed — Truncheons and Tyrants* (Malta, Union, 1958) for developments of an economic nature, see D. Mintoff (ed.), *Malta Demands Independence.*

20. W.F. Stolper et al., *Economic Adaptation and Development in Malta* (United Nations, 64-3557, 1964).
21. M.M. Metwally *Structure and Performance of The Maltese Economy* (Malta. A.C. Aquilina & Co., 1977), p. 51.
22. *Outline of Development Plan for Malta* 1973-1980, par. 1.
23. Stolper, *Economic Adaption and Development in Malta,* par. 525.
24. Lord Robens et al., *The Second Progress Report for January* 1969 — *September* 1970 (Malta, 'The Bulletin', 24 November 1970), p.8.
25. For details. see T. Zammit, *L'Università di Malta — Origine e Sviluppo* (Malta, Tipografia S. Cretien, 1913), pp. 3-4. This is the text of an oration delivered on 5 August 1913. Zammit says the Bulls were signed on 29 August 1561, by Pius IV, and on 9 May 1578, by Gregory XIII.
26. Deed signed on 14 November 1592. R.M. Library, *Università* (Notabile), Vol. XV ff.267r-269v. See also *Archivio Storico di Malta*, Vol. VIII, p. 28; and A. Vella, *The University of Malta* (Malta, National, 1969), pp. 8-9.
27. Parl. Papers 140, *Report of the Commissioners on the Affairs of the Island of Malta* 1838, II, 19, p.14; and III, p.12. In their report the Commissioners distinguished sharply between the educational facilities in the area around Valletta from that in the 'casals', where they said hardly any provision for education existed. In a footnote to their report, the Commissioners said they had been told that of a total population of 115,570 in the Maltese islands. only about 10,165 were calculated to be able to read and write (III, p.12).
28. P.J. Keenan, *Report upon the Educatinal System of Malta* (Dublin. Alexander Thom, 1879).
29. S. Savona, *Report on the Educational Institutions of Malta and Gozo,* (Malta, Govt. Printing Press, 1885), par. 38.
30. *The Primary Schools: Report of the Committee appointed by the Hon. the Minister of Education in* 1948 (Malta, Govt. Printing Office, 1949), p.v., par.3
31. *Ibid.,* p.v., par. 2.
32. D. Crichton Miller, *Report on Education in Malta* (cyclostyled, 1957), par. 28.
33. *Ibid.,* par. 41.
34. A detailed historical account of the development of Techincal Education in Malta up to 1968 was given by J.A. Myers in a talk delivered to the Malta Joint Group of the Council of Engineering Institutions on Thursday, 31 October 1968 at the M.C.A.S.T. See also J.A. Gatt, 'Technical Education in Malta' (Malta Univ. B.Educ. thesis, 1954).
35. I.L. Evans, *Report on Higher Education in Malta* (Malta, Govt. Printing Press. 1946), par. 45.
36. Cmd. 6647, *Report of the [Asquith] Commission on Higher Education in the Colonies* (London, HMSO, 1945), Ch.VII, p.35, especially para. 3 & 4.
37. I.L. Evans, *Report on Higher Educatiion in Malta,* par. 17.
38. *Ibid.,* par. 28-45.
39. H. Heattherington et al., *The Royal University of Malta — Report of the Commission* (Malta, Dept. of Information, 1957), par. 1.
40. *Ibid.,* par. 5. Among other things, the Commissioners explained what is meant by the autonomy of universities in England in the following words: 'In ordinary circumstances, no University is required to do what, deliberately, it does

not wish to do. But equally no University is left in doubt as to the Government's assessment of the whole national need, or of the Government's expectation that each University will make its appropriate contribution. Any University which elects a different line of policy — as for quite good reasons it may — must expect that the amount of its Treasury grant will thereby be affected......'

41. *Ibid.*, par. 6a.
42. *Ibid.*, par. 6c.
43. *Ibid.*, par. 6b
44. In the year preceding the 1957 Commissioners' report, the University's total expenditure had been £43,379, out of which £31,000 had come in the form of a government grant. In paragraph 24 of their report, the Commissioners estimated that future expenditure was expected to 'soon reach something over £81,000', a figure reached three years later. The University's vote continued to expand. and in 1970/71 had become £608,218.

    The University's sustained rate of growth was welcome and encouraged by occasional reports on the University. Both, the XI and the XIII report encouraged a continuation of the policies of development earlier adopted by a newly-appointed Rector, Edwin Borg Costanzi, and his associates. Both reports attempted to consolidate attainments, and to waive factors — such as under-payment — which were then undermining the success of the institution at such a critical stage of its development.

45. Most of the changes referred to have already been mentioned in this section, but could be summarised as: a) the introduction of free secondary schooling in government schools for all as from October 1970; b) the opening of new Trade Schools to complement the Technical Institutes in 1972; c) the fusion of two Teachers' Training Coleges into the 'Malta College of Education' as from September 1973; d) the separation of the Junior College from the University, and its changeover into an Upper Secondary School run by the Department of Education as from October 1973; and e) the raising of the school-leaving age to 16 as from 1974.

46. Education Bill, 1974, 'Objects and Reasons as in Supplement to *Govt. Gazette*. No. 12,975, p. 311.

47. The University's views were given in a press conference by Professor E. Borg Costanzi, Rector of the University, folowing a motion in Council to that effect, on Wednesday, 17 July 1974. On Thursday, most of the local papers carried a report on the Press Conference. The full text of the hand-out distributed by the University during the meeting with the Press, was published in *Malta News* of 25 July 1974, p.5.

48. *Malta Education Act* 1974, art. 33(6).

49. *Ibid.*, art. 29 (2a).

50. *Ibid.*, art. 30(a) & (4). A summary of how the three-tier system of 'Statutes, Regulations, and Bye-Laws' operating at the University prior to the new Act had come about as a result of the recommendations made earlier by the Heather_ington Commission and by the Evans Commission, was given in the University's Press Conference, and is summaried in the hand-out distributed by the University.

51. See *Il-Hajja* of 24 July 1974, *In-Nazzjon Tagħna* and *L-Orizzont* of the same date. See Mintof's 'winding up' in 'Debates tal-Kamra tad-Deputati' — Seduta Nru. 322 (22 July 1974), pp. 65 ff.

52. R. Dahrendorf et al., *The Royal University of Malta Commission* — *the XXth Report* I & II (Malta, cyclostyled, 1973 & 1974). Mintoff rejected this accusation in Debates, *op.cit.*, p.73 ff.

53. Government's views were published *officially* for the first time in the form of of a *White Paper* 'Tertiary Education — Proposed Reforms' in June 1978 (Malta, DOI, 1978). The amendments to the Education Act were given a first reading in Parliament on the same day.

54. Professor Dahrendorf resigned by letter of 6 June 1978, reported upon in *Times Higher Education Supplement* of 8 June 1978; Professor Horlock's resignation is reported in *Times Higher Education Supplement* of 18 August 1978.

55. 'Draft Report on some Restructuring Implications in Tertiary Education of the Student-Worker Concept' (*Għaqda Għalliema Università*, cyclostyled, December 1977).

56. For more details on events as they happened, cf. 'University Newsletter', a regular feature in the *Sunday Times of Malta* by 'Campusino'. See also the 1978 graduation oration by the Rector of the Old University in *Old University Gazzette* vol 11, 1, Supplement No. 1, pp. v-ix.

57. I.L. Evans, *Report on Higher Education in Malta*, par. 6.

58. *Ibid.*, par. 6b.

59. The term 'stratification' is purposely employed because of its wider extension than the over-used term 'class'. Some interpreters of Maltese social life (e.g. Boissevain) have suggested to the writer that 'classes' do exist in Malta; but in the absence of a specific social mobility study, and of statistics on the distribution and employment of wealth on the island, the author is inclined to reject the application of the term 'class' in the sense originally used by Marx: 'any aggregate of persons who perform the same function in the organization of production — freeman and slave, patrician and plebeian, lord and serf, guildmaster and journeyman, in a word, oppressor and oppressed' (Communist Manifesto). On the contrary, he is rather inclined to subscribe to a view that upholds the existence of a stratification system based on status 'status-groups', primarily, but not exclusively related to educational achievement (and hence in a way more amenable to study through the use of Weber's multidimensional approach), rather than on economic power in the Marxist sense. Talk of 'class distinctions' in Malta — especially over recent years — may generally be interpreted to be more of an attempt to politicize the issue, and legitimize the actions of political leaders — even though this itself, as Marx himself admitted, might create 'class consciousness', and may eventually give rise to class stratification, and the creation of *Klasse für sich* from the possible embryonic existence of *Klasse an sich* in the Marxist usage.

60. In this respect, the stream of short stories *Wenzu u Rożi* written by Dr. Ġorġ Zammit, on a typical village background, are a stark reminder of by-gone days.

61. *Radju ta' Malta* — *Listenership Survey, November* 1973 (Malta, Shaw Universal Marketing Services Ltd., 1973), p.14.

62. For documentation of this, see below Chapter IV, Sections 4.2 and 4.5.

NOTES TO CHAPTER 3: 'THE RESPONSE OF THE MALTESE TO RELIGION'

1. See, e.g., J. Wignacourt, *The Odd Man in Malta* (London, G. Bell & Son, 1914); unsigned articles in *Gentlemen's Magazine*, LXX.2 (1801), pp. 1044, 1802; and declaration of Blood Commission Cmnd. 1261, *Report of the Constitutional Commission*, 1960 (London, HMSO, 1961), par. 32.

2. G. Hasenhüttl's definition of institution given in *Concilium* New Series, 1, 10 (Jan. 1974), p.115 is followed here: 'An institution is a changeable but permanent, product of purposive social role behaviour which subjects the individual to obligations, gives him formal authority, and possesses legal sanctions.' The Church is here considered as such an institution. Hasenhüttle deals with the matter is more detail in *Kirche als Institution* (Freiburg, 1973).

3. G. Lenski, *The Religious Factor* (New York, Anchor Books, 1963).

4. Ch Y. Glock and R. Stark, *Religion and Society in Tension* (Chicago, Rand McNally, 1965), pp. 18-38.

5. L. Laeyendecker, *Investigating Religious Change: A Research Proposal*, in *CISR Acts* for 1973 (Editions du CISR, Lille), pp. 9-35; and handouts given during the Conference at The Hague.

6. A passing remark to this effect, specifically referring to Malta, is made by R. Towler *(Homo Religiosus: Sociological Problems in the Study of Religion* (London, Constable, 1974), p. 169.

7. Th. Luckmann, *The Invisible Religion* (New York, Collier-Macmillan, 1966).

8. Campbell understands 'irreligion' as 'any collective system of beliefs, feelings and actions which is expressive of hostility towards religion'. The elements he includes in his ideal-typical definition are: (a) active hostility to religion; (b)hostility to *all* forms of religious expression and commitment; (c) rejection of *all* faiths; (d) hostility to religion is expressed with the intention of eliminating religion altogether; and (e) the existence of a congruent identification of the expression of hostile rejection as irreligious by both the actor himself and by society at large. It is such irreligion that is excluded from this study. Campbell himself follows other writers (Glock and Stark, Damarath, etc.) and admits that irreligion is rarely found in this ideal-typical form. In Malta, as will be evident from subsequent pages, more specific types of 'irreligiosity' (what Campbell would call 'anti-Catholic irreligiosity') did exist in some aspects of the Dimechian, Stricklandian, and Mintoffian movements; and these elements will be analyzed in this book. See C. Campbell, *Towards a Sociology of Irreligion* (London, Macmillan, 1971); and C. Campbell, 'An Approach to the conceptualization of irreligion and irreligiosity', in *Acts of CISR - XI* (1971), pp. 485-502.

9. See *Acts of CISR* — 1973, pp. 37-106.

10. R. Towler, *Homo Religiosus: Sociological Problems in the Study of Religion*, pp. 128-44.

11. Th. Luckmann, 'Comments on the Laeyendecker et al. Research Proposal,' in *CISR Acts* — 1973, p.59.

12. See Appendix A on Religious Bodies in Malta, p. 213.

13. For a very interesting and well-documented instance of how true this is, see the description of what happened in the festivals of ancestor worship in *Nan-ching,* a village in China, in C.Y. Yang, *A Chinese Village in Early Communist Transition* (USA, Harvard Univ. Press, 1959), pp. 191-96.

14. The recent reforms in Catholic baptismal liturgical rites are intended to make the event even more communitarian.

15. Until the 1975   Marriage Act, the situation obtaining in Malta was that only 'religious' marriages can be validly contracted. Religion was not under-stood to be exclusively 'catholic'. Exceptional 'civil' celebrations before the Governor — allegedly contracted by persons not belonging to a religion with a proper official in Malta — are not documented.

16. Specific provision for this post is made in law. See *Laws of Malta,* Chapter XXVI (Addolorata Cemetery Ordinance), section 2. He is there referred to as 'Il-Kappillan taċ-Ċimiterju' (Cemetery Chaplain).

17. F. Houtart, *The Socio-Religious Study of Malta and Gozo* (Leuven, Centre de Recherches Socio-Religieuses, 1960), p. 121.

18. At the time when Houtart was in Malta, and up to 1969 in most parishes, Easter duties (confession and communion) could be checked and controlled by what was then known as the *bulettin.* This special ticket used to be distributed to each person over 14 by the parish priest in a special round of all the parish households before Easter, and was to be exchanged on the communion rail within a specified time in Eastertide.

19. Though not specifically referred to by Houtart, the latter's comments are evocative of J.H. Fichter' five-old typification of parishioners in *Social Rela-tions in the Urban Parish* (Chicago University, 1954). Within Fichter's frame-work, one would have to say that the 'potential parishioner' and the 'margin-al parishioner' categories were completely absent; that ten people would have had to be called 'dormant parishioners'; and that the remaining 1990 would be distributed between the 'nuclear' and the 'modal' categories, with the latter constituting the greater number.

20. Houtart, *The Socio-Religious Study of Malta and Gozo,* p.122.

21. B. Tonna and A. Depasquale, *Report on the Sunday Mass Census - December 17, 1967* (Malta, PRS, 1969), par.1.

22. *Ibid.,* par. 6.

23. *Ibid.,* par. 7.

24. *Ibid.,* par. 9.

25. B. Tonna, *Schoolgoing Adolescents* (Malta, Research Agency Malta, 1961), pp.64-74.

26. F. Houtart, *The Socio-religious Study of Malta and Gozo,* p.123. A note of caution on the preceding figures was included by Houtart himself (p.123); and therefore they must be carefully interpreted: 'These figures are of course only indications, but they are clear enough to allow the drawing of prudent con-clusions'.

27. B. Tonna, *Schoolgoing Adolescents,* p.69.

28. M. Vassallo, *Iż-Żgħażagħ Studenti Maltin u l-Qrar.* (Malta, Catechetical Com-mission, cyclostyled, 1972), chapter 5.

29. M. De Domenico, *Life from a Catholic Viewpoint* (Malta, Lux, 1938).

30. One instance, as funny as it is striking, was that of the Embassy of Communist China in Naxxar until 1973. The facade of this embassy was very often covered with photographs of Mao-Tse-tung and other political propaganda cartoons. In their midst one could notice the carved image of the Sacred Heart and a tiny electric light glowing beneath it.

31. F. Houtart, *The Socio-Religious Study of Malta and Gozo*, pp.123, 129.

32. B. Tonna, *Schoolgoing Adolescents*, Table 33.

33. B. Tonna, *Religious Attitudes and Behaviour of University Students in Malta* (Malta, PRS, 1968), especially pp. 10-17.

34. See report in *Sunday Times of Malta*, 27 May, 1973, p.8.

35. B. Tonna, *Lenten Sermons Census* (Malta, Research Agency Malta, 1964); and B. Tonna, *Lenten Sermons Census* (Malta, Research Agency Malta, 1965).

36. F. Houtart, *The Socio-Religious Study of Malta and Gozo*, p.111.

37. See account in *Dun Ġorġ* 1880-1962 (Malta, MUSEUM, 1965), unsigned, p.20, and letters in *Malta Tagħna* (23 May 1914), and in *Salib* (issues of 30 May 6 and 20 June, 1914).

38. See a collection of speeches by Archbishop Gonzi published in a series of pamphlets *Ir-Ragħaj lill-Merħla Tiegħu* (Malta, Lux, 1944), esp. No. 2.

40. *Ibid.*, par. 3.2.

41. *Ibid.*, pp.11-12.

42 *Ibid.*, p.22.

43. B. Tonna, *Maltese Catechists at Work* (Malta, Christus Rex, 1966).

44. J. Wignacourt, *The Odd Man in Malta* (London, G Bell & Son, 1914), p.129.

45. J.P. Forrestall, *Where are the Priests?* (India, St. Paul's Publications, 1970).

46. *The Clergy in the World* (Vatican, Congregation for the Clergy, 1970).

47. It is currently being observed that the situation is changing. Over the last decade, recruitment for the religious orders has been extremely low, and several orders — the Jesuits for example — have had no novices for some years. Recruitment for the secular clergy is more promising, even though diminishing too. Success in this latter case is attributable to the initiatives of Mgr V. Grech, Rector of the Malta Seminary, and to the Vocation Centre of the Archdiocese, the main preoccupation of which is the recruitment for the diocesan clergy ranks.

48. F.P. Mizzi, *Religious Vocations (Nuns and Sisters) in the Maltese Ecclesiastical Province* 1911-1966 (Malta, PRS & Social Research Centre, 1970).

NOTES TO CHAPTER 4: 'THE PLACE OF RELIGION IN MALTESE SOCIETAL ORGANIZATION'

1. E. Troeltsch, *The Social Teaching of the Christian Churches* (London, Macmillan, 1931), I, p.331.

2. Chapter II, section 2.3, *et seq.*

3. Already in Keenan's time (1879), it was realized that any expansion of the educational system would necessarily entail a greater participation by clergy-

men, as practically only priests were qualified enough to be recruited as teachers. Objections to such a development seem to have been raised with Keenan; but, after clearly stating that he did not in any way bear any special sympathy with any particular 'class' of people, Keenan refused to accept them, and very forcefully stated his position in his report: 'Priests are by vocation preeminently teachers, and therefore fit and proper persons to look after schools......' See: P.J. Keenan, *Report Upon the Educational System of Malta,* p.49, art. VI.

4. A number of the 560 teachers recruited in September 1955 when part-time education was abolished (see above p.54) were members of the clergy.

5. This is what appears to have lain behind the arguments brought forward in favour of the abolition of Religion as an entry requirement for the University in the years preceding the Education Act, 1974. Miss Agatha Barbara, Malta's Labour Minister of Education, was reported to have said in Parliament on 16 July 1974 — when the Bill was being discussed — that 'she knew many young men who were relieved because they had realised that the subject [Religion] would not be of much use on entering University, and they would be able to devote more time to other important subjects such as science'. *The Times of Malta* (18 July 1974). Previously, Dr V. Tabone, deputy leader of the Opposition, had lamented 'the elimination of religion [as an obligatory element] in the character formation of the Maltese student'.

6. For further details, see below, 4.5, p.111 *et seq.*

7. This assertion is based on the following facts:
   (i) The Church's share in the total provision of education in Malta is declining. The extraordinary rise in the number of rooms and provisions in state-run education has not been paralleled by Church-run institutions, the intake of which has remained relatively stable. This is especially significant in the secondary level, where enrolment in private schools went down from 51.0% of the total in 1957/58 to 26.6% in 1970/1. For details see *Table* 4.1-1 below.
   (ii) Since the traditional emphasis in Church schools has been on languages rather than on sciences, their students are liable to find their job opportunities in the emerging Malta quite limited. It has to be seen whether the 'classical' training provided in private schools will eventually channel itself into specific job categories, more related to administrative and 'service' (interpreters, tourist guides, etc.) positions rather than in the directly 'productive' sectors of the economy.

8. J.F. Boissevain, *Saints and Fireworks — Religion and Politics in Rural Malta* (London, Athlone Press, 1965).

9. J.F. Boissevain, *Hal-Farruġ — A Village in Malta* (USA, Holt, Rinehart & Winston, 1969).

10. J.F. Boissevain, *Hal-Farruġ,* p.79.

11. C. Freudenberg, *The Church and the Family in a Maltese Village,* (cyclostyled paper, 1966); A. Langenger, *The Parish Clergy — A study of Siġġiewi* (Sussex, cyclostyled paper, 1966).

Table 4.1-1   *The Participation of Private Schools in the Education System*

Year	Total School Population in Malta	Total School Population in Private Schools*	Total % Partic.	% in Primary Level	% in Second Level
1954/55	65,659	16,682	25.4	18.9	63.2
59/60	78,135	17,139	21.9	15.6	54.8
64/65	66,910	17,370	25.9	17.9	55.6
69/70	67,209	14,426	21.5	16.1	44.6
72/73	64,501	14,411	22.3	20.4	19.6
76/77	78,768	19,142	24.3	22.6	22.7

* Includes Nursery, Infant, Primary and School Sections of the School Population. Nursery schools in Malta were exclusively run by the Church; no privately-run Technical Schools or Institutes exist.

Source: *Education Statistics* (Malta, Central Office of Statistics), several issues.

12. This section is based on direct participant observation in December 1973 and January 1974.
13. It was very striking to note that even when people went out for a dinner-dance in one of Malta's hotels, most insisted that they should stay 'with their group', and asked that tables be set accordingly.
14. Echoing Canon 139 sec. 4 of the *Codex Iuris Canonici*, article 37 of the Regional Council of Malta (held in 1935 but promulgated in 1936) stated:
    '1. ... clerics, including Religious clerics, may not get involved with political parties, nor may they attend political meetings, nor may they solicit, or accept, either political or civil offices without the Ordinary's permission in writing;
    '2. ... nor may they make any written contributions in dailies, periodicals or magazines that might seem to serve in any way political ends, without the written permission of the Ordinary, under pain of automatic suspension *a divinis*.'
15. For a collection of relevant excerpts from official documents and brief explanatory notes, confer F.P. Mizzi, 'Religious Toleration and Political Activity of the Maltese Clergy in the Constitutions of Malta under British Rule', *Studia*, III (1966), 1-16

16. For a summary of what happened, see E. Dandria, *The Malta Crisis* (London, The Rotary Press, 1930), especially pp.5-18.

17. Extracts taken from the 1962 Electoral Manifesto of the MLP, sections 2-4, as in *The Voice of Malta* (MLP organ), 7 & 14 January, 1962.

18. Actual election results were: Nationalist Party: 25 candidates; Christian Workers Party: 4 candidates; Democratic Nationalist Party: 4 candidates; Progressive Constitutional Party: 1 candidate. This makes a total of 34 'loyal' candidates as against 16 MLP candidates returned.

19. The relevant details have already been discussed in Chapter 2.1, pp. 43-44.

20. For the reactions of the clergy to this agreement, and for their appreciation of it after some years since it was signed, see below, Chapter 6.42, pp. 172-179.

21. It is sad to note that this breakage of traditional family ties was legitimated by some church agencies themselves. The popularity of short stories with a background that clearly reflected the situation then current, known as *Baħar Qawwi — Ġrajja ta' llum* (Malta, Kollezzjoni R.E.M.A., undated), published with official church approval by a Jesuit-run group, definitely did not help to heal the then common family rifts.

22. See, e.g., 'Vox Conscientiae', *Il Gvern u il Cnisia F'Malta — Questionijet ta żmienna* (Malta, Stamperia Mifsud 1893), especially p.14.

23. *Report to the Socialist International by the Malta Labour Party April 1960 — October 1961*, photocopy in MVARC, p.4.

24. D. Mintoff (ed.), *Priests and Politics* (Malta, Union, 1961), p.5.

25. Transcript of public meeting held by MLP at Gzira Circus, Gzira on 21 January 1962 (2.30 p.m.), held in MVARC, pp.1-2.

26. Transcript of public meeting held by MLP in Transfiguration Avenue, Lija, on 28 January 1962 (2.30 p.m.), held in MVARC, pp. 3-4.

27. *Electoral Manifesto of the Malta Labour Party — 1962*, art. 4.

28. The relevant clause, Section 2 (2) of the *Malta Independence Constitution* (Malta, Supplement to the Malta Government Gazette, No. 11,688, 18 September 1964), stated: 'The State guarantees to the Roman Catholic Church the right freely to exercise her proper spiritual and ecclesiastical functions and duties and to manage her own affairs.'

29. In *A Reply to the Diocesan Commission's Pamphlet*, p.17, Mintoff had estimated the Church's property to be one-third by value of the entire property of these islands, and that its annual income was £2 million.

30. F.O. Buratto, B. Tonna and A. Depasquale, *Memorandum di progetti proposte su invito di S.E. Mons. M. Gonzi — Razionalizzazione di alcuni Servizi Pastorali* (Malta, PRS, 1967).

31. These intimate occasions tend to produce a very powerful mechanism that is capable of withstanding all kinds of change. On 12 November 1969, in an interview with P.A.C. Brockington, a reporter from *The Guardian*, Mintoff placed this kind of power mechanism second only to that accruing from the Church's presence in Maltese society, and insisted that a 'loosening of family ties' was

an essential pre-requisite for social advancement. For the reactions to this statement in Malta, see *Il-Qawmien* (Sunday paper, organ of the Social Action Movement) of 30 November 1969, 7 December 1969 and 14 December 1969; as well as *Leħen is-Sewwa* (a semi-official Church organ) of 3 Jaunary 1970.

32. C.G. Vella, 'The Spirit of Cana", *Kana* (Sept/Oct 1964), 14; and Cana Statutes, articles 3(i) and (ii).

33. Unsigned, 'A Providential Movement in Malta', *Kana* (Jan/Feb 1966), p.11.

34. P. Serracino Inglott, 'The Cana Movement: the Social Situation in Malta', *Kana* (Jan/Feb 1966), p.40.

35. *Il-Huġġieġa* V, No. 8 (February 1950), p.125.

36. *Archives of the Order in Malta* (AOM) 470 310r carries a letter to this effect. M. Miege, *Histoire de Malte* (Paris et Leipzig, Jules Renouard, 1841), p.238 asserts that the use of this press was severely restricted as the 'government of the Order had all the interests to keep the Maltese in ignorance'. The oldest book known to have been printed in Malta dates back to 1647: G.F. Abela, *Della Descrittione di Malta, isola nel mare siciliano con le sue antichità ed altre notizie* (Malta, Paola Buonacota, 1647). Printing permission was suspended for a time, and the first book printed after its introduction was the *Codex de Rohan* in 1723. According to AOM 470 280r, Pompeo del Fiore was the first person issued with a printing licence in Malta. The first 'journal' or 'leaflet' intended for a 'wide' circulation in Malta goes back to the period of the French occupation: *Journal de Malte, Feuille Nationale, Politique Morale,* and is mentioned by M. Miege, *Histoire de Malte,* p.239. See also D. Mintoff, 'Journalism in Malta — an account and an appreciation' (Malta University, MA thesis, 1971), esp. Ch. I.

37. *Il Giornale Cattolico in Malta* was first published in September 1840, and was soon to be followed by *L'Ape Religiosa* in October 1840, and by *Il Trionfo della Religione* in January 1843.

38. Parl. Paper, *Reports of the Commissioners appointed to Inquire into the Affairs of Malta* 1830 (140-1), pp.15-17. As examples of anti-Catholic newspapers one can mention: *The Harlequin or Anglo-Maltese Miscellany,* first published in July 1838; *Il Mediterraneo, Gazzetta di Malta,* starting August 1838; *The Critic,* starting June 1844, and *Il Vero Gesuita, Giornale Religioso,* which came out in May 1845.

39. First published on 1 September, 1928.

40. First issue dates back to February 1912.

41. See editorial of *Leħen is-Sewwa* of 31 August 1974, when the fortysixth anniversary of the paper was being celebrated.

42. *The Maltese Observer* started publication on 3 May 1964, and ceased on 27 July 1969.

43. The first issue of *Il-Ħaddiem* dates back to 15 May 1950; its first issue as a daily paper goes back to 30 March 1964. The paper stopped publication on 31 December 1969, and was replaced by *Il-Ħajja.* An earlier paper by the same

name (published regularly from 25 June 1926 till 12 December 1927) had been patronized by the Nationalist Party, and was not a forerunner of the Church-sponsored paper referred to here.

44. This is how David C.McClellan characterizes the 'need for achievement' (nA), in *The Achieving Society* (Princeton, N.J., Van Nostrand, 1961), p.334.

45. The extent to which this is so needs no further elaboration as it has been amply documented in chapters One and Two.

46. As distinguished from its *indirect* involvement, i.e. its effects on the parish level through the influence of diocesan structures like the Cana Movement.

47. *Taħlita tal-kulur* refers to colour petards. It is important to note that even leisure and free time, whenever organized, followed these parochial patterns. Football, the main winter sport, attracts large crowds, and is still very markedly parochial in spite of the fact that it is most popular in the more urbanized places like Sliema, Hamrun, Valletta and Paola. In summer, the same pattern is repeated in water-polo. The proximity to the sea of every town or village in Malta, and the existence of numerous creeks and small bays, makes it possible for the inhabitants of every village to have their 'own' place of relaxation on hot summer days, and thus tends to perpetuate the old pattern. Even though the popularity of the car had tended to disrupt this pattern, it was possible to note during summer 1974 that the increase in the cost of petrol as a result of the fuel crisis, these patterns have been somewhat re-enforced as people started to look again for the nearest place in which to enjoy the sun and the sea.

48. This was so because the change-inducing forces were mostly supra-village in nature, thus disrupting traditional societal organization as sanctioned by the Church. For an idea of the extent to which geographical divisions were important for the Church's organization of itself and of society, see 'Liber Secundus' of the *Codex Iuris Canonici* (promulgated in 1917, but still not repealed), and especially Canons 216 and 241, s.2.

49. One striking example is the reaction of some parish priests to the popularity of 'slacks' around the late-sixties and early seventies. In the official programme of the village festa of Siġġiewi for 1970, a prominent caption read: 'Mini-skirts, sleeveless dresses, slacks are forbidden in Church'. In 1971, the same caption read: 'Mini-skirts, sleeveless dresses and shorts are forbidden in Church'. By 1974, most girls attended Church for Mass wearing slacks and trouser suits, and were admired for their modesty in doing so!

50. According to these statutes, the role of the parish council was to be solely consultative; members were to be chosen exclusively at the discretion of the parish priest; and their real role was to help the parish priest enforce his control over the parish system, and to facilitate the diffusion of religious ideology as construed by him. See, in particular, articles 5 (iii); 10; 12; and 15 of the Statutes prepared by the College of Parish Priests.

51. This is not a strict rule which is enforced on the congregation. But some

parish priests argue they should not do anything to abolish the custom themselves.

52. The Social Action Movement (MAS) was founded in 1955 'with the aim of working for the cultural, economic and moral evaluation of society and especially of the workers'. It has interests in (a) social assistance; (b) economic activity (cooperatives, credit unions, and benefit schemes); (c) trade unionism; and (d) educational activities.

53. In 1966, the Archbishop set up a Committee for Diocesan Orphanages with a specific mandate to 'coordinate, help and advise' the Church's already existing charitable institutions for deprived children. In 1974 the number of these institutions was fifteen, including two specially dedicated for the care of the mentally handicapped.

54. A diocesan catechetical office had existed before under the direction of Fr. Anthony Vella. When for health reasons he had to retire, the office was closed down, and the work it began — consisting primarily in the publication of a series of catechisms especially written for the different age groups— had to be abandoned until it was taken up again by the new commission formed on the initiative of the priest society 'Christus Rex'.

55. A similar initiative, known as 'Teens and Twenties', was also started by a Jesuit Father, amongst others, and is very popular with Malta's youth.

56. When it was launched, *Il-Hajja* was to concern itself also with video and sound, and not just with printed matter. The attempts to do this — a joint effort promoted by Professors S. Busuttil and P. Serracino Inglott — never materialized.

57. The Church's direct involvement in seeking to lessen the housing shortage started in the mid-fifties when the Archbishop built several blocks of flats at Blata l-Bajda. The involvement was extended by the Church's policy to make its land more easily accessible to people who wanted to build their own homes. This development was intended to take a firm structural form through the creation of the *Malta Homes Society*. By 1974, the achievements of this society were already considerable, but several factors prevented the full realization of the aspirations of its founders.

58. Of some importance in the interpretation of events is recognition of the part played by Archbishop Gonzi, who, in his fifty-year tenure of that office (after which he was soon to retire), had witnessed the complete transformation of Maltese society and Church structure. He remained throughout open to change, and ready to adopt new approaches. His manner of control of his diocese appears to stem less from his particular ideological vision than from the supportive role that he has played whenever the weight of his status was neeeded to maintain or restore balance in a situation in which, without him, new initiatives might at times have got out of control, or in which existing arrangements would have persisted and become antiquated.

59. See the controversy started by a letter from Dom Mintoff on 16 December

1938, in *The Malta Chronicle and Imperial Services Gazette,* and especially his letter of 9 January 1939, and the editorial of *Leħen is-Sewwa* of 11 January 1939.

60. PRS statute, art. 2.

61. Even though planning — mostly economic — has recently come to be very popular, and in many ways the fashionable word for the progressively aligned and future oriented person in almost any sphere of life, the philosophy of planning remains largely undeveloped; and its particular application to religion not closely scrutinized. Planning bases itself on specific knowledge of problems, on the clear delineation of objectives, goals and targets, and on the adoption of one (or of a mixture) of the various planning techniques (e.g. top-down versus bottom-up planning; outside-in versus inside-out planning); so that the known problems could be solved; and the objectives, goals and targets could be achieved. Planning therefore is based on the rationalist ethic *par excellence,* and is best suited to an organization that allows itself to be tailored to meet the needs of a particular situation such that the ends, the resources, and the means could be coordinated. The realm of religion, which concerns itself with 'non-rational facts' only partially allows for planning. Pastoral planning cannot operate like economic planning, in which policies can be enforced by law. Nor are the competences of the priest comparable to those of production workers. They cannot be coordinated by preconceived plans to anything like the same degree. The priest has a wide measure of autonomy and discretion in the performance of his role, and especially so in its pastoral aspects. People cannot be processed like materials, and the priests' labours cannot easily be rationalized by time-and-motion studies, nor even stimulated and regulated by incentive schemes, and productivity bonuses. Nor is there a measurable 'output' to be controlled. All that can be relied upon is the effectiveness of early socialization, selection, and secondary socialization for the priestly role, under the very general control of Church authorities. That control cannot in itself operate mechanically, but must share in the general humane, affective and diffuse dimensions of the priests' own role performances. Lack of understanding of these considerations has made diffficult the translation of the concept of pastoral planning — which has indeed become too popular a slogan — into realities in Malta.

For a brief, but succinct, analysis of these problems, see the criticisms levied by B.R. Wilson on the Paul Report: B.R. Wilson, 'The Paul Report Examined', *Theology,* LXVIII, No. 536 (1965); for an examination of a role similar to that of the priest, see B.R. Wilson, 'The Teacher's Role', *Youth Culture and the Universities* (London, Faber & Faber, 1970), pp.51-72.

62. The first article of the conclusions arrived at in December 1973 by the members of the Third Commission for the Pastoral Plan after three days of talks with Don Pietro Pace, the man responsible for pastoral planning in Italy, stated: 'The actual historical situation of society, and of the Church in Malta... makes the adoption of pastoral planning a matter of extreme urgency'.

63. Many factors contributed to the difficulties in implementing such a plan: not least among them the perspectives and situations of some of those who had, earlier in life, initiated new social concerns in the Church. They, after all, had

as individuals promoted action to meet certain needs. Their conceptions of the causes they had helped to start were conditioned by the style of the Church at the time at which they had introduced their new ideas. They had themselves done much by private initiatives; and they were disposed to favour such initiatives rather than public planning, and their conception of what the Church might do was more dependent on ideals of dedicated individual priests acting from personal conviction, rather than on formally rational planning procedures and bureaucratically structured patterns of action.

NOTES TO CHAPTER 5: 'THE DIOCESAN CLERGY'

1. T. Parsons, *The Social System* (London, Routledge & Kegan Paul, 1967), pp.480-535.
2. This chapter and the following one refer specifically to the diocesan clergy incardinated in the diocese of Malta. The diocesan clergy of Malta's sister diocese, Gozo, have been excluded from this study altogether.
3. Each diocesan priest was served with a questionnaire, hereafter reproduced as Appendix B. All the following tables on Malta's diocesan clergy were worked out on the basis of returns (response was 100%), but were updated up to 31 December 1972.
4. A few more parishes have been set up since the 1973 census; but these have been discounted in the present analysis.
5. It was alleged during my interviews — for the purposes of Chapter VI — that pressure by the Council of Parish Priests on the Archbishop not to abandon this practice, was the cause of some friction and a number of protests in the press against the nomination, in April 1974, of the parish priest of Dingli to the vacant post in Naxxar, in preference to somebody who had been acting as parish priest there for some time.
6. *Codex Iuris Canonici,* Canons 739 and 1094.
7. For a brief, but cogent, description of this model of parish priest, see E. Magri, *Min hu l-Kappillan* (Malta, Muscat, 1960). Among other things E. Magri says, 'In other words, in front of us we have the representative of Christ, of the Pope, and of the Archbishop, and we should obey him... without reserves, excuses, or protests...' (p.5).
8. For further details see above, the sections on the influence of the church in village life, pp. 96-104. A very interesting account of what the relationship of the *kappillan* with his parishioners could be like is to be found in N. Monsarrat, *The Kappillan of Malta* (London, Cassell, 1973). It is to be noted that times have changed considerably since the second world war, during which Monsarrat's novel is set.
9. Detailed research into the image portrayed by ̣ιe *Viči* may show that it differs fundamentally from that of the *kappillan.* The latter plays a predominantly 'paternal' role, the *Viči* a 'maternal' role. It would be interesting to correlate the changes currently occurring in relationships within the Maltese

family, and the possibly changing ideas about the roles of the *kappillan* and his *viċi* in the larger, similarly changing 'parish family'.

10. This is changing rapidly as a result of a revaluation of the importance of 'direct' pastoral work, and also as a result of improved work conditions for the *Viċi*. For details, see below pp. 275-76.

11. M. Vassallo, *The Work of Malta's Vice-Parish Priests* (Malta, College of Vice-Parish Priests, cyclostyled, Oct, 1970), par. 19. (The report was not published· but was circulated among the *Viċijiet*.)

12. *Ibid.*, par. 20.

13. See above, pp. 111-113 for details on the Cana Movement; p. 122 for Catechetical Commission; and pp. 113-116 for details on the Emigrants' Commission.

14. Unfortunately no clear distinction results from the Census returns between the more important clerical jobs at the Curia, and the less important ones in the same place, or somewhere else. The number 25 incorporates both categories. It is worth noting that Church 'bureaucracy' differs extensively from normal, more rationalized bureaucratic systems of other organizations — like Trade Unions, Insurance Companies and the State bureaucracy — even in Malta. In the Church, the secretarial tasks which in other organizations would be undertaken by specialized but 'non-executive' personnel are often undertaken by priests, because the labour of priests can be obtained at low cost; celibacy makes possible relatively low stipends; the priestly vocation makes for a 'tractable' labour force; dedication can be assumed in whatever line of service the priest is called to undertake. The relative inertia, and feeling of content in spite of obvious underemployment, undoubtedly militates against immediate adoption of more rationalized deployment; and further explains the difficulties encountered by those who launched the idea of pastoral planning.

This somewhat schematized presentation leaves out completely the one or two individual priests whose main day-time duty falls neither under the category of teachers nor under the heading of ecclesiastical specialist. Such would be the case of the chief librarian at the Malta Public Library. The small incidence of these cases did not warrant inclusion of yet another category.

15. Archbishop Gonzi was made Archbishop of Malta in 1943. It is said, however, that from the time of his election to the Bishopric of Gozo in 1924 he had played a very influential role in developments in the Malta diocese. Considerations of his role in the Strickland affair tend to confirm this suggestion. Archbishop Gonzi was appointed Archbishop Emeritus in 1976, and replaced by Mgr G. Mercieca.

NOTES TO CHAPTER 6: 'THE WORLDVIEW OF MALTA'S DIOCESAN PRIEST-HOOD IN A PERIOD OF GENERAL UPHEAVAL'

1 The inspiration to diversify one's research methods was heavily influenced by discussions held with Dr K. Hope of Nuffield College, Oxford; and by a reading of J. Webb *et al.*, *Unobtrusive Measures: Nonreactive Research in the*

Social Sciences (U.S.A., Northwestern University, 1966). The data for this section of the book was collected in 1974.

2. Homans' hypothesis that 'the higher the social rank, the wider will be the range of his interactions' was here taken as the basis for research. Some priests were obviously more influential than others in the opinion-forming and decision-taking processes in the diocese; and an attempt was made to include as many of these as possible in the interviews. See *The Human Group* (London, Routledge & Kegan Paul, 1959), p.145.

3. Interviews were carried out in Maltese, but some interviewees preferred to dictate their answers in English; or at times to write them down themselves in that language. In such instances, the quality of the style and grammar has not been improved. Quotations were generally taken from the most articulated opinions offered, but care was given to make sure that these were truly representative.

4. The letter and number which follow direct quotations from the interview data indicate the group of which the respondent is a member, and the number of years since his ordination at the time of the interview. The letters, ranging from A to F, indicate the groups as given above (Chapter 5, 5.4, pp. 133-143) : A = Parish Priest   B = *Viċi*;   C = Ecclesiastical   Assistant;   D = Teacher-priest; E = Parish Helper; and F = Student-priest.

5. A policeman's salary, in March 1948, amounted to £109 per annum; that of a hospital attendant £70 per annum; a postman's ranged from £60 to £120 per annum; and that of a secondary schoolmaster from £150 to £350 per annum. (Source: *Annual Abstract of Statistics*.)

6. This and subsequent quotations from this letter are taken from a copy of the letter sent to the Archbishop in 1946, which was shown to me by the priest in question. The letter was originally written in English, and hence is uncorrected.

7. *Il-Hajja*, 11 November 1973.

8. The interdiocesan council was announced as part of the pastoral plan, and as means whereby Vatican II *aggiornamento* could be brought about. Up to 1978, the plans to hold such a council had not been realized.

9. No specific examples were given by contributors; but the 'Saydon incident' must have been still fresh in the priests' memories. On the eve of the 1966 general elections, Mgr P.P. Saydon, an internationally renowned biblical and semitic languages scholar, made a declaration to the effect that voters for the Malta Labour Party committed no mortal sin. He was immediately suspended *a divinis* and had to leave the island immediately because of mounting social pressures.

10. The Ligutti affair has already been discussed in a preceding section, Chapter 5, 4.4, pp. 110-111. For a selection of letters on the issue, see *The Bulletin* (the paper that broke the news in Malta) as from 23 March 1971, and *Il-Hajja* of the same period.

11. Many priests I interviewed insisted that the widespread impression in Malta that priests earn a lot of money is incorrect. It was mostly parish priests, they insisted, who used to benefit from the generosity of the people, and who could, especially in rural villages, live off the gifts in kind which they received. The

priests who did not go into teaching usually had to rely on their family's **wealth** **and** well-being for their daily living.

12. One particular response elicited from another old priest with a university career behind him was unique. Because it is so evocative of the old language dispute (see above, pp.40,65) it is reproduced in full: 'The intelligentsia still dislikes Maltese, and prefers services held in Latin, English or Italian. It is not difficult at all for me to preach in Maltese, because I hate purism. I do not stupidly try to avoid the many non-Semitic words and expressions commonly used in Malta' [C.39].

13. See above, pp. 98, 97 *et seq.*

14   It is to be recalled that the interviews were carried out in Maltese.

15. See articles 94, 97-103, and especially footnote 32 of the *Abbozz ta' Direttorju dwar il-Festi ippreparat mill-Kummissjoni tal-Festi* (Malta, Liturgical Commission, cyclostyled, 1968). Footnote 32 states in Maltese: 'the procession should return to Church in the indicated time, so that enough time could be left for the unperturbed continuance of "external" festivities: the band concert in the parish square, fireworks, etc. It is not deemed fit for these outdoor celebrations to be held during the procession because they distract the people's devotion, and lengthen the duration of the procession'

16. Articles 93-109 of the *Direttorju dwar il-Festi etc.* have a special significance. They prescribed the separation of the parts to be played by civil and ecclesiastical authorities. In them, greater importance was given to the role of civil regulations to control 'external manifestations', even though this control had to be exercised in collaboration with Church authorities. This separation of powers, which implied a relaxation of the influence enjoyed by the parish priest, was heavily criticized in the amendments and comments eventually submitted by the College of Parish Priests. See in particular the amendments by the parish priests to articles 94, 96 and 97-103, to be found, with the comments of the Cathedral Chapter, in *Direttorju tal-Festi (Osservazzjonijiet Generali)*, another report by the Liturgical Commission.

17. See *Codex Iuris* Canonici, canons 904; 2368 (1) & (2); 2369.

18. B. Tonna, *Preliminary Report on the Diocesan Clergy* (Malta, PRS, 1964), pp.33-34.

19. *Regional Council — Clergy* (original manuscripts held at the PRS), f.142a.

20. *Ibid.,* f.338h.

21. B. Tonna, *The Image of the Priest in Malta* (Malta, PRS, 1967), p.19

22. *Ibid.,* p.20.

23. M. Vassallo, *The Work of Malta's Vice-Parish Priests* (Private Report to the Council of Vice-Parish Priests, 1970), par. 20c.

24. For further details, see above, Chapter 5, pp. 108-111.

25. *Il-Hajja,* 19 August 1971, p.1.

26. The declaration was reproduced in all the papers on the following day, 1 April 1971. See also the editorial comments of *The Bulletin* of the same day.

27. *Il-Hajja,* 26 May 1971.

28. *Ibid.,* 9 June 1971.

29. The actual announcement came through a letter written by Mgr Sapiano himself in the Church paper *Il-Hajja* on 20 June 1972.

30. *Pastor*, No. 52 (July 1972), p.35.
31. Article 1 of the regulations of the 'Parish Presbyterium' states: 'In every parish, or vice-parish, where there are at least three priests, including the parish priests, or "vicar curate" or "vicar substitute", the parish presbyterium should be set up as a consultative body for the parish priest, "vicar curate", or "vicar substitute".' See also criticism of the regulations in the clergy review *Pastor* (no. 58), editorial.
32. It is to be recalled that these interviews were carried out during summer 1973. An attempt to solve problems of disharmony at the headship of the Maltese Church was made in November 1973 when Mgr E. Gerada, then Co-adjutor, was asked to return to the Vatican Diplomatic Corps as Apostolic Nuntio to Guatemala and El Salvador.
33. See, e.g., *l-Orizzont* of 9 April, and 29 April 1974, and *Il-Hajja* of 29 April 1974.
34. A. Depasquale, *Relations between Church and State* (Malta, RUM, cyclostyled, 1974). The five theories range from (a) Regalism and Gallicanism; (b) the Theory of Coordination; (c) Fenelon's theory on the moral authority of the Church; (d) the theory of the Church's truly juridical but indirect authority over the State in mixed matters; and (e) the theory of the Church's direct authority over the State.
35. It is important to recall that the politico-religious dispute during the 1960s had been based on this particular view of Church-State relationships. A pamphlet written by a leading lay leader, Mr. Paul Saliba, then President of the men's section of the Catholic Action, stated that: 'Socialism does not recognise Mother Church as the juridical and perfect society, established by Jesus Christ the Son of God; and does not recognise the authority given by God to the Pope, to the bishops, and to priests. Socialism wants to annihilate the church's authority, and to replace it with an international society with only material ends in view... Socialism wants complete and permanent separation between state and church. Socialism does not want the church to speak on daily life, neither on individual matters nor on society's life... they want the Church to be completely subject to the State... they want to damp its voice which is none else but the voice of Christ...' P. Saliba, *Is-Soċjaliżmu* (Malta, Muscat, 1992), pp.28-29. This pamphlet carried a *Nihil Obstat* and an *Imprimatur*

   See also the 1956 Lenten Pastoral Letters (also published in *Times of Malta*, 7 March 1956), for an enunciation of the view that the Church's right to interfere in 'mixed matters' is supreme, and for a vigorous attack on the so-called 'liberal philosophers' who were then promoting novel ideas about Church-State relationships.
36. This was confirmed to me in writing by Archbishop Gonzi himself. To the question 'What did the dispute with the Malta Labour Party exactly consist of?' he replied, 'Il-ġlieda mal-MLP kienet dwar ċerti punti li kienu jhambqu hafna fuqhom u li ma kienux jaqblu mal-ispirtu tal-Knisja; u mil-banda l-ohra is-Soċjaliżmu, li dak iż-żmien kien iġġudikat skond il-prinċipju ammess mill-Papiet: li wieħed ma jistax ikun kattoliku veru u soċjalista. Illum dawn iż-żewġ raġunijiet naqsu hafna'. ['The dispute with the MLP was about certain

points about which they used to insist a great deal, and which could not fit with the teaching of the Church; and on the other hand Socialism, which, at the time, was judged according to the principle proposed by the Pope: one could not be a true Catholic and a Socialist.'] See also P. Saliba, *Is-Soċjaliżmu*, pp.16-31.

37. See, e.g., the articles in *Leħen is-Sewwa* of February 1962 by P.P. Spiteri, the frequent articles by 'Gladiator' and 'Don Camillo' in the same paper, and especially the pamphlet *Il-Verita dwar l-A.A.P.S.O.* (Malta, M.A.S., 1961).

38. See 'L-Istorja ta' Mintoff: Is-Soċjaliżmu ikkundannat ta' Mintoff, Bidu u Żvilupp bil-fatti u bid-dokumenti', in *Leħen is-Sewwa* (February 15, 1962). (The title means: 'The history of Mintoff: Mintoff's condemned socialism: origin and developments with facts and documents'.) See the polemic with Mr Scully in *The Daily Malta Chronicle* and *Government Services Gazette* of December 1938 and Jan/Feb 1939, and especially Mintoff's contributions of 16 and 24 December, 1938. *Leħen is-Sewwa* commented editorially on 11 January 1939.

39. Further research into this matter disclosed another point of view. Sources close to the people involved in the MLP-Church negotiations in 1969 suggested that Bishop Gerada took the initiative to seek a *modus vivendi* with the MLP following a call from the Archbishop; that the peace agreement was not signed in a haphazard way and without full prior consultation with the Archbishop; and that Bishop Gerada entered the scene after other abortive attempts by other people. The comments of this section are however illuminative in some respects: they at least indicate that what could have been false impressions entertained by some of the clergy were never corrected, and hence that proper communications between clergy and bishops either did not exist, or did not function properly in this particular case.

40. This is a fact in Malta. For the reaction of MLP supporters to the active part played by individual priests in Nationalist-organized Independence celebrations in 1973, see editorial in *l-Orizzont* of 25 September 1973. *L-Orizzont* is published daily by the General Workers' Union, an organization which always supports MLP policies.

41. The Church had strongly opposed the setting up of the Casino during the MLP administration of 1955-58. During the Nationalist administration, it is alleged that the Church reluctantly agreed not to openly oppose the venture after a report submitted by a layman (sent by the Church to investigate the operation of Casinos in other countries) on condition that certain entry rules were observed.

42. After Independence, Dr G. Borg Olivier changed the order of precedence, and put himself before the Archbishop.

43. A note of protest was published by the Church then, but many priests considered it inappropriate. The Czech Minister was an ex-priest.

44. Some examples were given by interviewees: the silence of the Church on the morality of strikes when a politically inspired strike had brought the dry-docks to a standstill for six months; and its silence on increased prostitution as a result of more frequent visits by the American Sixth Fleet.

45. Homosexuality between two consenting adults is no longer a crime. The bias in favour of men in the criminal code relative to adultery has been removed.

46. For more details on the extent of the Services' importance for the islands' economic viability, see above, Chapter 2, pp. 45 *et seq.*

47. In a private discussion I had with the Archbishop soon after his return to Malta, he told me that the Defence Secretary did suggest to him a figure well above the one earlier offered to Mintoff, and one which was not far below the figure on which settlement was finally reached.

48. This is important: many priests insisted that they did not mind Gonzi doing something because of his personality and history; but they would not consider his action as apt for *any* bishop who happened to be leading the diocese.

49 It is interesting to note that a few months after the interviews had been carried out, a Franciscan friar left the order to form a new party. Dr Colombo had been a medical practitioner and Minister of Finance in the 1947 Labour administration before joining the Capuchins.

50. See, e.g., the letter of Mgr E. Coleiro in *The Sunday Times of Malta*, 13 January 1974, p.15.

51. Mgr. J. Mercieca is a Gozitan, and had been very active in Malta's sister diocese when Mgr Pace was still Bishop there. It was alleged that he left Gozo when Mgr N. Cauchi was nominated Apostolic Administrator in that diocese and thus blocked him the chances of being nominated bishop there himself. From Gozo he went to Rome where he took up an appointment as Judge of the *Sacra Romana Rota*. Soon after his nomination as Auxiliary to Archbishop Gonzi in Malta, it was being alleged in clerical circles that the Vatican had made the appointment without prior consultation with Archbishop Gonzi. Mgr Mercieca was appointed Archbishop of Malta in 1976. Archbishop Gonzi was simultaneously nominated 'Archbishop Emeritus of Malta'.

52. See *l-Orizzont* of 1 August, 1974. A few days later, an unsigned circular, making fun of the situation, was received by a group of 'chosen priests'.

53. Even a decade ago, the concept of resignation from a job to which a priest would have been assigned by the Archbishop would have been differently received in the Maltese Church. Resignations from important positions within the Church, allegedly as a result of situations created, or endorsed, by official decisions taken by the Ecclesiastical Authorities, have recently become more common. The new sense of independence within the Church and from the Bishop's 'missio', which these priests are demonstrating, is a clear departure from the traditional tenet that 'a priest is meaningless unless fully united with the Bishop'. The decision to resign from a specific appointment, yet at the same time to remain a priest, and to take up other work without being asked to do so specifically by the Bishop — at a time when there is also a conscious demand for the reform of the old system — suggests that these priests may be distinguishing between allegiance to the Church leadership and allegiance to what they consider to be the pristine kernel of truths as revealed by Christ, and suggests that a complete revaluation of the most important features of traditional Catholic ideology is in the making.

54. See, e.g., A.J. Russell, 'A Sociological Analysis of the Clergyman's Role with special reference to its development in the early nineteenth century' (Oxford Univ. D.Phil. thesis, 1970); M.G. Daniel, 'London clergymen: the ways in which their attitudes to themselves have changed in the first ten years of

their ministry' (London School of Economics M.Phil. thesis, 1968) and M. J. Woolgar, 'The Development of the Anglican and Roman Catholic Clergy as a Profession' (Leicester University Ph.D. thesis, 1960).

55. A profession is here understood according to the model provided by Russell, *ibid.*, p.4, and is meant to comprise the following elements: an occupational group that has (a) specialist functions; (b) a prolonged period of training; (c) a monopoly of legitimate performance; (d) self-regulating mechanisms with regard to entry and expulsion; (e) a fiduciary relationship between practitioner and client; (f) a distinctive professional ethic; (g) a reward structure and career pattern; and (h) a research orientation and (i) control of the institution within which the professional role is legitimated.

56. Perhaps the clearest instance of the institutional expression of such collaboration on a wide scale in Malta is provided by the diocesan commissions, and notably by the Cana Movement in which members of the various professions cooperate, each according to his distinctive specialization, for the perpetuation of Maltese family traditions and ideals. For further details, see above, Chapter 4, 4,5, pp. 111-113.

57. For an explanation of this assertion, see above, pp. 187-188.

58. All the priests who had been ordained in 1972 were served with a questionnaire which they were asked to return through the post. Fourteen out of the seventeen replied. The aim of this short questionnaire was to provide some sort of check on what other priests were saying on some aspects of the priest's life in Malta. A translation of the questionnaire is included as Appendix D.

59. A translation of the questionnaire distributed to each Seminarian in October 1973 is included as Appendix E.

60. This was the precise purpose of the 'Paul Report' in 1964. See L. Paul, *The Deployment and Payment of the Clergy* (London, Church Information Office, 1964). For reactions to it, see G.E. Duffield (ed.), *The Paul Report Considered* (Marcham, The Marcham Manor Press, 1964); and B.R. Wilson, 'The Paul Report Examined', *Theology*, LXVIII (1965),, pp.89 *et seq.*

NOTES TO 'CONCLUSION'

1. Various examples could be cited. At a time when M.A. Vassalli believed that the Order of the Knights was in serious difficulties, rather than joining the subversive elements then being cultivated on the island by the French, he wrote an important memorandum to the Grandmaster in which he advocated that the Order should rationalize her activity and develop relationships with the East. His ideas were considered impractical, however, and he eventually joined the Jacobite faction. See F. Panzavecchia, *L'Ultimo Periodo della Storia di Malta sotto il Governo dell'Ordine Gerosolomita* (Malta, Stamperia del Governo, 1835), pp.342-47. See also G. Mitrovich, *The Claims of the Maltese founded upon the Principles of Justice* (London, Mills & Son, 1835); and his *Indirizzo ai Maltesi* (Londra, dai Torchj di Mills e Figlio, 1835) in which he made substantial claims for better salaries and pensions for the Maltese. Similarly, see N. Zammit, *Malta*

e Sue Industrie (Malta, Stamperia di Governo, 1886), pp.33-42, 116-22, and especially 123-26. Zammit criticizes the widespread belief in luck among the Maltese; and insists that it is necessary to 'destroy the superstition of luck from the people's minds'. For an account of similar calls by M. Dimech, see H. Frendo, *Birth Pangs of a Nation — Manwel Dimech's Malta* (Malta, Mediterranean Publications Ltd., 1972), Ch. VII. The above names have been given by way of an indication, and others — like G. Ellul Mercer, F. Mizzi, N. Mizzi, S. Savona and P. Boffa — could also be cited to similar effect.

2. The debate was conducted in the columns of *The Daily Malta Chronicle and Imperial Services Gazette* in December 1938 and January 1939. On 9 January 1939, Mintoff wrote that he believed 'workers' should have the same economic rights as the peers and the judges... and anything that will help to put that ideal in practice, whether it comes from the Pope or from any other source, is welcome to us...' He later commented on how he understood Malta's social structure since 1500 AD, and divided it into three social strata: (a) the Knights, (b) the 'professionists', an (c) the workers and peasants. He commented: 'The "professionists" licked the Knights' boots whilst the workers and peasants licked the boots of their fellow citizens, the "professionists". Captain Ball occupied Malta by request of these "professionists" who had worked up the workers and the peasants to a red-hot religious fanaticism. Thus the Knights left the island and in their stead ruled the British who, being interested nn the island from a strategic point of view, gave all the desired privileges to the "professionists" who later on developed into ultra-patriots, and became pro-Italian...'

3. The need to extend their social base, in spite of the fact that suffrage was not yet universal, had been felt by the leaders of the Nationalist Party, particularly in 1927 when, in an attempt to woo voters from the then still nascent Labour Party (it had been formed on 12 April 1921), and while retaining the language question issue as the basis of their electoral programme, the Nationalists proposed social reforms more extensive than those of the Labour Party itself. The election was won by the Compact formed by Sir G. Strickland, leader of the Constitutional Party, and by Dr. P. Boffa, leader of the Labour Party.

4. For an attempt to understand Maltese rural politics (in the early sixties) in this manner, see J.F. Boissevain, *Saints and Fireworks*. Direct connections between the social roots of religious and political extremism have been observed in a number of countries. S.M. Lipset, *Political Man* (London, Mercury, 1960), pp.107-108, refers to the success of young Trotsky in Czarist Russia as dependent on the support he got from religious sects; to the extent to which Communists in Holland and Sweden are more numerous in centres which once were the basis of fundamentalist religious revivalism; and to how, in Finland, Communism and revivalist Christianity are often strong in the same areas. The Maltese case is however very different from the instances mentioned by Lipset: in Malta the opposition between the patron saint and the secondary saint as it existed in some villages (and as it still does even if with diminishing relevance) is best understood as a form of institutional opposition within the same broad framework of belief; and so as opposition mostly of a formal kind. In the cases mentioned by Lipset, the opposition between the beliefs of

the people of different groups are real, and differ fundamentally in their content.

5. G. Kester, *Workers' Participation in Malta, Issues and Opinions* (Malta, R.U.M. Press, 1964), pp.30 and 99.

6. *Ibid.*, p.118.

7. Many Maltese were greatly impressed when, during a TV series *Għad-dell tal-Ħasira* (televised during summer 1974), an elderly couple from Imtaħleb were interviewed and their life portrayed. Many were struck by the sharp contrast between the world-views, life-patterns, and even the 'habitation' of that couple who withstood change and that of the normal contemporary Maltese family.

8. The incidence of this process is even more striking in Malta than it is in all except very densely populated parts of western society: the countryman need not emigrate to an urban centre, but is able simply to visit the town for work and to return home in the evenings.

9. See above, p.   , for a quotation from this debate which Mintoff had with a few others, the most important of whom was a person called Mr Scully.

10. For references to the works of Vasselli, Zammit and Dimech, who are three examples, see above, p.   , footnote 1, and Bibliography.

11. K. Davis, 'Political Ambivalence in Latin America', *Journal of Legal and Political Sociology*, 1-2 (October 1942), p. 143. Davis' reference to Catholicism in these terms might not stand the test in a contemporary Latin American context, now world renowned for its avid promotion of the Theology of Liberation!

12. *Leħen is-Sewwa,* 11 January 1939. The strange adjective 'pecked-out' loses its force in translation. In the Maltese original, the word *mintuf* is used as a pun on the surname *Mintoff*.

13. Some historical examples illustrate this point:
(a) In 1838, when the Royal Commissioners were investigating the prospects of relaxing press censorship on the island, one of the objections to which they gave serious consideration was whether more liberty to the press could offend religious feelings in Malta. So great was the turmoil in clerical circles then, that about the time of the Commissioners' arrival, 'a meeting of the secular clergy, attended by more than 250 persons, and including most parish priests, elected a committee of eight from their own body, to consider the affairs of their own order. This committee of eight approved of the introduction of a liberty of printing, but qualified their approbation by the following resolution: "That every printed attack, direct or indirect, upon the Catholic, Apostolic, Roman religion, as determined by the sacred canons of the church, ought to be prohibited under the severest penalties...".' The agreement which the Commissioners eventually reached with the elected group of priests still suggested that the priests expected civil authority to punish anybody who 'indecently offended or insulted our dominant religion'. See Parl. Papers 141-I, *Report of the Commissioners Appointed to Inquire into the Affairs of the Island of Malta* 1838, pp.16-17.
(b) In one of the issues of *Il-Bandiera tal-Maltin,* M. Dimech had written 'Who has seen to it that the people be given this light? Nobody. They allow the people to be mistaken in everything, and they want to extend the peace [*hena*] of their birthplace! We have said this repeatedly, and we will repeat it:

those men who do not make sure to enlighten the people are traitors!' In a handwritten note adjacent to this text, the Vicar General wrote: 'Non si può far peggio che insegnare il popolo dottrine tali eretiche!' AAC, *Čirkularijiet P. Pace*, 1911, 86 (xvii),

14. For details of the conflict, see above, Chapter 4.3, pp.
15. The relationship between extensive use of the products of technology and the process of rationalization is made by B.R. Wilson, 'Sociological Methods in in the Study of History', *Transactions of the Royal Historical Society*, 5th Series, vol. 21 (197), pp. 102-103.
16. Parl. Paper 140-I, *Reports of the Commissioners*, 1838, p. 16.
17. The term is borrowed from C. Campbell who distinguishes clearly between 'ir-religion', 'irreligiosity' and various kinds of irreligion, such as 'anti-clerical', 'anti-ritualistic' and 'anti-ecclesiastical' religion. See C. Campbell, 'An Approach to the Conceptualization of Irreligion and Irreligiosity', in *Acts of CISR*, 1971, pp. 485-501
18. Cmnd. 1261 *Report of the Malta Constitutional Commission*, 1960 (London, HMSO, 1961), par. 32.
19. See, merely by way of example, the debate in the letters' column of *The Sunday Times of Malta*, as from September 1974.
20. Repeatedly, Dom Mintoff publicly uses religious values to legitimize his actions. On October 29, 1974, e.g., he sought to have people endorse the proposed changes in the constitution, by referring explicitly to one of the basic tenets of Christianity: equality of all men before God. In that same meeting, too, he explicitly distinguished between two types of Christians: 'stamped Christians (*tal-bolla*), and 'real Christians', and insisted that only those in the second category are true Christians. See *l-Orizzont*, 28 October 1974. In the Education Debate in July 1978, to mention just one more case, a similar approach was adopted.

Bibliography

MANUSCRIPT SOURCES

ARCHIVES

AAC — *Archives of the Curia of the Archbishop,* especially *Acta Civilia.*
AEC — *Archives of the Emigrants' Commission.*
ACM — *Archives of the Cana Movement.*
AOM — *Archives of the Order of Malta* held in Malta Public Library).
AOPRS — *Archives of the Pastoral Research Services,* especially the collection of letters sent in 1966 in preparation for the Interdiocesan Council.
MVARC — Archives of the writer, which include a collection of private documents given to him by priests, a collection of newspaper cuttings on debated issues, and transcripts of a number of meetings held by MLP leaders in the 1960s.

UNPUBLISHED WORKS

BARETJE, R. 'La Démande Touristique' (Université d'Aix-Marseille, thesis for the Doctorat Science Economique, 1968).
BUGEJA, J. 'British Influence on Maltese Development 1919—1933' (Oxford Univ. B. Litt. thesis, 1973).
COOPER, R.J. 'An Analysis of Some Aspects of Social Change and Adaptation to Tourism on Ibiża' (Oxford Univ. D. Phil. thesis).
COXON, A.P.M. 'A Sociological Study of the Social Recruitment, Selection, and Professional Socialization of Anglican Ordinands' (Leeds Univ. Ph.D. thesis, 1965).
DANIEL, M.G. 'London Clergymen — The Ways in which their Attitudes to themselves and their Work have changed in the First Ten Years of their Ministry' (London Univ. M.Phil.thesis, 1967, 1967).
FRENDO, H. 'Language of a Colony' (Malta Univ. M.A. thesis, 1974)
FREUDENBERG, C.D. 'The Church and the Family in a Maltese Village) (Sussex Univ. B.A. dissertation, 1966).
GATT, J.A. 'Technical Education in Malta' (Malta Univ. B. Educ. thesis, 1954).

LANGENGER, A. 'The Parish Clergy: The Parish of Siggiewi' (Sussex Univ. B.A. dissertation, 1966).

MINTOFF, D. 'Journalism in Malta — an account and an appreciation' (Malta Univ. M.A. thesis, 1971).

MUNOZ-HERNANDEZ, M. 'The Idea of Social Change in the Philosophy of Jean-Jacques Rousseau' (Oxford Univ. B. Litt. thesis, 1967).

RAWIN, S.J. 'Changes in Social Structure in Poland under Conditions of Industrialization 1945—1963' (London Univ. Ph.D. thesis, 1965).

RICHARDSON, M. 'Aspects of the Demography of Malta' (Univ. of Durham Ph.D. thesis, 1960).

ROBERTSON, A.F. 'The Dynamic Process of Change in a Mediterranean Island Community' (Edinburgh Univ. M.A. thesis, 1964).

RUSSELL, A.J. 'A Sociological Analysis of the Clergyman's Role' (Oxford Univ. P.Phill. thesis, 1970).

SCEBERRAS TRIGONA, A. 'Constitutional Change and the Maltese Constitution' (Malta Univ. L.L.D. thesis, 1973).

WOOLGAR, M.J. 'The Development of the Anglican and Roman Catholic Clergy as a Profession' (Leicester Univ. Ph.D. thesis, 1960).

ZAMMIT MANGION, J. 'Landmarks in the Development of Education in Malta' (Malta Univ. B.Educ. thesis, 1952).

PRINTED SOURCES

MALTESE NEWSPAPERS

Il-Berqa (The Lightning) 1939—1971 [for a long time daily, then weekly, renamed *Berqa u Telstar*: stressed the views of the CP, eventually of the PCP].

The Bulletin 1955—   [evening daily, independent].

The Daily Malta Chronicle and Government Services Gazette [daily, 1938 & 1939 issues only referred to in this thesis].

The Government Gazette 1813—   [published in Italian between 1813—16 as *Gazzetta di Malta*; ceased to be a newspaper as from 1839, now used solely for publishing laws and government regulations].

Il-Habib (The Friend) 1912—1928 [Church weekly, replaced by *Leħen is-Sewwa*].

Il-Haddiem (The Worker) 1950—1969 [weekly until 1964, thereafter daily; replaced by *Il-Hajja*].

Il-Hajja (Life) 1969—   [Church daily].

Il-Helsien (Liberation) 1958—1967 [daily, intermittently weekly; MLP publication].

Leħen is-Sewwa (The Voice of the Truth) 1928—   [weekly, with periods when issued daily; organ of Malta Catholic Action, semi-official Church paper].

Malta News 1965— [daily; GWU publication, now *The News*].

The Maltese Economist 1969—1974 [monthly; intermittently weekly].

The Maltese Observer 1964—1969 [weekly; Church publication].

Il-Mument (The Moment) 1972— [weekly; NP publication].

In-Nazzjon Tagħna (Our Nation) 1969— [daily; NP publication].

L-Orizzont (The Horizon) 1964— [daily; GWU publication].

Il-Qawmien (The Rising) 1958— [weekly; MAS publication].

Is-Sebħ (Dawn) 1973—1976 [daily, intermittently weekly; MLP publication].

The Sunday Times of Malta 1920— [weekly; stresses point of view of PCP, and formerly that of the CP, now *The Sunday Times*].

The Times of Malta 1935— [daily; stresses point of view of the PCP, and formerly that of the CP, now *The Times*].

It-Torċa 1944— [weekly; GWU publication].

The Voice of Malta 1959—1972 [weekly; MLP publication].

IMPORTANT GOVERNMENT PUBLICATIONS/REPORTS

Parl. Papers 140 & 141, Reports of the Commissioners on the Affairs of the Island of Malta — 1838.

C. 5975 Correspondence respecting Sir L. Simmons' Special Mission to the Vatican — 1890.

Cd. 6090 Report of the Royal Commission on the Finances, Economic Position and Judicial Procedure of Malta — 1912.

Cmd. 3588 Correspondence with the Holy See relative to Maltese Affairs (Jan 1929-May 1930).

Cmd. 6647 Report of the Commission on Higher Education in the Colonies 1945.

Cmd. 9657 Malta Round Table Conference — 1955.

Cmnd. 1261 Report of the Malta Constitutional Commission — 1961.

Cmnd. 2121 Malta Independence Conference — 1963.

Cmnd. 2406 Malta Independence Constitution — 1964.

Cmnd. 2423 Proposed Agreement on Malta's Defence and Assistance — 1966.

Cmnd. 4943 Agreement with respect to the Use of Military Facilities in Malta — 1972.

BRUCE, W.N. *Report on the Re-organization of Education in Malta* — *1921* (Supplement to *Govt. Gazette* XII, 1921).

CRICHTON-MILLER, D. *Report on Education in Malta* (cyclostyled, 1957).

DAHRENDORF, R. et al. *The RUM Commission XV Report*, Parts I & II (cyclostyled, 1974 & 1974).

EDUCATION COMMITTEE, The Primary Schools (Govt. Printing Office, 1949).
ELLIS, C. 'Report on the Education of Malta' (Times of Malta, 13 & 14 Jan. 1943).
EVANS, I.L. Report on Higher Education in Malta (Govt. Printing Press, 1946).
HEATHERINGTON, H. et al. The RUM — Report of the Commission (Dept. of Information, 1957).
KEENAN, P.J. Report upon the Educational System of Malta (Dublin, Alex. Thom., 1879).
ROBENS, Lord, et al. Joint Mission for Malta Report (DOI, 1967).
SCHUSTER, G.E. Interim Report on the Financial and Economic Structure of the Maltese Islands (Govt. Printing Office, 1950).
STOLPER, W.F. et al. Economic Adaptation and Development in Malta (United Nations, 64 — 3557, 1964).
WOODS, W. Report on the Finances of the Government of Malta (HMSO, Col. 196, 1946).

IMPORTANT CHURCH REPORTS

BURATTO, F.O., TONNA, B & DEPASQUALE, A. Razionalizazione di Alcuni Servizi Pastorali (PRS, 1967). *
BUSUTTIL, F. Rapport dwar il-Hidma Karitativa u Assistenzjali f'Malta u Ghawdex (PRS, 1971).
DEGUARA, A. (ed.) Seminar Pastorali (Kulleġġ tal-Kappillani/PRS, 1966).
DEPASQUALE, A. Statistical Tables: Maltese Priests 1911-1970 (PRS, 1970).
Inventory of Church Property (PRS, 1970). *
HOUTART, F. The Socio-Religious Study of Malta and Gozo (Leuven, Centre de Recherches Socio-Religieuse, 1960). *
McKINSEY & Co. Financial Administration of the Diocese — The Church of Malta (PRS, 1970).
MIZZI, F.O. Priestly Vocations 1911 — 1964 (PRS & Social Research Centre, 1966).
Religious Vocations: Nuns and Sisters (PRS & Social Research Centre, 1970).
Rapporti dwar il-Konsultazzjoni dwar is-Saċerdozju Ministerjali f'Malta u f'Ghawdex (PRS, 1971).
PACE, C. Maltese Lay Associations in Profile (PRS, 1972).
PACE, P. Pastorale Organica per Malta (PRS, 1967). *
PIN, E. Aspetti Sociologici del Rinnovamento Pastorale in Malta (PRS, 1967). *

TONNA, B. *Schoolgoing Adolcents* (RAM, 1961).
  The Parish of Floriana (RAM, 1961).
  The Maltese Vice-Parrocco (RAM, 1963). *
  The Cana Clinic (RAM, 1963). *
  Preliminary Report on the Diocesan Clergy (PRS, 1964). *
  Lenten Sermons Census 1964 & 1965 (RAM, 1964 & 1965). *
  Census of Maltese Sisters (PRS, 1966). *
  What is happening to Religion in Malta? (PRS, 1969). *
TONNA, B. & DEPASQUALE, A. *L-Ewwel Abbozz tal-Pjan Pastorali* (PRS,
  1966).
  The Image of the Priest in Malta (PRS, 1967).
  Reaction to the Liturgical Renewal (PRS, 1967). *
  Religious Attitudes and Behaviour of University Students in Malta
  PRS/RUSTA, 1968).
  Census of Sunday Mass Attendance: 17.12.67 (PRS, 1969).
VASSALLO, M. *The Work of the Vice-Parish Priests* (Kulleġġ tal-Viċijiet,
  1970). *
  Iż-żgħażagħ Maltin u l-Qrar (Catechetical Commission, 1973). *
  Those Men in Black (PRS, 1973).
  * Those marked (*) were never officially published.

SELECTED BOOKS AND ARTICLES

ABELA, M. *Malta: un' economia in via di sviluppo* (Malta, COS, 1962).
  An Enquiry into Family Size in Malta and Gozo (Malta, COS, 1963).
ABRECHT, P. *The Church and Rapid Social Change* (London, SCM, 1961).
Anon. *Il-Gvern u il Cnisja* (Malta, Stamperia Mifsud, 1893).
  Lill-Haddiema (Malta, Għaqda Soċjalista Maltija, 1927).
  L-Iskandlu (Malta, Salesian Press, 1941).
  Għawdex jiddefendu lill-Knisja (Malta, 1961).
  Dun Ġorġ Preca: Is-Serv t'Alla (Malta, MUSEUM, 1965).
Anon. *Baħar Qawwi I & II* (Malta, REMA, undated).
  Il-Qawmien tal-Haddiem Malti: Storja tal-Partit Laburista 1920 — 1970,
  I (Malta, Freedom, 1971).
AQUILINA, J. *Papers in Maltese Linguistics* (Malta, MUP, 1972).
ARGYLE, M. *Religious Behaviour* (London, Routledge & Kegan Paul, 1958).
ATTARD, L. *Conferenzi fuq il-Haddiema* (Malta, E. Lombardi, 1921).
AUSTIN, D. *Malta and the End of the Empire* (London, Frank Cass, 1971).
BARRINGER, H.R. et al. *Social Change in Developing Areas* (Cambridge,
  Mass., Schenkman, 1965).
BARRINGTON, L. (ed.) *Malta Year Book* (Malta, Lux, annually 1953 —
BENDIX, R. & LIPSET, S.M. 'Karl Marx' Theory of Classes', in R. Bendix

& S.M. Lipset (eds), *Class, Status and Power* (Glencoe, Free Press, 1957), pp. 26-35.

Class, Status and Power (Glencoe, Free Press, 1957).

BERGER, P.L. *The Noise of Solemn Assemblies* (NY, Doubleday, 1961).

The Precarious Vision (NY, Doubleday, 1961).

Invitation to Sociology (London, Penguin, 1966).

Rumor of Angels — *Modern Society and the Rediscovery of the Supernatural* (London, Allen Lane, 1969).

The Social Reality of Religion (London, Faber, 1969).

BERGER, P.L. & LUCKMANN, Th. *The Social Construction of Reality*: *Treatise in the Sociology of Knowledge* (London, Penguin, 1971).

BILLIET, J. 'Secularization and Compartmentalization in the Belgian Educational System', *Social Compass*, XX, 4, pp. 569-92.

BLAU, P.N. *Bureaucracy in Modern Society* (NY, Random House, 1956).

Exchange and Power in Social Life (NY, Wiley, 1964).

BLIZZARD, S.W. 'The Minister's Dilemma', *Christian Century* (25 April 1956), pp. 508-10.

'Role Conflicts of the Urban Parish Minister', *City Church* VII(4), (Sept. 1956), p.11 *et seq.*

'The Protestant Minister's Integrating Roles', *Religious Education* (July-Aug. 1958), p.1 *et seq.*

'The Parish Minister's Self-Image of his Master Role', *Pastoral Psychology* (Dec. 1958), p. 25 *et seq.*

'The Parish Minister's Self-Image and Variability in Community Culture', *Pastoral Psychology* (Oct. 1959).

BLOUET, B. *The Story of Malta* (London, Faber & Faber, 1972).

BOGAN, R. 'Priests, Alienation and Hope', *The Month*, CCXXXIV, 1270 (June 1973), pp. 195-201.

BOISSEVAIN, J.F. *Saints and Fireworks* — *Religion and Politics in Rural Malta* (London, Athlone Press, 1965).

Hal-Farruġ: a Village in Malta (USA, Holt, Rinehart & Winston, 1969).

Friends of Friends (Oxford, Blackwell, 1974).

BORZOMATI, P. *Studi Storici sulla Calabria Contemporanea* (Chiaravalle Centrali, Framas, 1972).

BOWEN-JONES, H. *Malta: Background for Development* (Durham Univ. Press, 1960).

BROTHERS, J. 'Social Change and the Role of the Priest', *Social Compass*, X.6 (1963), pp.477-89.

BUDD, S. *Sociologists and Religion* (London, Collier, 1973).

BURGALASSI, S. *Preti in Crisi: Tendenze sociologiche del' Clero Italiano* (Fossano, Editrice Esperienze, 1972).

Il Comportamento Religioso degli Italiani (Firenze, Vallecchi Editore, 1968).

BUSUTTIL, S. *Malta's Economy in the Nineteenth Century* (Malta, MUP, 1969).

BUTLER, G. *Coffin in Malta* (London, Geoffrey Blas, 1964).

BRUCE, M.W. *Malta, A Geographical Monograph* (Malta, Progress Press, 1965).

CAMPBELL, C. *Towards a Sociology of Irreligion* (London, Macmillan, 1971.

CHRISTIAN, W.A. Jr. *God and Person in a Spanish Valley* (London, Seminar Press, 1972).

COLEIRO, E. *Kors ta' Soċjoloġija* (Malta, Dar S. Ġużepp, 1947).

CREMONA, J.J. *Human Rights Documentation in Malta* (Malta, MUP, 1966).
An Outline of the Constitutional Development of Malta under British Rule (Malta, MUP, 1963).

DAHRENDORF, R. *Homo Sociologicus* (London, Routledge & Kegan Paul, 1973).
Class and Class Conflict in Industrial Society (London, Routledge & Kegan Paul, 1959).

DANDRIA, E. *The Malta Crisis* (London, The Rotary Press, 1930).

DAVIS, J. *People of the Mediterranean* (London, Routledge & Kegan Paul, 1977).

DAVIS, P. *Akarva: Emergence of Community?* (Dept. of Psychol. & Sociol., Univ. of Canterbury, New Zealand, Research Project 22, 1972).

DAVIS, K. 'Political Ambivalence in Latin America', *Journal of Legal and Political Sociology* 1-2 (Oct. 1942).
Human Society (NY, Macmillan, 1959).

DAVIES, E.T. *Religion in the Industrial Revolution in South Wales* (Cardiff, UK: Univ. of Wales Press, 1965).

DE DOMENICO, M. *The Malta Crisis* (Malta, Lux, 1938).
Life from a Catholic Viewpoint (Malta, Lux, 1938).

DELIA, E.P. *Focus on Aspects of the Maltese Economy* (Malta, Midsea Books, 1978).

DELLEPORT, J., et al. 'Bibliographie annotée pour une sociologie du clergé', *Social Compass*, VIII.4 (1961), 355-65.

DELLEPORT, J.J. (ed.) *The Priest in a Secularized World: Conferences of the III International Congress at Lucerne, 18-22 September 1967* Maastricht, NL, Institute for Intereuropean Sacerdotal Exchange, 1968).

DE NEVE, A. 'Secularization in Russian Sociology of Religion', *Social Compass*, XX.4 (1973), 593-602.

DOBIE, E. *Malta's Road to Independence* (Norman, Univ. of Oklahoma Press, 1967).

DORE, R.P. *Aspects of Social Change in Modern Japan* (N.J., Princeton Univ. Press, 1967).

DUFFIELD, G.E. (ed.) *The Paul Report Considered* (Marcham, The Marcham Manor Press, 1964).

DURKHEIM, E. *The Division of Labour in Society* (Glencoe, The Pure Press, 1933).

The Elementary Forms of the Religious Life (NY, Collin Books, 1961).

DUVERGER, M. *Political Parties* (London, Methuen, 1967).

EISENSTADT, S.N. *The Protestant Ethic and Modernization: A Comparative View* (NY, Basic Books, 1968).

Comparative Perspectives on Social Change (Boston, Little & Co., 1968).

Social Differentiation and Stratification (Illinois, Scott, Foresman & Co., 1971).

EPSTEIN, T.S. *South India: Yesterday, Today and Tomorrow* (London, Macmillan, 1973).

ETZIONI, A. *A Sociological Reader on Complex Organization* (Glencoe, The Free Press, 1961).

A Comparative Analysis of Complex Organization (Glencoe, The Free Press, 1961).

ETZIONI, A. & ETZIONI, E. *Social Change* (London, Basic Books, 1964).

FENN, R.K. 'The Secularization of Values: An Analytical Framework for the Study of Secularization', *Journal for the Sc. Study of Religion*, VIII. 1 (1969), 112-24.

FICHTER, J.H. *Social Relations in the Urban Parish* (Chicago, Chicago Univ., 1954).

Religion as an Occupation (Notre Dame, Ind., 1961).

'A Comparative View of the Parish Priest', *Archives de la Sociologie des Religions*, 8.16 (1963), p.44 et seq.

Priest and People (NY, Sheed & Ward, 1964).

America's Forgotten Priests (NY, Harper & Row, 1968).

FRENDO, H. *Birth Pangs of a Nation: Manwel Dimech's Malta 1860-1921* Malta, Mediterranean Publication, 1972).

FREUD, S. *The Future of an Illusion* (London, Hogarth Press, 1962).

GALEA, E. (Mgr. Bishop) *Frak tad-Deheb* (Progress, A.K.M., 1962).

Inħarsu dak li hu tagħna (Malta, A.K.M., undated).

GALEA, P.P. *Il-Kerk ta' d-Demoniu micxuf f'Malta* (Malta, Stamperia Giuseppe Cumbo, 1912).

GANADO, H. *Rajt Malta Tinbidel*, I (Malta, Il-Hajja, 1974).

GIDDINS, A. *The Class Structure of the Advanced Societies* (London, Hutchinson Univ. Library, 1973).

GLOCK, C.Y. & STARK, R. *Religion and Society in Tension* (Chicago, Rand McNally, 1965).
American Piety (Berkeley & Los Angeles, Univ. of California Press, 1960).

GLOCK, C.Y., et al. *To Comfort and to Challenge* (Berkeley & Los Angeles. Univ. of California Press, 1967).

GOFFMAN, E. *Asylums* (London, Anchor Books, 1961).

GOLLIN, G.L. 'Theories of the Good Society: Four Views on Religion and Social Change', *Journal for the Sc. Study of Religion*, IX.1 (1970), p.1 *et seq.*

GONZI, G. *Il-Cnisja u l-Ħaddiem (Żmien il-Jasar)* (Malta, Cathloic Social Guild, undated).

GONZI, M. *Ir-Ragħaj lill-Merħla Tiegħu* (Malta, Għaqda ta' Qari Malti, 1944).

GOODE, E. 'Some Sociological Implications of Religious Secularization', *Social Compass*, XVI.2 (1969), 265-73.

GREELEY, A.M. *The Persistence of Religion* (London, SCM Press, 1973).

GUIZZARDI, G. 'New Religious Phenomena in Italy: Towards a Post-Catholic Era' (Toronto, VIII World Congress of Sociology, 1974).

HALL, D.T. & SCHNEIDER, B. *Organizational Climates and Careers: the Work Lives of Priests* (NY, Seminar Press, 1973).

HILL, M. *A Sociology of Religion* (London, Heinemann Educational, 1973).

HILLERY, G.A. (Jr.) 'Definitions of Community: Areas of Agreement', *Rural Sociology*, 20 (June 1955), p.111 *et seq.*
'The Convent: Community, Prison or Task Force', *Journal for the Sc. Study of Religion*, VIII.1 (1969), 140-51.

HOGBIN, I. *Social Change* (Melbourne, Melbourne Univ. Press, 1971).

HOMANS, G.C. *The Human Group* (London, Routledge & Kegan Paul, 1951).

HOSELITZ, B.F. *Sociological Aspects of Economic Growth* (Glencoe, The Free Press, 1962).

HOUTART, F. 'La Vocation au Sacerdoce comme perception collective de valeurs', *Arch. de Soc. des Rel.* 16 (1965), 39-43.

HUIZING, P. 'Church and State in Public Ecclesistical Law', *Concilium*, VIII. 6 (Oct. 1970), 126-35.

HASENHUTTL, G. 'The Church as an Institution', *Concilium*, New Series, I. 10 (Jan. 1974).

INKELES, A. *Social Change in Soviet Russia* (Cambridge, Mass., Harvard Univ. Press, 1968).

JARVIE, I.C. & AGASSI, J. *Hong Kong: a Society in Transition* (London, Routledge & Kegan Paul, 1969).

KAVANAH, J. *A Modern Priest looks at his Outdated Church* (NY, Trident Press, 1967).

KENNY, M. *A Spanish Tapestry — Town and Country in Castile* (London, Cohen & West, 1961).

Kunsill tal-Provinċjali, Kulleġġ tal-Kappillani, Ġunta Djoċesana, *Il-Protesta ta' Malta Kattolika: 5 ta' Marzu, 1961* (Malta, Empire, 1961).

LAEYENDECKER, L. 'Investigating Religious Change: a Research Proposal' *Acts of CISR* — XII (1973), pp. 9-35.

LAFERLA, A.V. *British Malta* I & II (Malta, Aquilina, 1946).

LAURENZA, V. *Ciò che l'istruzione in Malta deve alla Chiesa* (Malta, Empire Press, 1939).

LAUWERS, J. 'Les théories sociologique concernant la secularisation — Typologie et critique', *Social Compass*, XX.4 (1973), 523-34.

LAVAGNA, C. *Le Costituzioni Rigide* (Roma, Edizioni Richerche, 1964).

LEE, H.I. *A Study in Constitutional and Strategic Development* (Malta, Progress, 1972).

Leħen is-Sewwa, leaflets No. 2 & 3, *'Ġabra tal-Pastorali tar-Randan'* and 'L-Interdett: għaliex qabel 1-10 ta' April? (Malta, AKM, 196).

LENSKI, G. *The Religious Factor* (NY, Anchor Books, 1963).

LIPSET, S.M. *Political Man* (London, Mercury Books, 1963).

LOEWENSTEIN, K. *Political Power and the Governmental Process* (Chicago, Univ. of Chicago Press, 1957).

LUCKMANN, Th. *The Invisible Religion* (NY, Macmillan, 1966).
'Comments on the Laeyendecker et al. research proposal', *Acts of CISR* — *XII* (1973), pp. 55-68.

MAGRI, E. *Min hu l-Kappillan* (Malta, Muscat, 1960).
Ma' l-Arċisqof fit-Triq għall-Hajja (Malta, Muscat, 1961).

MAITRE, J. *Les Prêtres Ruraux* (Paris, Editions du Centurion, 1967).

MARTIN, D. *The Religious and the Secular* (London, Routledge & Kegan Paul, 1969).
The Sociology of English Religion (London, SCM Press, 1967).
'Notes for a General Theory of Secularization', *(European) J. of Sociology*, 10.2 (1969), 192-201.
'An Essay in Conceptual and Empirical Synthesis', in *Acts of CISR* — *XII* (1973), pp. 517-28.
Tracts against the Times (London, Lutterworth Press, 1973).
A General Theory of Secularization (Oxford, Basil Blackwell, 1978).

MARX, K. & ENGELS, F. *On Religion* (Moscow, 1957).

MATRAS, J. *Social Change in Israel* (Chicago, Aldine, 1965).

McLEISH, J. *The Theory of Social Change — Four Views Considered* (London, Routledge & Kegan Paul, 1969).

MEISSNER, B. (ed.) *Social Change in the Soviet Union* (Notre Dame, Ind., Univ. of Notre Dame Press, 1972).

MERTON, R.K. *Social Theory and Social Structure* (NY, Free Press, 1965).

METWALLY, M.M. *Structure and Performance of the Maltese Economy* (Malta, A.C. Aquilina, 1977).

MEYRIAT, J., et al. *La Calabrie, une région sous-developpée de l'Europe Mediterranéene* (Paris, Colin, 1960).

MICHALLEF, G.A. *Alcune Osservazioni Economico-Politiche sull'Isola di Malta* (Livorno, Dai Torchj di Glauco Masi e Compagno, 1825).

MICHEL, B. *Les Ressources du clergé et de l'Eglise en France* (Paris, Editions du Cerf, 1971).

MIEGE, M. *Histoire de Malte* (Paris et Leipzig, Jukes Renouard, 1841).

MILLS, T.M. *The Sociology of Small Groups* (N.J., Prentice Hall, 1967).

MILNE, R.G. 'Family Planning in Malta', *Population Studies*, XXVII.2 (1973), 373-86.

MINTOFF, D. *Malta's Struggle for Survival* (Malta, Lux, 1949).

Malta u l-Gvern Ingliż (Malta, Muscat, 1950).

(ed.) *Malta First and Foremost: The Malta Labour Party Re-affirms its Faith* (Malta, Muscat, 1950).

Malta u l-United Nations (Malta, Muscat, 1950).

Malta u l-Patt ta' l-Atlantiku (Malta, Muscat, 1950).

(ed.) *Malta Betrayed: Truncheons and Tyrants* (Malta, Union, undated).

(ed.) *Malta Demands Independence* (Malta, MLP, 1959).

(ed.) How Britain Rules Malta (Malta, Union, 1960).

(ed.) *Priests and Politics in Malta* (Malta, Union, 1961).

Il-Prinċipji Fundamentali tal-Partit tal-Haddiema (Malta, Żgħażagħ Laburisti, 1961).

(ed.) *United Nations Committee of 24 Debate Independence for Malta* (Malta, Freedom, 1964).

(ed.) *Il-Kalvarju tal-Haddiem* (Malta, Freedom, 1964).

(ed.) *Malta-Church-State-Labour* (Malta, Freedom, 1964).

(ed.) *A Reply to the Diocesan Commission's Pamphlet* (Malta, Freedom, 1966).

MITROVICH, G. *The Claims of the Maltese founded upon the Principles of Justice* (London, Mills & Son, 1835).

MIZZI, F.P. 'Church-State Relations in Malta', *The American Ecclesiastical Review*, CLII.4 (April 1965).

'Religious Toleration and Political Activity of the Maltese Clergy in the Constitutions of Malta under British Rule', *Studia*, 3 (Dec. 1966).

MOL, H. (ed.) *Western Religion* (The Hague, Mouton, 1972).

MORGAN, J. Review of A.M. Greeley's *The Persistence of Religion*, in *Crucible* (Jan. 1974), pp. 51-52.

NEAL, M.A. *Values and Interests in Social Change* (Englewood Cliffs, N.J.: Prentice-Hall, 1965).

O'DEA, T.F. *The Sociology of Religion* (N.J., Prentice Hall, 1966).
'Five Dilemmas in the Institutionalization of Religion', *J. for the Sc. Study of Religion*, I.1 (Oct. 1961), 30-39.
Sociology ana the Study of Religion (NY, Basic Books, 1970).

O'NEILL, D.P. *The Priest in Crisis — a Study in Role Change* (London, Chapman, 1968).
The Social System (London, Routledge & Kegan Paul, 1967).

PAUL, L. *The Deployment and Payment of the Clergy* (London, Church Information Office, 1964).

PERISTIANY, J.G. *Honour and Shame* (London, Weidenfeld & Nicolson, 1965).
Sociology in Greece (Rome, 1960).

PESCI, G. *Aħwa fi Cristu* (Malta, Mercuris Press, 1930).

PITT-RIVERS, J. *Mediterranean Countrymen* (The Hagne, Mouton & Co., 1963).

POPLIN, D.E. *Communities: a Survey of Theories and Methods of Research* NY, Macmillan, 1972).

POTEL, J. et al. *Le clergé francais, évolution demographique ... images de l'opinion publique* (Paris, Centurion, 1967).

PUCCIO, G. *Il Conflitto Anglo-Maltese* (Milano, Treves-Treccain-Tumminelli, 1933).

REMY, J. & HAMBYE, I. 'L'appartenance religieuse comme expression de structures culturelles latentes: problème de méthode', *Social Compass*, XVI. 3, pp. 327-42.

ROBERTSON, R. (ed). *The Sociology of Religion* (London, Penguin, 1969).
A Sociological Interpretation of Religion (Oxford, Blackwell, 1970).

ROSE, A.M. *Human Behaviour and Social Processes* (London, Routledge & Kegan Paul, 1972).

SALIBA, P. *Min hu l-Isqof* (Malta, Empire Press, 1961).
Is-Soċjaliżmu (Malta, Fergħa Rġiel — AKM, 1962).
L-Arċisqof Gonzi: Ġrajjiet mill-Hajja u l-Hidma Tiegħu (Malta, Lux, 1965).

SAMUELSSON, K. *Religion and Economic Action* (London, Heinemann, 1961).

SAPIANO, G. 'Il-Prinċipji Fondamentali tal-Malta Labour Party u l-Verità Kattolika Kuntrarja', *Leħen is-Sewwa*, 22 Sept. 1961.

SCHREUDER, O. 'Where are the Priests?', *Seminarium* (Oct/Nov 1965), pp. 816-94.
'Types of Catholic Priests', *Acts of CISR — IX* (1967), pp. 33-35.
'The Structure of the Ministry in the Contemporary Church: a Socio-

logical Study', *News Bulletin of the Institute for Interueropean Sacerdotal Exchange*, II.1/2, pp. 54-64.
Metamorfosi della Chiesa (Brescia, Queriniana, 1969).
SEASTON, G. *The Catholic 'New Order'* (Malta, Catholic Social Giuld, 1941).
SEGRETERIA DI STATO (ed.) *Esposizione Documentata della Questione Maltese (Febbraio 1929-Cinquo 1930)* (Vatican, Tipografia Poliglotta, 1930).
SERRACINO INGLOTT, P. 'Why am I ... *? Does it really matter what?' *Ferment* (Oct. 1966).
Introduction in: R. England (ed.), *Contemporary Art in Malta* (Malta, A Malta Arts Festival Publication, 1973), pp. 7-16.
SERVAIS, E. & BONMARIAGE, J. 'Sunday Mass Attendance as a Cultural Institution', *Social Compass*, XVI.3, pp. 369-86.
SHINER, L. 'The Meanings of Secularization', *International Yearbook for the Sociology of Religion*, Band III, Vol. III, pp. 51-59.
'The Concept of Secularization in Empirical Research', *Journal for the Sc. Study of Religion*, 67 (19   ), 207-20.
SPITERI, L. *The Development of Industry in Malta* (Malta, Lux, 1969).
SMELSER, N.J. *Theory of Collective Behaviour* (London, Routledge & Kegan Paul, 1962).
SMITH, D.E. (ed.) *Religion, Politics and Social Change in the Third World* (London, Collier-Macmillan, 1971).
STAHMER, H. *Religion and Contemporary Society* (NY, Macmillan, 1963).
STACEY, M. *Tradition and Change* (Oxford, O.U.P., 1970).
SHANIN, T. (ed.) *Peasants and Peasant Societies* (London, Penguin, 1971).
Special Diocesan Commission, Malta. *The Quarrel of the Malta Labour Party with the Church* (Malta, Empire Press, 1966).
STEPHAN, K.H. & STEPHAN, G.E. 'Religion and the Survival of Utopian Communities', *Journal for the Sc. Study of Religion*, XII.1 (1973), 89-100.
STROZZO, J.A. 'Professionalism and the Resolution of Conflicts among the Catholic Clergy', *Sociological Analysis* 31.2 (1970), 92-106.
STYS, W. 'The Influence of Economic Conditions on the Fertility of Peasant Women', *Population Studies*, XI.2 (Nov. 1957), 136-48.
TARROW, S.G. *Peasant Communism in Southern Italy* (New Haven, Yale U.P., 1967).
TAWNEY, R.H. *Religion and the Rise of Capitalism* (London, Penguin, 1969).
TAYLOR, R.F. *Christians in an Industrial Society* (London, SCM Press, 1961).
TILLICH, P. *Theology of Culture* (NY, Oxford U.P., 1959).

TONNIES, F. *Community and Association* (London, Routledge & Kegan Paul, 1955).

TONNA, B. 'The Allocation of Time Among Clerical Activities', *Social Compass*, X.I (1963), 93-106.

Sociologia nella Pastorale della Parocchia e della Diocesi (Roma, Centro Orientamenti Pastorali, 1970).

TOWLER, R. *Homo Religiosus: Sociological Problems in the Study of Religion* (London, Constable, 1974).

TROELTSCH, E. *The Social Teaching of the Christian Churches* I & II (London, Macmillan, 1931).

VALLIER, I. *Catholicism, Social Control and Modernization in Latin America* (Santa Cruz, Univ. of California, 1970).

VASSALLO, M. (ed.) *Contributions to Mediterranean Studies* (Malta, MUP, 1977).

VELLA, A.P. 'The Role of Private Schools in Maltese Education', *Malta Yearbook* (1961), pp. 135-38.

VORGRIMLER, H. (ed.) *Commentary on the Documents of Vatican II*, I-V (London, Burns & Oates/Herder & Herder, 1969).

'VOX CONSCIENTIAE' *Il Gvern u il Cnisja f'Malta — Questionijiet ta żmienna* (Malta, Stamperia Mifsud, 1893).

VRCAN, S. 'Some Theoretical Implications of the Religiosity as a Mass Phenomenon in a Socialist Society', in *Acts of the CISR — XI* (1971), pp. 503-524.

WACH, J. *The Sociology of Religion* (Chicago, Phoenix Books, 1944).

WALCOT, P. *Greek Peasants, Ancient and Modern: a Comparison of Social and Moral Values* (Manchester, Manchester Univ. Press, 1970).

WALLERSTEIM, I. (ed.) *Social Change, the Colonial Situation* (NY, John Wiley & Son Inc., 1966).

WATT, L. *Communiżmu* (Malta, Għakda ta' Qari Tajjeb, 1935).

WEBER, M. *The Protestant Ethic and Spirit of Capitalism* (London, G. G. Allen & Unwin Ltd., 1930).

The Sociology of Religion (London, Methuen, 1965).

WERTHEIM, W.F. *Indonesian Society in Transition* (The Hague, W. van Hoeve Ltd., 1959).

WIGNACOURT, J. *The Odd Man in Malta* (London, G. Bell & Son, 1914).

WILLIAMS, P. 'The Nature of Religion', *Journal for the Sc. Study of Religion*, II.1 (1962).

WILSON, B.R. 'The Pentecostalist Minister: Role Conflicts and Sociological Status', *American Journal of Sociology*, XLIV.5 (March 1959).

'The Paul Report Examined', *Theology*, LXVIII.536 (Feb. 1965), p. 89 et seq.

Religion in a Secular Society (London, C.A. Watts, 1966).

'Sociological Methods in the Study of History', in *Transactions of the Royal Historical Society*, 5th Series, 21, pp. 101-18.

Patterns of Sectrianism (London, Heinemann, 1967).

The Youth Culture and the Universities (London, Faber & Faber, 1970).

Religious Sects (London, World Univ. Library, 1970).

(ed.) *Rationality* (Oxford, Blackwell, 1970).

Magic and the Millenium (London, Heinemann Educational, 1973).

The Noble Savages (Berkeley, Univ. of California Press, 1975).

WILSON, M. *Religion and the Transformation of Society* (Cambridge, Cambridge Univ. Press, 1971).

WINDISCH, U. 'Societé rurale, développement touristique, pouvoir politique et conscience de classe', *Cahiers Vilfredo Pareto*, 25 (1971), 121-183.

WOLF, C.P. 'The Durkheim Thesis: Occupational Groups and Moral Integration', *Journal for the Sc. Study of Religion*, IX.1 (1970).

WORSLEY, P. *The Trumpet shall Sound* (London, Paladin, 1970).

WOSSNER, J. (ed.) *Religion im Umbruch* (Stuttgart, Ferdinand Enke Verlag, 1972).

YANG, C.K. *A Chinese Village in Early Communist Transition* (Harward Univ. Press, 1959).

YINGER, J.M. *Religion, Society and the Individual* (NY, Macmiilan, 1957).

Index

INDEX OF SUBJECTS

RELIGION AND SOCIETY

Already published
1. M. U. Memon, *Ibn Taimiya's Struggle against Popular Religion.* 1976. XXII + 424 pages.
2. R. de Nebesky-Wojkowitz, *Tibetan Religious Dances.* 1976, VIII+320 pages.
3. W. Grossmann, *Johann Christian Edelmann: From Orthodoxy to Enlightenment.* 1976, XII+210 pages.
4. B. B. Lawrence. *Shahrastani on the Indian Religions.* 1976, 300 pages.
5. M. A. Thung. *The Precarious Organisation: Sociological Explorations of the Church's Mission and Structure.* 1976, XIV+348 pages.
6. F. W. Clothey, *The Many Faces of Murukan. The History and Meaning of a South Indian God.* 1978, XVI+252 pages.
7. W. A. Graham, *Divine Word and Prophetic Word in Early Islam. A Reconsideration of the Sources.* 1977, XVIII+266 pages.
8. A. Jackson, *Na-khi Religion. An Analytical Appraisal of the Na-khi Ritual Texts.* 1979, XXII+366 pages; 16 plates.
10. M. Ayoub, *Redemptive Suffering in Islam. A Study of the Devotional Aspects of Ashura' in Twelver Shi'ism.* 1978, 304 pages.
11. J. H. Stewart, *American Catholic Leadership: A Decade of Turmoil, 1966-1976. A Sociological Analysis of the NFPC's* 1978, XX+200 pages.

In preparation:
9. J. van Kessel, *Danseurs dans le désert (en Chili). Une étude de dynamique Sociale.* With a Summary in English.
12. J.Y. Lee, *Korean Shamanistic Rituals.* With photographs.
13. B.L. Goff, *Symbols of Ancient Egypt in the Late Period.* With photographs.
14. J. P. Deconchy, *Orthodoxie religieuse et sciences humaines.* With a summary in English.
16. H. W. Turner, *From Temple to Meeting House. The Phenomenology and Theology of Places of Worship.*
17. J. Pérez-Demon, *Self and Non-self in Eearly Buddhism.*
18. J. Thrower, *The Alternative Tradition. A Study of Unbelief in the Ancient World.*
19. *Official and Popular Religion. Analysis of a Theme for Religious Studies,* ed. by P. H. Vrijhof and J. Waardenburg.

MOUTON PUBLISHERS · THE HAGUE · PARIS · NEW YORK